CRAFT BRITAIN

CRAFT BRITAIN

WHY MAKING MATTERS

Helen Chislett & David Linley

To Rosie and Florence. I might not be a Master maker but I am grateful I made you.
– Helen Chislett

To all those who have touched my spirit and my soul.
– David Linley

6   Foreword by Stephen Bayley

10   Introduction

12   1 Past & Present

32   2 Heritage & History

54   3 Rare & Endangered

76   4 Roots & Region

98   5 Kind & Sustainable

118 6 Useful & Beautiful

136 7 Health & Wellbeing

150 8 Unique & Personal

170 9 Masterful & Magical

190 10 Collected & Curated

212 11 Inspirational & Aspirational

234 12 Innovative & Collaborative

252 Index

Contents

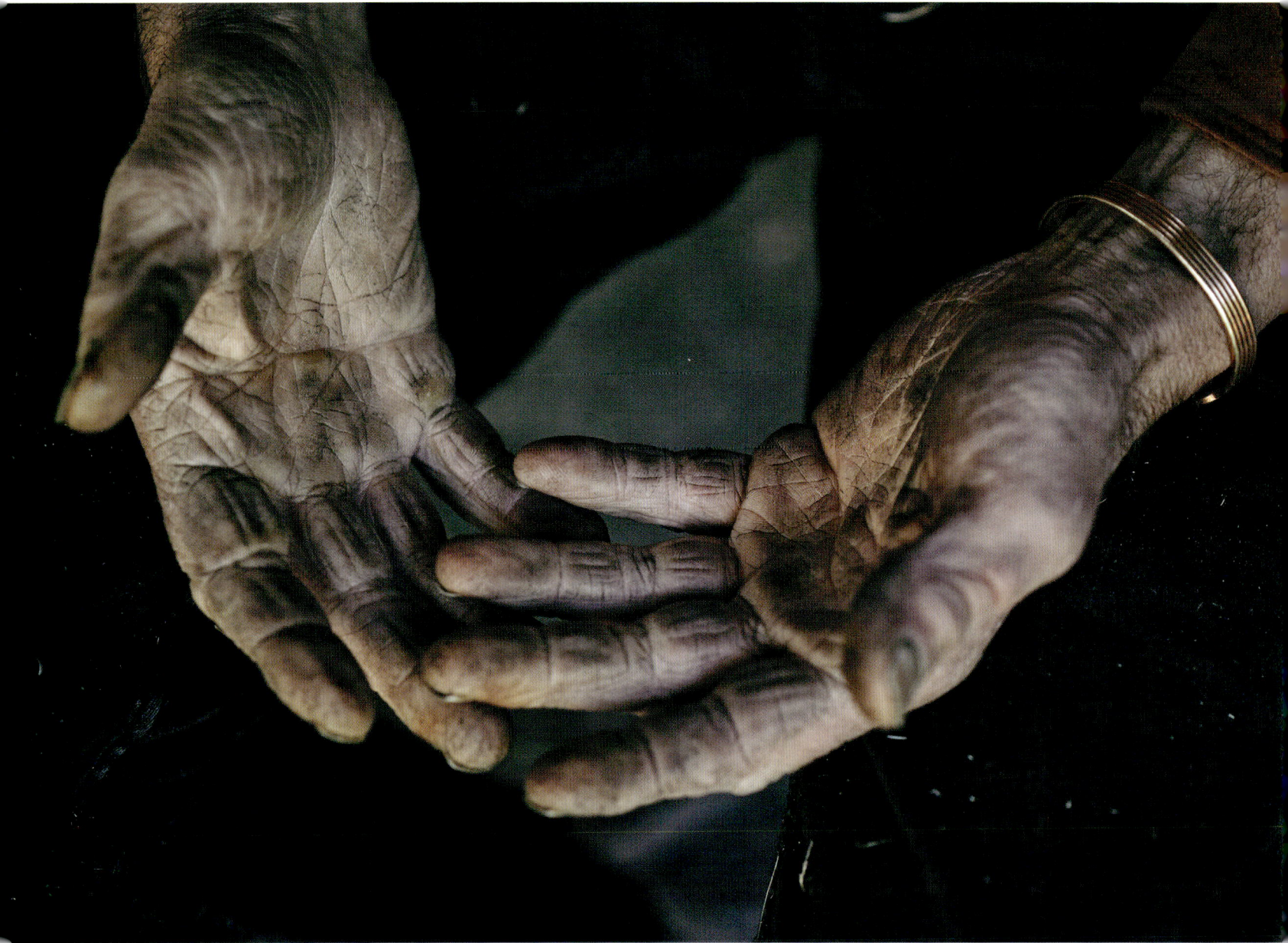

The tannin-stained hands
of oak swill maker Owen
Jones (see pages 70–73).

Foreword by Stephen Bayley

WHAT ABOUT SOME GOOD NEWS? The first inspiring truth of our precarious historic moment is that quality is, at last, becoming valued above quantity and novelty.

The second is that the era of restless change, a compulsion that animated so much of modern design, is over. The taste for the-next-new-thing is now only a very weak current.

There's a substantial backstory of richness in our culture which needs to be appreciated and exploited, not undermined by meretricious change. This applies, for example, to food as well as furniture. When a 'progressive' Chicago chef says he wants to create 'floating cheese', we groan and ask 'why?'

And significantly, in furniture retail, distinctions between old and new are blurring too. 'Mid-century modern' now looks like an historical style label, the equivalent of baroque or rococo. London's most *chic* decorator neighbourhood is Pimlico where shops once specialising in expensively shabby antiques are now manufacturing new furniture to old designs. And no-one bothers about the distinction. They only want to know if it is good.

Technology, so long the motivating force in the designer mentality, has not always enriched us: the smartphone has, along with its daily betrayals of our tastes and whereabouts, made hi-fi, television, cameras, books, calculators, inch-tapes, spirit-levels, clocks, telescopes, paintboxes, watches, thermometers and radios redundant. But smartphones cannot replace furniture.

During The Great Isolation, when a medieval plague shut down even the most shiny and confident technopolis, we maintained exiguous contact with the external world through devices of which we are becoming ever more suspicious – our smartphone is very clever, but it is not to be trusted. Besides, Netflix only gets you so far.

Instead, people found great comfort not in mystifying and invisible gigabytes, but in simple daily rituals. It was not just the uptick in sourdough baking that changed perceptions of life's options, but the discovery that sweeping the floor or cleaning the fridge could, given the right attitude, achieve something of the character of a spiritual exercise.

And people incarcerated at home learnt also to appreciate their surroundings more critically than ever before. In the early twenty-first century, the orotund Biblical cadences of John Ruskin echoed down the centuries like a New Testament prophet using a megaphone. Yes! There is nobility in manual work. And, for sure, anything that is made acquires a moral character which it's our duty to understand.

It was not just the spirit of Ruskin that was revived, but Henry David Thoreau's too. This poet of solitude warned us from his cabin in a Massachusetts forest to beware of any enterprise requiring new clothes. He preached an austere self-reliance, probably making his own shoes; his biographer said he lived his entire life as performance art. Thoreau, quite correctly, believed an 'unnecessary' doormat was 'the beginnings of evil'.

Thus, the context of this book. Craft would be marginal if it were only a minority activity involving introspective and archaic hobbyists. Instead, it's a larger concern of caring about the nature of things, being suspicious of meretricious novelty, of investing passion in the everyday and enjoying absolutely everything every day because every day is all we've got. Plus, worrying about what's truly necessary. An act of love, perhaps.

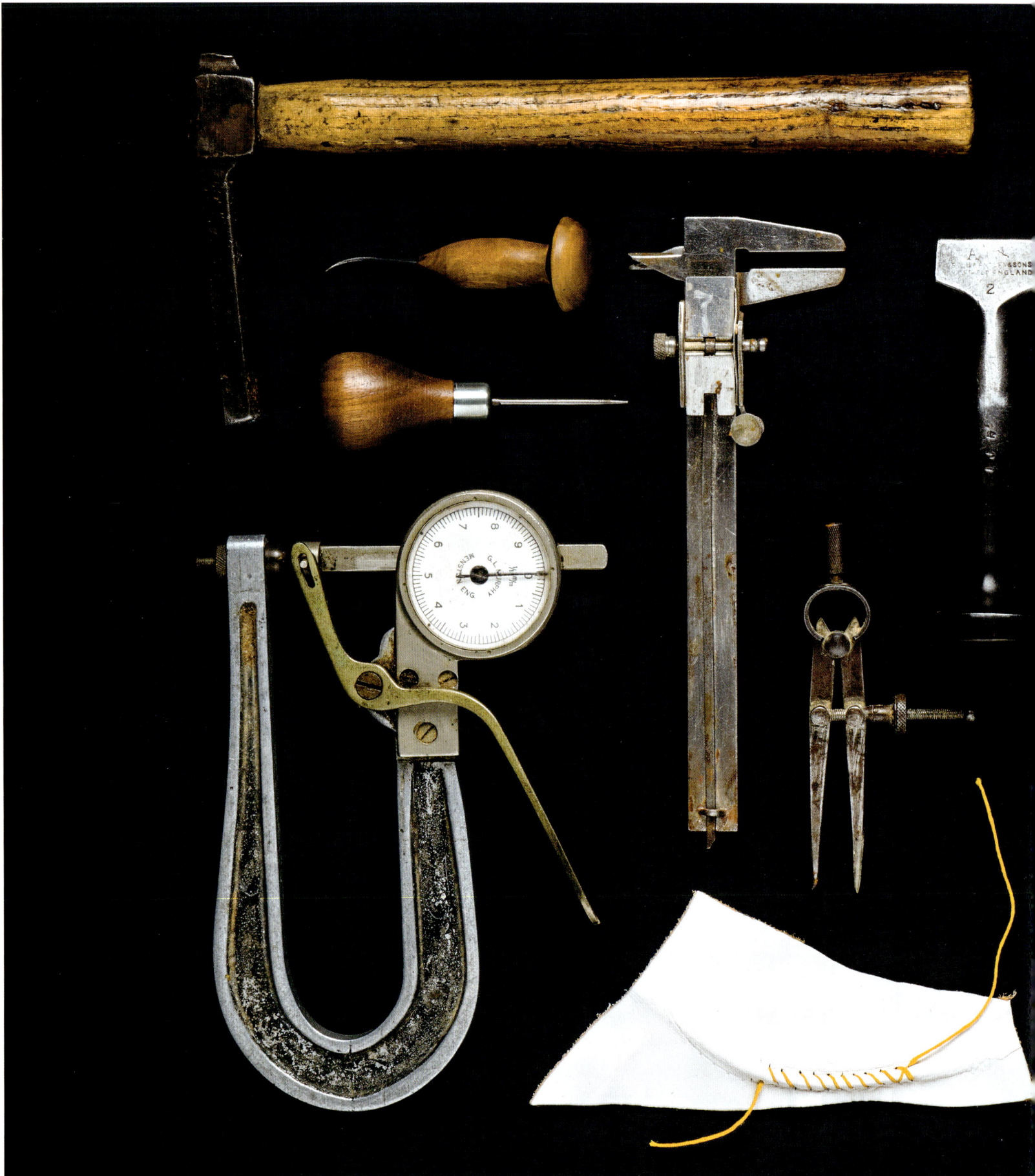

A variety of tools
from the shoemaker's
workshop, courtesy
of bespoke shoemaker
Caroline Groves
(see page 162).

The Philosophy of Thinking, of Dreaming, of Creating...

This book has been a long time in the making.

WE MET IN 1998 at a workshop in Whitby, North Yorkshire where we ate fish and chips out of newspaper with the sound of sawing and hammering all around us. It was an interview for a Sunday newspaper and once the copy was filed, we might never have met again. Yet we discovered an affinity that day for all things craft, which nearly a quarter of a century later has come to fruition here.

At the time, craft was far from popular. It had rather twee and nostalgic connotations, far removed from the shiny wenge-and-taupe interiors so fashionable at the turn of the century. While David had the practical experience of a maker from his time at the bench in his workshop (Whitby was part of a network of highly-skilled craftspeople used to make Linley furniture), Helen simply admired the time, talent and dedication it took to make something from raw materials.

After all, there is something primeval in our love of craft and the objects it produces. Craft is the genus of all cultures, as can be seen in the cathedrals, mosques, temples, synagogues, palaces and ancient cities across the globe. It was the use of tools that first marked Man out as something special in the aniWmal kingdom and without tools and the techniques to use them, we would not have cars, computers, phones or space stations. Everything we take for granted started with someone tinkering around in a workshop, yet by the late twentieth century – as society became more ubiquitously mechanised – that basic truth appeared forgotten.

Then, slowly the tide began to change, as craft began to hold its own with art and design. Artists such as Damien Hirst, Grayson Perry, Tracey Emin and Gavin Turk began to blur the boundaries with art works that encompassed taxidermy, pottery, appliqué and needlework respectively. Slowly, other sectors – particularly that of food and drink – began to appropriate words such as craft and artisan. We now had craft beer, craft coffee, craft chocolate, artisan cheese and artisan bread.

And then craft exploded into contemporary consciousness in a way we would never have thought possible. It was thrilling to see craft and craftsmanship celebrated – not just for its influence on our past, but as something unique, exciting and dynamic.

It also raised the question, What is craft? As this book illustrates, it is not a word that is as easy to define as people might think. Craft forms a triumvirate with art and design, each overlapping into the other like a three-set Venn diagram. There is nothing new in this blurring of the boundaries. Craft and design are an essential part of the language of the decorative arts; it is only in recent decades that each dialect has splintered off into its own region.

Craft is often defined as the skill of making something by hand, but if the resulting object is a dry-stone wall on a Derbyshire dale, it is perceived as something quite different from a hand-blown glass vessel in an international art fair. Both are craft, but one is seen as purely functional, whereas the other is seen as akin to fine art. If a table is made by a local carpenter, it is craft. If it is made in a workshop headed by a designer-artist (who may or may not be personally involved with its making), it is perceived as a piece of custom design. The fact is that – like art – craft is a word that people use in different contexts to mean different things to different people. Our own view is that it is all valid and valuable; that the whole is greater than the sum of the parts.

Happily, craft has not only survived, but positively thrived in a way we might not have thought possible twenty-five years ago. Within these pages, we have tried to bring together all aspects of craft from traditional, heritage skills to the most contemporary and collectible examples; from makers with decades of experience to those who have only recently discovered that using their hands quietens the mind and frees the spirit. We are immensely grateful to everyone who has helped and encouraged us with this project. Our only regret is that a book gives limited space and we were unable to include all the talented craftspeople we so admire. We dedicate it to the next generation of artists and craftspeople, bringing their love, passion and commitment for what they do into a new dawn of creativity. The post-War industrialised world may have driven a wedge between us and the natural, human process of making, but we can learn from the past, recognising that skills which harness the mind, imagination, hand and eyes are as relevant and important to our future as ever before.

It seems to us that there is no better time than this to celebrate British makers and making, and everything craft does to heal and nurture the human spirit.

HELEN CHISLETT & DAVID LINLEY

I

PAST & PRESENT

Let's start with some good news. There are *a lot* of initiatives happening right here, right now that are strengthening the craft sector for future generations. We want to pay tribute to a few of these.

First of all, we have the Victoria & Albert (V&A) Museum in London, which is the world's largest museum of applied arts, decorative arts and design, with a permanent collection of over 2.27 million objects. For anyone seeking to learn more about the UK's craft heritage – either past or present – there is no better place to begin than here.

We are also fortunate to have a dedicated body, the Crafts Council, which was set up in 1971 to advise the government 'on the needs of the artist craftsman and to promote a nation-wide interest and improvement in their products'. Its sister bodies are Craft Scotland and Craft NI (Northern Ireland). In 2021, it marked its fiftieth anniversary with the opening of a new gallery space in North London and an exciting programme of exhibitions and events across the UK. The Crafts Council launched the Collect fair in 2004, now one of the most important and influential events internationally to be focused on contemporary craft and design. In order for the fair to be enjoyed by craft enthusiasts across the world, participating galleries are gifted an online presence on Artsy.net while the programme of talks includes both a live and a virtual audience.

The Queen Elizabeth Scholarship Trust (QEST) also deserves special mention. Founded by the Royal Warrant Holders Association in 1990, both to commemorate its own 150th anniversary and the 90th birthday of HM Queen Elizabeth, The Queen Mother, it has, since its inception, awarded over £5 million (about $7 million) to around 650 QEST Scholars. These alumni work across the UK in a multitude of disciplines ranging from embroidery, armoury and silversmithing to bookbinding, millinery and guitar making. Once accepted into the QEST family, Scholars are further supported through opportunities for exhibitions, networking, collaborations and commissions. In addition, QEST runs a professional business development programme with Cockpit Arts. The organisation is a valuable resource for anyone searching for a particular craft skill, with an online directory of all its Scholars.

The Society for the Protection of Ancient Buildings (SPAB) was founded by William Morris in 1877 and is still playing an active part through training schemes, courses, advice and research. The SPAB William Morris Craft Fellowship was founded in 1987 to address the shortage of craft skills needed to conserve and repair historic buildings – still an ongoing concern today. Many SPAB Fellows are now working in the heritage sector maintaining and restoring cathedrals, castles and country estates.

The Artworkers' Guild is a body of around 400 leading artists, craftspeople, architects and academics, which represents over 60 creative disciplines. Its aim is to support the visual arts and crafts in any way that might be beneficial to the community. It encourages cross-discipline collaborations and has an impressive programme of events, mentoring and outreach projects. Founded in 1844 by young architects and designers, many of them prominent in the Arts and Crafts movement, work by Guild members can be seen all over Britain in country

Above: Matthew Hensby, one half of Bibbings & Hensby – preparing furniture components with a drawknife and shave horse.

Opposite: Work in progress by renowned wood sculptor, Eleanor Lakelin, who has also been championed by the Michelangelo Foundation (see also page 180).

estates, historic houses, cathedrals, churches – and the objects within them. At the root of its ethos is a recognition of the healing, humane value of craftsmanship.

Equally significant is Heritage Crafts (formerly known as the Heritage Crafts Association), which was founded in 2010 to 'safeguard traditional craft skills for the future'. Working in partnership with government and key agencies, it provides a focus for individual craftspeople, groups, societies and guilds, and is an accredited NGO for UNESCO's Convention for the Safeguarding of Intangible Cultural Heritage. This states:

'Any efforts to safeguard traditional craftsmanship must focus not on preserving craft objects – no matter how beautiful, precious, rare or important they might be – but on creating conditions that will encourage artisans to continue to produce crafts of all kinds, and to transmit their skills and knowledge to others.'

So far, around 180 countries from Albania and Algeria to Zambia and Zimbabwe have signed up to the Convention, effectively making intangible cultural heritage part of their cultural policy. Unfortunately, at the time of writing the UK is not yet one of them.

As well as continuing to advocate for this change, Heritage Crafts offers invaluable resources to the heritage crafts community, including the publication every two years of the Red List of Endangered Crafts (see chapter 3). It also provided practical assistance through the pandemic, with a COVID-19 Hardship Grants Scheme that awarded a combined £50,000 (almost $70,000) to 53 makers over six months through the generosity of its donors and supporters. As with QEST, the Crafts Council and The Art Workers' Guild, it provides a directory of affiliated craftspeople.

The work of The Creative Dimension Trust (TCDT) includes free workshops (some online), tuition and materials to young people between the ages of fourteen and nineteen across the UK

in a bid to show them the potential in forging a career pathway linked to precise hand-eye co-ordination. Founded by Penny Bendall, a Royal Warrant holder and leading conservator of ceramics, all workshops are taught by world-class tutors. Subjects are as diverse as costume making, floral work, gilding, leather working, metal chasing, puppet making and signwriting. The emphasis is on transferable skills that could change the direction of a young person's life, with a variety of work placements also organised. TCDT is actively involved in trying to inspire young people from every walk of life, cutting across barriers of income, colour and class.

Other bright spots include London Craft Week (LCW), the Great Northern Contemporary Craft Fair (GNCCF) and Crafty Fox Market. LCW was established in 2015 by Guy Salter OBE and brings together over 250 established makers, designers, brands and galleries within the capital each May. Visitors can choose from an extensive programme of exhibitions, talks, workshop tours, demonstrations and masterclasses. Its sister event, Create Day, is held each September and is a twenty-four-hour opportunity to engage with over 300 artists, makers, designers and creators across the globe through exclusive video content. GNCCF was founded in 2008 and is held each autumn at Manchester's iconic Victoria Baths, with an impressive and carefully selected line-up of around 160 UK designer-makers, including contemporary ceramicists, jewellers, textile designers, woodworkers, metalsmiths, glass makers, furniture makers and printmakers. Crafty Fox Market was established in 2010 and supports emerging designer-makers with opportunities to showcase their work in venues across London and beyond, including in nightclubs, museums, major city landmarks and community spaces.

The Prince's Foundation

The Prince's Foundation reflects HRH The Prince of Wales's commitment to championing holistic and sustainable solutions to the challenges the world faces today. Working with satellite bodies both nationally and internationally, its base is Dumfries House in East Ayrshire, where philosophies and principles are put into practice.

The Building Craft Programme was set up by The Prince's Foundation in 2006. Each year, it brings together twelve students on an eight-month course, providing an opportunity to gain practical experience in traditional building skills. Participants are drawn from many trades, including stonemasonry, joinery, bricklaying, blacksmithing, plastering, thatching, roofing, tiling and specialist decorating, with the aim of elevating them to the next level of craftsmanship.

The programme includes a live project, often at the Dumfries House estate. In 2020, students created a shepherd's hut, and the following year they built a new outdoor classroom to support the Foundation's STEM education initiative.

Its sister project, the Building Arts Programme, aims to inspire a future generation of artists, craftspeople, designers and makers to promote a built environment that draws on an extensive range of skills, materials and processes. Launched in February 2020 – just before the pandemic hit – it is a collaboration between The Prince's Foundation and QEST. Focusing on those that 'think with their hands', it aims to encourage students to utilise their skills within the human-made landscape of architecture, design and placemaking, challenging the preconception that 'craft' is confined purely to the past. During a period of industry placements, participants have the opportunity to learn first-hand from Master craftspeople across the UK, including some of the wonderful Master craftspeople featured in this book, such as basket weaver Annemarie O'Sullivan (see pages 107–110), wood sculptor Eleanor Lakelin (see page 180) and Kevin Gauld, aka The Orkney Furniture Maker (see pages 105–106).

In 2018, the Foundation collaborated with the Historic Environment Division (HED) and

Left and below: QEST Scholar Rob Walker, founder of Signs by Umberto, is one of the last practitioners of reverse-glass writing. This verre églomisé panel was exhibited at Fortnum & Mason in London.

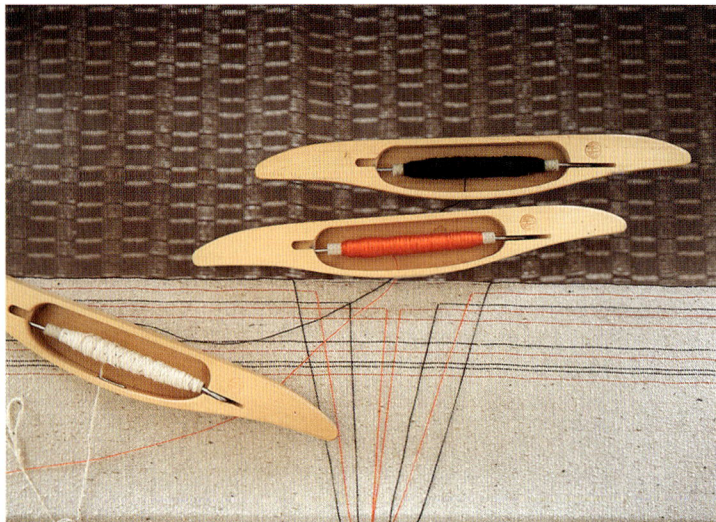

Above: Detail shot of the loom used by weaver, Emily Mackey, one of the craftspeople promoted by the Michelangelo Foundation. The cloth is a mix of silk noil and bespoke-dyed wool.

Above right: Tracey Whalen, maker of bespoke womenswear, is also tutor at the Modern Artisan programme initiated by The Prince's Foundation in collaboration with Yoox Net-A-Porter.

Hillsborough Castle on a live construction training programme in Northern Ireland, which in turn led to a new qualifications-based training course in building skills in the region. In 2021, it announced plans to expand this training across the border with a programme supported by The Heritage Council and the Benefact Trust, giving aspiring craftspeople both from the Republic of Ireland and Northern Ireland the opportunity to hone heritage craft skills.

The Prince's Foundation School for Traditional Arts was founded in 2005. It offers pioneering post-graduate programmes for those interested in the artistic practice of the traditional arts. The Foundation also has a base at Trinity Buoy Wharf in East London, where it runs a Diploma Year course in fine and applied art, a dynamic skills-based course unique in its focus on the interplay between traditional skills, innovation and creativity. Its Future Textiles programme has been expanded to the Wharf, where it aims to fill the hole caused by sewing and textiles being largely dropped from the school curriculum.

The new training and education base within the Highgrove estate in Gloucestershire complements the work of Dumfries House. This offers a programme of textile production skills and a number of craft residencies. Highgrove is also the site of the annual Snowdon Summer School. Set up in 2016, this ten-day programme allows students to learn traditional cabinet making and marquetry techniques from Master craftspeople. In 2021, The Prince's Foundation announced a new partnership with City & Guilds, giving students graduating from its courses internationally recognised qualifications.

The Philanthropists

Support for crafts has also come from international bodies such as the Michelangelo Foundation for Creativity and Craftsmanship. This not-for-profit organisation aims to champion craftsmanship, endorse and enable its artisans to sell their work, and help them sustain and grow their businesses. Founded in 2016, it is the brainchild of Johann Rupert and Franco Cologni. In

1988, Rupert established Compagnie Financière Richemont, which today includes brands such as Cartier, Van Cleef & Arpels, Dunhill and Purdey. Cologni was previously Managing Director and Chairman of Cartier International. Together, they recognise that the luxury sector could not exist without the commitment, time and dedication of generations of craftspeople.

The work of the Foundation includes the *Homo Faber Guide*, a digital platform that highlights craftspeople, ateliers and small manufacturers across Europe – from Master artisans to rising stars. As well as providing a directory of makers for those interested in buying or commissioning craft (including several featured in this book), it promotes special events, masterclasses, workshop tours and curated museum experiences. It also hosts a flagship event at the Fondazione Giorgio Cini in Venice, presenting the work of hundreds of artisans and designers and giving visitors the opportunity to discover the skill, talent and time that goes into crafting exquisite objects by hand. Its Doppia Firma (Double Signature) initiative pairs top designers with Master craftspeople to produce a collection of unique objects that are shown at the Salone del Mobile each spring. The youth development programme includes a summer school that funds short courses across Europe aimed at students and recent graduates to inspire and enable a new generation to enter craft and fulfil their potential within the sector.

Crafts are also benefiting from the generosity of private investors. At Marchmont House, an eighteenth-century Palladian mansion in the Scottish Borders, director Hugo Burge has determined to make the estate usable in a practical way. Marchmont was awarded the prestigious Sotheby's Restoration Award in 2018 after an eight-year restoration programme. It now seeks to inspire and celebrate creativity by supporting artists, hosting open studios and offering studios and residencies. The Marchmont Workshop – which makes rush-seated ladderback chairs in the style of Ernest Gimson and Philip Clissett (see page 105) – is one of eleven units available for makers and creators on the estate.

At the other end of the country, Grandey's Place in Hertfordshire is dedicated to supporting heritage crafts through twenty studio spaces, many of them generously subsidised. Founded by philanthropist Clive Beecham in 2019, with the active support of QEST and Heritage Crafts, it recognises that craftspeople often struggle to survive financially, given escalating rents and a dwindling number of customers. Patronage is the life blood of craft success, so would-be clients are invited to come on a 'journey of creation', designed to show that commissioning a work of craft excellence is a two-way process that can, and should, be shared. Craftspeople at Grandey's

Above left: The many types of chisel used by stone sculptor, Michelle de Bruin, whose studio is based at Marchmont House in the Scottish Borders.

Above right: Inside Michelle de Bruin's Marchmont studio with works in progress that include a lion intended for a gatepost and a sculpture of a wolf.

Opposite: De Bruin was commissioned by Hugo Burge of Marchmont to design and make the emblem for the Marchmont Makers Foundation, carved onto the gable end of the artists' studios.

include saddlers, luthiers (who make or restore stringed instruments), specialist upholsterers, tailors, horologists and furniture makers (some of whom we have highlighted within this book).

There are also many wonderful individuals working hard to safeguard craft. Potter Lisa Hammond MBE founded Clay College in Stoke-on-Trent in 2017 with the support of the ceramics community worldwide. Its aim is to protect the future of studio pottery by providing a forum in which the current generation of Master craftspeople can pass on their wisdom and skills to the emerging generation, against a backdrop of the closure of many leading ceramic departments. Alongside the two-year diploma, Clay College provides evening and short courses for the local community. This initiative follows on from the highly successful Adopt a Potter scheme, which was established by Hammond in 2009 to help bridge the gap between the completion of higher education courses and the setting up of individual studios by teaching technical and business skills.

Craft Design House in Edinburgh was founded by craft *aficionado* Gillian Scott in 2016 and provides a unique opportunity for both corporate clients and the public to access the skills of an array of hand-picked designer-makers. Services include creating eco-conscious and individual collections for hospitality, retail and gifting partners, while its popular Mending Boutique teaches skills such as embroidery, patchwork, darning and quilting. By creating experiences that engage its audience, it communicates messages concerning provenance, materials, sustainability and the value of nurturing up-and-coming designer-makers.

Many interior design studios also go above and beyond to support the craftspeople and workshops with whom they collaborate. Under Winch's Wing was established as a direct response to the struggle of craftspeople to survive the COVID pandemic. Founded by Andrew Winch, a

Richard Platt (left) of The
Marchmont Workshop
shows a volunteer
how to harvest the raw
material with which to
make traditional rush-
seated chairs.

supporter of QEST and Trustee Director of Winch Design (a key player in the super-yacht industry), he and his team hand-select talented makers who are promoted through the company's website and offered help in terms of business development, marketing and improved social media.

Moving Forward

In 2020, the Crafts Council produced *Market for Craft*, its third report analysing the state of the craft market (the previous two were in 2006 and 2010). This proved to be a useful snapshot of how the sector is doing, and it included some encouraging statistics. The British continuing love and appreciation of craft generated sales of around £3 billion (about $4 billion) in 2019. The findings also revealed a growing new generation of younger craft consumers searching for ethical and sustainable products. The ease of online shopping had resulted in online craft purchases accounting for thirty-three per cent of the market in 2020, as opposed to five per cent back in 2006.

However, look closely at the figures and the picture distorts. While more people are buying crafts, they are buying them at a lower value. The challenges faced by Master craftspeople and established makers have changed little since 2006. The work of bodies such as QEST and Heritage Crafts continues to be crucial in promoting and supporting the cream of crafts professionals, who have dedicated many years to mastering their skills. Only sixteen per cent in this category reported profits in excess of £30,000 ($39,000).

The international market for British craft is also a mixed picture. Next to the home market, Europe has traditionally been the biggest importer of British craft (particularly France and Switzerland). While EU countries continue to account for around forty per cent of British craft exports, twenty-six per cent of makers said that Brexit had already had a negative impact on their sales, while a further twenty-two per cent said they expected this to be the case in the future. However, on a more positive note, the USA is the third largest importer of British craft. In 2020, sales of craft to the USA accounted for £517 million ($700 million) – about eleven per cent of the total value of the crafts sector. However, there is an estimated untapped market of nearly four million people in NYC and three million people in LA who are yet to buy from a UK maker but would 'definitely' or 'probably' consider doing so in the future. There is real room for potential here, particularly if supported at government level through practical help with shipping, customs and local agents.

Room for Improvement

According to the *Market for Craft* report mentioned above, the demographic of makers is showing signs of becoming more inclusive, with around a quarter of makers in 2020 having a disability – double the number recorded in the 2006 survey. However, the proportion of black, Asian and ethnically diverse makers is unchanged since 2006, with only two to four per cent identifying within these groups.

Nobody can question the need to improve diversity within the craft sector. In 2021, a two-year AHRC-funded UKRI/RCUK Innovation Fellowship, led by Dr Karen Patel of Birmingham City University in collaboration with the Crafts Council UK, entitled *Supporting Diversity and Expertise Development in the Contemporary Craft Economy* was published. This research project reported barriers

Right: Kilt making is now listed as Endangered on the Red List produced by Heritage Craft. Nikki Laird (shown here) founder of The Kiltmakery runs courses to pass on the skill.

Far right: Potter Chris Bramble captured on film by Jo Sealy for The Black Artisans project that she initiated to celebrate and make visible UK-based black craftspeople.

for black, Asian and ethnically diverse communities to become professional makers. These included college and university curricula that create a sense of 'otherness' by failing to address cultural histories of craft and craft techniques from around the world. When the Crafts Council opened the doors of its new gallery in 2021, one of its first exhibitions was *We Gather*, featuring five female makers of black and Asian heritage. New works featured in the exhibition were commissioned by Dr Patel and were a response to her research project. In tandem with *We Gather*, the Crafts Council showcased *The Black Artisans*, a travelling photography exhibition by Jo Sealy that showcases and celebrates UK-based black craftspeople working in heritage crafts and other areas of cultural heritage.

In 2021, Heritage Crafts – a partner of *The Black Artisans* – announced a training bursary for ethnically diverse makers, recognising this is still an under-represented group within the sector. This first bursary was sponsored by DCA Consulting, but the hope is to provide at least one bursary every year if reliable funding can be found.

All this shows that craft isn't something to be moth-balled and marginalised: it is a force that is energetic, relevant, dynamic and passionate. If it is to stay that way, it must inspire, welcome and connect with all those who have the potential to be the skilled makers of the future. There might still be work to do, but right now there is optimism and the future looks bright.

MARY WING TO:
Whip Maker and Leather Artisan

Right: Hand-cutting the leather ready for braiding or plaiting the whip. It was Mary Wing To's love of leather that first inspired her to take a saddlery course to perfect her techniques.

Opposite: Here she plaits the whip core with kangaroo leather lace. Inside every whip handle, she rolls a piece of newspaper to mark the date when the whip was completed.

Having always loved watching horses as a child, Mary Wing To was inspired by this emotional connection to focus on leather during her MA in Fashion Design and Technology at the London College of Fashion (she had previously trained as a bespoke coat maker in Savile Row). Having graduated with Distinction in 2007, she embarked on a two-year saddlery course at Capel Manor College to hone her leather working skills. Her original intention was to use this experience to incorporate leather into her fashion work, but she excelled at the craft and spent a further three years as an apprentice harness maker at the Royal Mews of Buckingham Palace, under the discerning eye of Frances Roche, HM The Queen's Master saddler, and Catrien Coppens, Master harness maker.

Having qualified as a harness maker and Member of The Society of Master Saddlers, she was awarded a QEST Scholarship in 2012, which enabled her to study with Master whip maker, Dennis Walmsley. Dennis was a self-taught Master who, unusually, made every part of a whip from scratch. He had never agreed to share his skills with anyone before, but Wing To

'My mission is to ensure that the centuries of development that have made whip making an art continues onwards.'

persuaded him and, over a year, he taught her how to prepare the cane; techniques for plaiting and braiding the leather around the core; and the silverwork craft needed for the collar. When he passed away, she was determined not to let this knowledge die with him, but to continue his unique methods of working.

In 2016, she founded Whip in Hand, creating bespoke whips for her niche clients. Inside every whip handle, she rolls a part of a newspaper – *The Times* – showing the date of when the whip was created; this was something Dennis had passed on to her so that the date could eventually be discovered far into the future. Notable equestrian clients have included Charlotte Dujardin CBE, multiple World and Olympic champion in the field of dressage (including three gold medals); and Nick Skelton CBE, show jumper and Olympic gold medal winner. In 2022, she was one of four QEST Scholars chosen to take part in the Michelangelo Foundation exhibition, *Crafting a More Human Future* in Venice.

In addition to Whip in Hand, Wing To is Chanel's Master of Atelier in the UK, responsible for the running of its leather repair and restoration service. She also creates her own leather fashion collections, sculpting, moulding, carving, dyeing and stitching the material to create dramatic, sculptural garments.

Of her whip making craft, she says, 'Whips are made by hand, and held in the hand and so there is an intimate connection between the craftsperson and the rider – both are Masters of their discipline: one in the making and one of the horse. My mission is to ensure that the centuries of development that make it an art continues onwards, so I hope to take on my own apprentices eventually.'

LUCY McGRATH:
Paper Marbler

Artist, designer and paper marbler, Lucy McGrath founded her studio, Marmor Paperie, in 2015. Seeing shops saturated with digitally printed, mass-produced products, she wanted to herald a return to quality, craftsmanship and individuality. She first discovered marbling – and other bookbinding techniques – when studying Illustration at the University of Brighton. Subsequently, a holiday to Istanbul ignited her discovery of *ebru*, the art of traditional Turkish marbling dating from the fifteenth century, which in turn led to her embarking on a short course to learn the technique on her return to the UK.

Marbling is classified as Endangered on the Heritage Crafts' Red List (see page 56), with fewer than ten professional paper marblers left in the UK. Its heyday was the nineteenth century when it was a technique commonly used for making end-papers in books. We were delighted we were able to use some of McGrath's designs for this one.

She uses methods that have barely changed for centuries. First, a shallow dish is filled with size (water thickened with seaweed extract) and acrylic paints are mixed to the correct shades for

Right: Lucy McGrath in her Cockpits Arts' studio, from where she runs Marmor Paperie, a business dedicated to keeping alive the Endangered craft of paper marbling.

> 'There is something magical about how marbling interacts with the natural chaos of water – like harnessing some wild force you can never fully control.'

the chosen design. When everything is ready, the paints are carefully dripped onto the size using stiff brushes or pipettes. Because of the strong surface tension, colours spread across its surface rather than dispersing. The surface is then manipulated using traditional tools, such as bamboo skewers, to create elegant and intricate patterns. Once the design is complete, paper is carefully laid onto the size, picking up the colours and capturing the pattern. Once the size is rinsed off, the sheet of paper is hung up to dry.

If the marbled paper is to be used for bookbinding, a template is then drawn onto the sheet of paper. This process needs careful consideration, as the aim is to capture the most beautiful part of the pattern onto the cover of the book. Boards are then cut to fit, glued to the marbled paper, weighted down and left to dry. It takes a full day to press a book if it is to be perfect.

Being passionate about her craft, McGrath organises her own in-person and online workshops to teach the skill to craft enthusiasts. As well as creating her own collections of marbled journals, diaries, paper and gifts, she is much in demand for bespoke commissions, both from luxury brands and private individuals. Marbling made to order in this way means that Marmor Paperie is a naturally sustainable business, but McGrath goes above and beyond to improve this side of things further, recycling papers, offcuts and packaging wherever possible.

Of her chosen craft, she says, 'Now is an exciting time for the craft, as it is moving away from the traditional association of bookbinding into large-scale artworks and fashion. There is something magical about how marbling interacts with the natural chaos of water – like harnessing some wild force you can never fully control.'

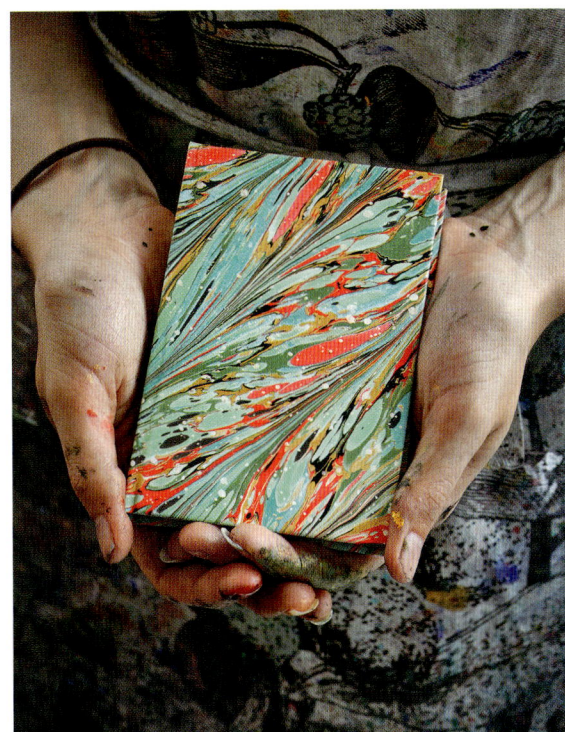

Above and left: McGrath sprinkles paint over the thickened water before manipulating it into the effect she wants, as shown on the finished notebook.

2

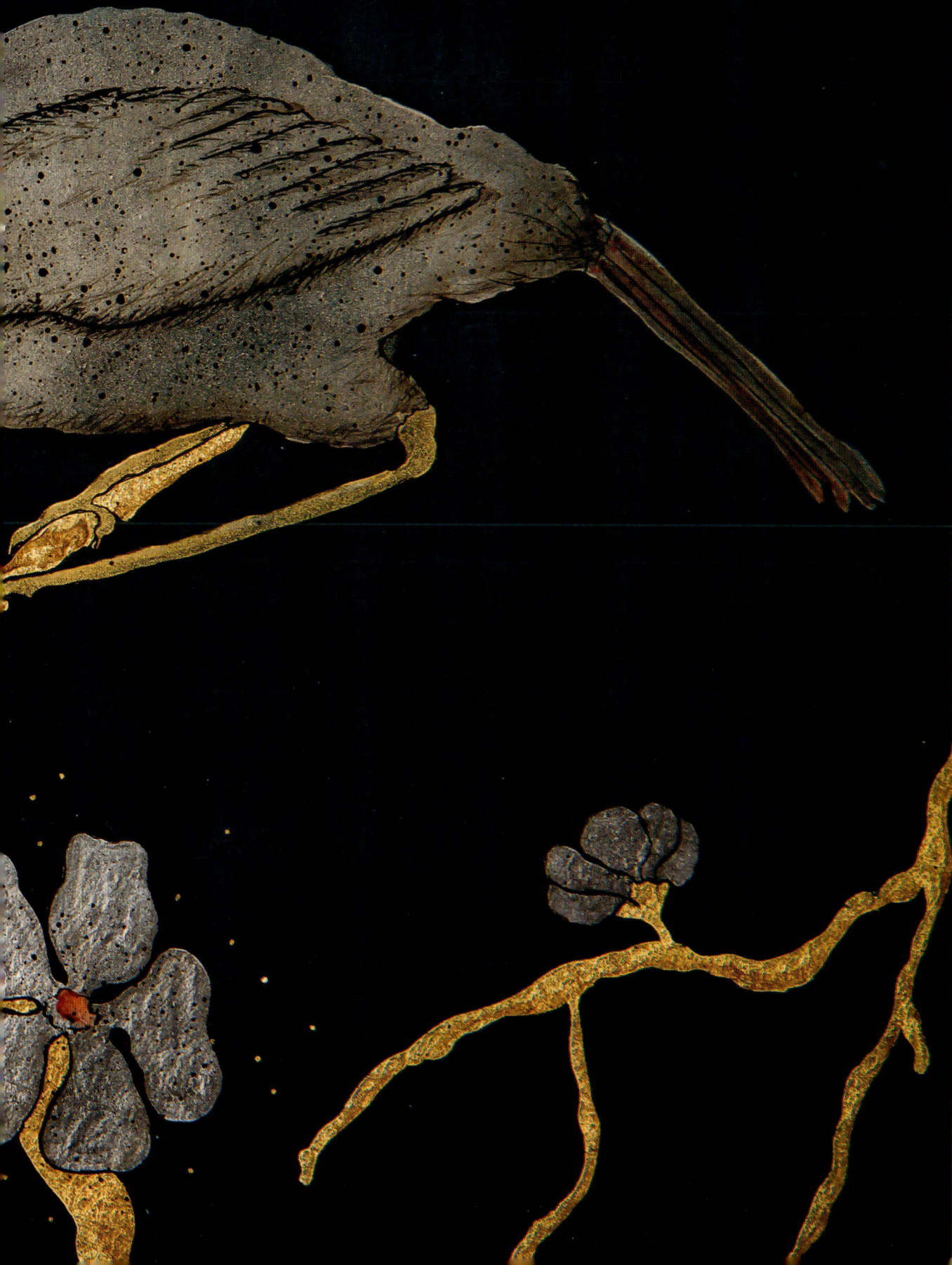

Previous spread: Detail
of a pair of lacquer
cabinets by Pedro da
Costa Felgueiras, founder
of Lacquer Studios, with
motifs of 24 carat-gold,
platinum, palladium and
dots of Japanese junkin-
hiramefun.

Our cities, towns and villages are crammed with portals to the past in the shape of cathedrals, castles, palaces and monuments. We are blessed to live in a place where we are never very far from a piece of our human history, from the stateliest of country houses to the humblest of parish churches. We have around 20,000 scheduled monuments; upwards of 1,600 registered parks and gardens; over thirty World Heritage sites and almost half a million listed buildings. These add up to a built heritage of cultural, religious, archaeological and industrial significance, dating from circa 4000BCE to the twentieth century. The fact is we are awash with history to the point we barely register it.

While it is true that tourism does play a significant part in our national economy – pre-pandemic it contributed about £237 billion ($316 billion) to the UK's GDP – it would be cynical to think that this is the only role our built heritage plays. In fact, we are a country that takes enormous pride in the history that has shaped us. The National Trust membership alone is bigger than the entire populations of countries such as Costa Rica, Norway and New Zealand – currently heading towards the six million mark.

Happily, we take the business of conservation seriously, with responsibility spread over a number of statutory organisations including English Heritage, Historic Environment Scotland, Cadw (Wales) and the Historic Monuments Council (Northern Ireland). In addition, there are non-statutory bodies that include the National Trust and its sister, National Trust Scotland, as well as the amenity societies that local authorities are obliged to consult when taking decisions on partial or total demolition of listed buildings. The story does not end there, given the plethora of specialist preservation groups dedicated to conserving historical buildings and their landscape.

The Royal Collection is one of the largest and most important art collections in the world, and one of the last great European Royal collections to remain intact. It includes priceless works held in Buckingham Palace, Windsor Castle, Clarence House, Frogmore House, the Royal Pavilion, Brighton and the Palace of Holyroodhouse. What is less visible to visitors is the enormous effort, skill and dedication that goes into maintaining the Collection and preserving it for future generations. The Royal Collection Trust includes the combined efforts of fine art conservators, ceramic specialists, chandelier restorers, gilders, horologists, book binders, embroiderers, armourers, carpenters and jewellers, to name but a few.

Repair and Restore

With all this passion and dedication swirling around our historic houses and monuments, it seems strange that the spotlight rarely falls on those whose life's work has been to maintain the fabric of these structures: people such as stonemasons, carpenters, roofers, tilers, lime plasterers, thatchers, bricklayers, pargetters, gilders, blacksmiths, wood carvers and specialist decorators. For too long, we have ignored the problem of dwindling numbers of people taking up these specialist trades, but there are signs of optimism that this is changing. Bodies such as The Prince's Foundation, the Queen Elizabeth Trust (QEST), Heritage Crafts, the SPAB and others are all working to turn the tide and save vital master craft skills from disappearing for ever.

Right: The rich, ochre colours and intricate patterns of Makins Paisley damask by silk-weavers Gainsborough, shown here in the loom (see page 84).

Left: Artist Hugh Dunford Wood creates lino-cut collections of hand-printed wallpaper, which are made to order, allowing the client to choose both the ground colour and the print colour.

Opposite top: A carved cherry wood block used by Allyson McDermott to create one of her hand-blocked and flocked wallpaper designs suitable for historic interiors.

Opposite below: Sheets of bespoke, hand-blocked wallpaper are hung up to dry in McDermott's studio. Greater lengths are needed to fit the height of rooms in many grand heritage buildings.

A property such as a palace or grand country home is actually constructed from hundreds of individually crafted components, yet when we look, we see only the spectacular whole. The problem lies in maintaining each component, extending its life well beyond what the original maker might have thought possible. Plasterwork crumbles, ancient wallpaper peels, stained-glass windows crack, carpets are faded by sunlight, fabrics are assaulted by moths, chairs collapse with age – a myriad factors conspire to destroy furnishings that were once the height of fashion and gloriously colourful.

Allyson McDermott is one of the world's leading authorities on recreating historic wallpapers. A conservator, scientist, historian, designer and maker, she is expert in working from the tiniest shred of evidence and rediscovering age-old processes of traditional woodblock printing, varnishing, gilding, embossing, hand-painting and flocking. She heads up a team of talented conservators and designers working on architectural gems such as the Royal Pavilion, Brighton and the Palace of Westminster, as well as museums, royal palaces, historic houses and private homes. In addition, her studio holds an important archive of both European and Oriental designs dating from the seventeenth to the twentieth century, any of which can be recreated to order, often combining historic patterns and techniques with contemporary ideas and colourways.

Tristram Bainbridge was the furniture conservator at the V&A Museum in London and was also Associate Tutor for the Furniture Conservation programme at West Dean College in Sussex (see page 144), where he himself studied for a MA in Conservation Studies as a QEST Scholar after graduating with a degree in History of Art from the Courtauld Institute. Today, he runs his own company, Bainbridge Conservation, with his wife, Abigail – herself a renowned paper and book conservator. Bainbridge and his highly skilled team offer a range of services across

Left: Conservator Tristram Bainbridge uses the ancient art of urushi lacquering to repair and protect the light-damaged surface of an eighteenth-century Chinese Export lacquer table.

Left below: The decoration on this table is very fine. After filling micro cracks with diluted applications of lacquer, gold and silver powders are sprinkled on to the wet surface and then polished.

numerous materials, including the conservation of wood, gilding, lacquer, historic interiors, books and works of art on paper. Asian lacquer (*urushi*-based) is a personal specialisation of his.

Where possible, he endeavours to preserve objects for as long as possible, but subtle intervention is sometimes unavoidable if a particular item is to survive. While his repairs are aesthetically pleasing and sympathetic – in fact, often invisible to the untrained eye – Bainbridge always makes clear what is original and what has been repaired in order to help the conservators and researchers of the future.

Pride and Patronage

For many working in the heritage sector, it is Britain's rich wealth of centuries-old traditions that allow them to survive, with many proudly bearing their Royal Warrants. The Royal School of Needlework (RSN), for example, celebrated its 150th anniversary in 2022. Originally named the School of Art Needlework, it was able to add its royal prefix in 1875, when Queen Victoria became its first royal patron. Currently based at Hampton Court Palace, its world-renowned embroidery studio restores historical textiles and creates bespoke new embroidery for interiors, fashion, art and, of course, royalty. From Queen Victoria's funeral pall through to successive coronation robes of state and the royal wedding dress of HRH the Duchess of Cambridge, it has played its part in many important royal occasions. In recent years, it has also worked on commissions for clients as diverse as Sir Paul McCartney, *Game of Thrones*, Vivienne Westwood and artist Cornelia Parker.

Its archive contains more than 4,000 embroidered objects and many thousands of designs. Interestingly, the RSN is currently compiling a world directory of stitch called RSN Stitch Bank, which aims to digitally conserve and preserve every stitch around the globe. Stitches can fall into obscurity if they are not used, which means that when an older embroidered piece is discovered,

curators cannot always recognise the stitches. In addition, textiles throughout the world continue to be threatened by wars and other critical events – as well as changes in manufacturing processes – so this project goes to the heart of the RSN's purpose.

Hand & Lock has a similarly rich history. It was founded by a young Huguenot refugee from France called Monsieur Hand in 1767. Many Protestants fled to Britain in the late seventeenth century to escape religious persecution, taking their highly evolved craft skills with them. Hand began by manufacturing and selling lace to military tailors, later adapting his eye for design into military badges and the accoutrements of officers' dress uniforms. The business flourished for 200 years. Separately, in the 1950s, a young designer called Stanley Lock was employed by the specialist embroidery house of CE Phipps & Co. When Mr Phipps retired, Lock took over the company and gave it his own name. His vision was to turn

Above: A raised and metal-thread embroidered brooch worked by the Royal School of Needlework. The techniques include wired petals embellished with metal threads, spangles and pearls.

Left: A hand-embroidered goldwork design by Hand & Lock inspired by the work of Gustav Klimt. Metallic threads reflect light and create these dazzling effects.

it into a couture house of embroidery, and it subsequently collaborated with fashion houses such as Christian Dior, Norman Hartnell and Hardy Amies. In 1998, both companies were acquired by Alastair MacLeod and merged into Hand & Lock.

William Cowley is the last surviving parchment and vellum maker in the UK, and one of the very few worldwide. The family business was founded in 1850, has been passed down for five generations and is still owned by the family today. Apprentices typically require seven years of training, mastering a craft that has been unchanged for millennia. Made using the hides of calf, goat and sheep, parchment and vellum (which uses the skin of young animals, such as lambs and calves)

are natural by-products of the meat, milk and wool industries. Cowley's sources its hides from farms known for their high animal welfare standards, and no animals are bred specifically for this purpose. Every skin is hand-selected from the abattoir, with skins discarded if they are marked – for example, with piercings from barbed-wire or tick bites. Occasionally, ancient manuscripts feature these sorts of scar, with writing curved around them. It takes months of hard work to transform the rough hide into smooth, silky parchment or vellum.

It is a sobering thought that without the making of parchment and vellum, we would have had very little written history until comparatively recently. Unlike paper made of plant pulp – a method not widespread until the end of the fifteenth century – parchment and vellum take many centuries to degrade. The *Domesday Book* of 1086 was written on parchment, as was the United States' *Declaration of Independence*. The Instrument of Consent signed by HM The Queen for the marriage of HRH Prince William to Catherine Middleton was written on vellum made at Cowley's. Long after we have gone, these nuggets of history will survive. That is why many believe it was misguided of the House of Lords to end the printing of laws onto vellum in 2016, breaking with a thousand-year-old tradition and placing an ancient craft into an even more precarious situation.

Time and Timelessness

Walk around the St James's area of London and it is hard to go more than a few paces without encountering one of the numerous Royal Warrant-holding companies that are the beating heart of this corner of Westminster. St James's Palace was built in the 1530s on the orders of King Henry VIII, but was then secondary in importance to the Palace of Whitehall. For more than 100 years, very little was built here, but in 1665 Charles II granted Henry Jermyn, the first Earl of St Albans, the right to develop the land south of Piccadilly into a grand new residential neighbourhood for London, beginning with fourteen grand houses in what became St James's Square. By 1662, the dirt track that led to the gates of St James's Palace was paved and given a name: St James's Street. Before long it was an area made fashionable by coffee houses, chocolate houses, taverns, tailors and gentlemen's clubs, attracting style-setting aristocracy, who in turn inspired a wealth of elegant shops keen to attract the attention of the wealthy elite.

Lock & Co. is one of the oldest businesses in the area. In 1676, hatter Robert Davis opened a shop on St James's Street to cater for the bur-

Above: In medieval Europe, goldwork was used on religious vestments to inspire devotion and awe. This goldwork design uses coloured purl bullion to create a design that is vivid with colour.

Left: Two examples of calligraphy by heraldic artist and medieval illuminator, Neil Bromley, on fine vellum from William Cowley: one showing a heraldic beast bearing the arms of Richardson; the other a detail from an illuminated heraldic panel detailing the Royal Arms of Scotland.

Opposite: Rolls of sinamay fabric in the Lock & Co. workshops. Woven from the stalks of the abaca tree, it is lightweight and easily moulded making it ideal for millinery.

geoning upper classes, such as the great Whig families of Marlborough, Bedford, Devonshire and Walpole. In 1686, George Lock – importer of coffee, chocolate and tobacco – opened a coffee house a few doors away on the same street. His grandson, James, married Charles's sister, Mary, and in 1765, they moved – with their four children – to number six St James's Street and established Lock & Co., today the oldest hat shop in the world. Soon it was attracting patrons of note, including the Prime Minister, Lord Grenville. However, one of its most famous customers was Admiral Lord Nelson who visited Lock just before the Battle of Trafalgar and ordered

a 'cocked hat and cockade 7 1/8 full', a cockade being a rosette of ribbons worn in the hat as a badge of office. Other signature Lock hats include the black fedora that Oscar Wilde wore on his 1882 US lecture tour; the Coke hat (originally created for gamekeepers on the Holkham Hall estate) that Bond villain, Oddjob, wore in *Goldfinger*; and the top hat of *Alice in Wonderland*'s Mad Hatter, a character claimed to have been inspired by James Benning, the shop manager of Lock at the time.

Swaine Adeney Brigg, makers of fine leather goods and umbrellas, can trace its roots back to around 1760 when a saddler by the name of

Left: The *Conformateur*, invented by Allie Maillard in Paris in the 1840s, is used to measure the head size and shape of a person's head. It is still used by Lock & Co.'s hatters to fit hard hats.

Opposite: One of Lock & Co.'s longest serving hatters, Mr. Andrew Baselgia, steaming and shaping a felt trilby in preparation for its delivery to the fortunate customer.

Right: Considered the pinnacle of a gentleman's formal wardrobe, Lock & Co.'s lovingly restored, antique silk toppers are made from rare Parisian silk and finished with a crepe band.

Opposite: A master craftsperson in the Swaine Adeney Brigg workshops secures the small but essential 'stop pin' into the shaft of a solid oak Brigg umbrella to prevent the user opening the umbrella too far.

John Ross chose to specialise in whip making. An astute businessman as well as Master craftsman, he sold not only complete whips but also their individual components, such as the eye or loop for attaching to a crop. His work was exceptionally fine and over time he opened premises on Piccadilly and became official whip maker first to the Duke of Cumberland and later to King George III. However, when he died without heirs in 1798, he left the business to his friends and associates, James Swaine and Benjamin Slocock. In time, Slocock was replaced by Adeney (the married name of James's daughter), trading as Swaine & Adeney until 1943, when it formed a partnership with Thomas Brigg & Sons, umbrella makers of St James's.

The 1960s gave the company a welcome burst of publicity, first with *The Avengers*, which catapulted the Brigg umbrella favoured by John Steed (actor Patrick Macnee) to a new market overseas, and second with Sean Connery's debut as James Bond in *From Russia with Love*, for which the company made Bond's box-of-secrets briefcase. (Ian Fleming had, in fact, name-checked

Opposite: These traditional metal cutters are used to shape the various sizes of wallet made by Ettinger. They are decades-old and considered an important part of the company's heritage.

Right: Each Ettinger wallet is made by hand using materials, tools and hand skills that have changed little over the last hundred years. The awl used here gathers leather together into very precise pleating.

Far right: Once complete, the bifold wallet can be personalised with the client's initials embossed in gold or silver. For this, Ettinger uses a forty-year old Franklin Regal Stamping Machine.

Swaine & Adeney in his 1957 novel when describing what the briefcase contained.) Today, the company is still both manufacturer and retailer of its products, combining the skills of UK-based milliners, leather workers and umbrella framers to produce both its standard ranges and fully bespoke services.

Ettinger was founded in 1934 by Gerald Ettinger, an émigré from Germany. Having previously represented a German leather goods maker, selling their products to the UK, he moved to London and set up an office just off Regent Street. He arrived with a list of contacts from his previous role, including names of skilled leather workers in Clerkenwell. Back then, leather was a local economy with hides sourced from nearby Smithfield market and tanned with water from the river Thames, before being delivered to makers a horse-and-carriage ride away. Ettinger was ambitious to produce leather goods of exceptional quality and began by commissioning the ancient firm of Prestwick, makers of fine leather suitcases, to make prestige items to his own design. Thirty years later he was able to buy the Prestwick company and its workshops outright, and thirty years after that the firm of Ettinger was awarded a Royal Warrant to The Prince of Wales.

PEDRO DA COSTA FELGUEIRAS:
Lacquer Expert

Right: Pedro da Costa Felgueiras, founder of Lacquer Studios, surrounded by the pigments, tools and brushes of his ancient craft.

Opposite top: Ultramarine blue is ground by hand in preparation for distemper. All the pigments used are as close to the historic originals as possible.

Opposite below: A detail of one of the 80 dragons da Costa Felgueiras helped to create for the Great Pagoda of Kew, to replace those long vanished in time.

Pedro da Costa Felgueiras is a historic paint, lacquer and japanning expert, who founded Lacquer Studios in 1995 in Hoxton, London. The studio specialises in *urushi*-based Oriental lacquer and shellac-based European lacquer. Having completed his studies at the Sir John Cass School of Art, Architecture and Design (now the London Metropolitan University), where he studied for a BSc in the Conservation and Restoration of Decorative Surfaces, he soon established a repu-

tation among antiques dealers and museums for his exhaustive research and scrupulous attention to detail.

Today, as well as restoring objects for museums such as The Wallace Collection, Strawberry Hill House and the 1762 Great Pagoda of Kew (where he played a key role in the reinstatement of 80 dazzlingly iridescent dragons), da Costa Felgueiras creates bespoke work for private clients (including artists Gilbert and George) using

'What keeps me fascinated is the possibility of always being able
to create a better piece, an even more beautiful surface.'

centuries-old methods and the rarest of materials. His particular area of expertise is the history of traditional pigments, from the blue of lapis lazuli mined from a single quarry in Afghanistan and the red of crushed cochineal beetles to *caput mortuum*, a mineral purple that in the nineteenth century was briefly substituted with material made from grinding up the bodies of Egyptian mummified cats. His craft is slow and laborious, with hand-ground paints sometimes taking a month to dry and harden. Lacquering and japanning may require thirty individual layers of shellac (which is made from the *Kerria lacca* beetle), each one rubbed down before the next is applied. He favours traditional handmade tools, such as Japanese lacquer brushes made from the tails of rats or the hair of pearl divers.

None of this is born out of pretension, but is part of da Costa Felgueiras's mission to keep the skills and high standards of the past alive by restoring and creating objects of exceptional refinement and feeling.

One of his favourite projects was Strawberry Hill House. 'I worked with architectural historian, Kevin Rogers, and together we had to get into the mindset of Horace Walpole. Through historic and scientific research, we managed to find out exactly which materials and pigments were used in the mid-eighteenth century. Then my expertise was to put into practice what we had discovered, using only what would have been available at that time. It was back-breaking work but such a joy to do.

'What keeps me fascinated is the possibility of always being able to create a better piece, an even more beautiful surface. I want to know that I have created something that will hopefully outlive me and be enjoyed by others for generations to come.'

TOYE, KENNING & SPENCER:
Insignia & Regalia Maker

Opposite top left: The embroiderer follows the design by stitching the silk plate down. Embroideries such as these were supplied to European royalties at the heights of their power.

Opposite top right: Toye, Kenning & Spencer creates bespoke embroideries using Gold 2% plate wire, which is wrapped in coloured silks to recreate and match the quality of historic embroideries.

Opposite below: The company holds a Royal Warrant from HM The Queen Elizabeth II, which is testament to its expertise in gold-wire embroidery.

Toye, Kenning & Spencer has a history that goes back to 1685 when Guillaume Henri Toyé fled to Britain, disguised as a cattle dealer, after the Catholic King of France, Louis XIV, revoked the Edict of Nantes in 1685, which had previously protected those of the Protestant faith. Toyé was part of a mass exodus of around 200,000 Protestant Huguenots who fled to neighbouring countries. The Huguenots were known for their many arts and craft skills, including silk weaving, and their arrival in Britain enriched our culture enormously.

Toyé settled with his family in Bethnal Green – then aptly named Hope Town – and began weaving silk, velvet, silver lace and gold lace for the gentry. By the time his great grandson moved the business to a factory in Camden Town in 1793, the business was specialising in naval and military accoutrements. In 1835, another descendant – the now anglicised William Toye – established Toye & Co. By the 1860s, Toye commissions had spread to the USA, including (controversially and in secret) supplying uniform and accoutrements to both sides of the American Civil War. When khaki was introduced to the British army, it forced the business to look for new clients – which it found in the shape of masonic lodges and the banners and sashes of the newly emerging trades unions. However, it was the coronation of King George VI and Queen Elizabeth that gave the company a huge boost, with a six-month intensive period of producing banners, emblems, robes and insignia for the occasion. In fact, the velvet cushions on which the royal crowns were carried were made by the women of Toye's in conjunction with those from the Royal School of Needlework.

By the 1950s and the coronation of our own Queen Elizabeth II, the company was trading under the name of Toye, Kenning & Spencer. Once again, it was asked to supply banners, robes and regalia suitable for the new Elizabethan era. Toye also owns the factory of WJ Dingley in Birmingham's Jewellery Quarter, from where it has spread its offering to cover all manner of ceremonial works of art, including standards, flags and maces. Its exquisite metalwork can be seen on medals, trophies and insignia, as well as in its many collaborations with elite jewellery and fashion houses worldwide.

Deputy Chairman Frederick Toye – twelfth generation since Guillaume Henri Toyé – says of its survival, 'Having survived two World Wars, eight recessions, and a fair few pandemics, Toye, Kenning & Spencer is no stranger to hard times. Being a small family firm with full ownership of production from start to finish, combined with diverse skills across metals and textiles, we have always been able to adapt quickly to changing circumstances. Today, as global supply chains creak, the company ethos of taking risks and owning the totality of its production in the United Kingdom is looking just as relevant now as it did in 1685.'

'As global supply chains creak, the company ethos of taking risks and owning the totality of its production ... is looking as relevant now as it did in 1685.'

3

RARE & ENDANGERED

There is a lot of attention paid, rightly so, to the flora and fauna we risk losing through loss of habitat, environmental pollution and climate change. Yet we are also at risk of losing a slice of our own human history and experience through disappearing craft skills. This is a worldwide problem, not just a British one, but the good news is that having recognised the danger, many organisations are now working together to turn the tide.

Heritage Crafts first produced its Red List of Endangered Crafts in 2017 and has now produced three editions at two-year intervals. It began as a grim recording of declining craft professions, but it has now ignited a conversation nationally about what can be done to support a sector that we are in danger of losing skill by skill. Of course, there are those who might argue, what does this matter? Crafts reflect the society we live in and if that society no longer needs or wants swill baskets, parchment, clogs or fans, then so be it. However, the response to that must surely be the sadness when a craft slips into invisibility. By the time people notice it has gone, it is too late.

In 2021, the Red List included 244 crafts. Of these, four are now officially extinct: cricket ball making, lacrosse stick making, paper mould and deckle making (a deckle being the wooden frame used in manual papermaking) and gold beating.

If the permanent loss of cricket ball making seems a tragedy in the country that gave the world this sport and considers it part of its national culture, even more shocking is the fact that cricket bat making seems set to join it before too long. The last lacrosse stick maker (a game appropriated by Europeans colonisers from indigenous people of Canada) was Tom Beckett of Hatters-leys, who retired in 2014. This Eccles-based company had begun by making cricket bats and then added lacrosse sticks to its offering in 1912, when the game was immensely popular.

The last paper mould and deckle maker in the UK was Ron McDonald, who passed away in 2017. He had served a five-year apprenticeship from the age of sixteen at his father's company, Amies & Son Ltd in Kent. The loss of this craft has had a knock-on effect on other crafts, including commercial, handmade paper making. Gold beating is the process of hammering gold into fine sheets of gold leaf, an extremely labour-intensive process. The last UK gold beaters were employed by Habberley Meadows of Birmingham, which tried unsuccessfully to keep the skill alive despite competition from abroad, but in the end was defeated by cheaper imports.

The Critically Endangered list – those with a shrinking base of makers, little financial liability, limited training opportunities or no mechanism to pass on skills and knowledge – include twenty newcomers. These range from barometer makers and sporran makers to horsehair weavers and pointe shoemakers (as worn by ballerinas).

The Endangered category – those with sufficient craft skills to transmit to the next generation of makers, but with an ageing demographic and shrinking market share – also included some 'new to 2021' categories. For the first time hat makers and kilt makers are listed, as are type founders and lithographers.

Overall, the world of music seems particularly badly hit, with British piano makers, harp makers, bagpipe makers, bow makers, brass instrument makers, free reed instrument makers (a category that includes accordions), keyboard

Right: Thomas Kennedy, one of the UK's last masters of the ancient art of *scagliola*, created this verdant woodland scene using little more than gypsum plaster, animal glue and raw pigments.

Above: Thomas Greenaway uses the traditional hand bowsaw – the *archetto* – to cut semi-precious stones and marbles into elaborate pietra dura designs.

instrument makers, percussion instrument makers, woodwind instrument makers and flute makers all either Endangered or Critically Endangered. The equestrian world fares little better with horse collar makers, side saddle makers and whip makers now in serious decline. There are also crafts here that many people might not even recognise as such, including neon benders, diamond cutters, surgical instrument makers and glass eye makers.

Just as species can only be saved by conserving habitats, crafts can only be saved if enough people make a positive choice to support them, by paying that little bit extra for handmade objects as opposed to mass-produced imports. It is also crucial to encourage a new generation of makers while there is still time, so they can learn skills from Master craftspeople, whether through apprenticeships or specialised training.

Heritage Crafts should be applauded for their trail-blazing work in this area, which has now been picked up and amplified by its collaboration with the Michelangelo Foundation (see page 21). It has led the way in showing how important it is to bang the drum for something in which one believes. Since 2019, it has provided grants of up to £2,000 ($2,600) to thirty-five individual practitioners through its Endangered Craft Fund. It has also campaigned for national recognition of the UK's National Living Treasures – a term first used by the Japanese government for individuals recognised as Preservers of Important Intangible Cultural Properties.

The Good News

It is understandable when confronted by the hard facts of Heritage Crafts' Red List to assume it is one-way traffic only. In fact, there are exam-

Above: Greenaway at work on the restoration of a William Burgess *pietra dura* table from Lotherton Hall, carefully using a needle to remove the remains of pine resin.

ples of crafts that have gone from endangered to viable in recent years.

Gilding is one example. Having appeared on the Red List of 2017 and 2019, it has been removed from the latest edition thanks to renewed interest in its use in restoration, lettering and signage. More surprisingly, rug tufting has also been taken off the list, thanks largely to a surge of popularity amongst a younger generation who have taken it up and shared their creations on Instagram and Tik Tok. Devon stave baskets are similar to the Sussex trug insofar as they are made from split staves bound by a wooden rim and handle, but unlike their Sussex counterparts, whose staves are bent into place, the staves remain rigid. When they were listed in 2017, they were very nearly extinct, but there are now five professional makers, one trainee and a variety of stave basket courses.

Occasionally, latent crafts can even be revived. One such example is wooden bowl turning using a pole lathe, a technique which had virtually disappeared by the 1950s. It was revived by Robin Wood MBE, Trustee of Heritage Arts, and is now a thriving and viable craft with many professional makers, keen amateurs and students.

Rare Crafts

Not all crafts fall within the confines of the heritage sector. Some are labelled rare rather than endangered.

Thomas Kennedy, for example, has spent over twenty-five years perfecting the craft of *scagliola*, a sixteenth-century plasterwork technique practised by only a handful of artists in the world today. *Scagliola* is thought to have originated in southern Germany as a direct response to the growing obsession among Europeans for coloured marbles, inspired by the first excavations of Ancient Rome. The technique replicates marble and other stones but is, in fact, comprised of gypsum plaster, animal glue and raw pigments in a process that is almost entirely intuitive. It proved to be a highly effective way of imitating marble inlaid with precious stones: the *pietra dura* (translated as hard stone) with which wealthy Romans decorated their floors and walls.

Initially fascinated with the traditional use of the material, Kennedy now focuses on using it in a more contemporary setting. Together with his sculptor wife, Louisa, he runs his own workshop, Kennedy Design Studios, creating unique furniture and sculptural pieces that give new relevance to this rare and beautiful technique. Designers often commission him to create a unique marble surface that still looks natural despite being unlike anything that can be found at the marble quarries. Such a finish can only be made in *scagliola* and furthermore can only be made to the recipe that is unique to Kennedy. The client will not be able to obtain the same finish from any other *scagliola* studio, either in the UK or internationally.

In his view, *scagliola* is in a healthier position than it was fifty years ago, in part because of the efforts of firms such as Hayles & Howe who have championed the art and raised its profile.

It is a similar story with Thomas Greenaway of Greenaway Mosaics, a specialist in hand-crafted *pietra dura*. While *scagliola* is a technique used to imitate *pietra dura*, Greenaway is one of the very few in the UK who has mastered the original skill, and thought to be the only person practising here to have been trained by Master craftsmen in Florence. Each piece of *pietra dura* is created by inlaying highly polished precious and semi-precious stones into marble, in effect 'painting with stone' – a technique similar to creating marquetry designs with wood. It was whilst visiting the Opificio delle Pietre Dure museum in Florence while on an Art History Abroad course

that his fascination with the craft began. This is where *pietra dura* flourished during the Renaissance, with Florentine artists in great demand as they travelled across Europe to work in royal and noble households. Greenaway later studied at the Chippendale International School of Furniture in Scotland, where he became passionate about marquetry work, and then worked as an apprentice in a number of *pietra dura* workshops in Florence, where he was trained by some of the most eminent Masters in Florentine mosaics. On his return to the UK, he established Greenaway Mosaics in 2010.

Always a slow and painstaking process, *pietra dura* requires tools and techniques of ancient origin, such as mastery of the traditional hand bow-saw – the *archetto*. It also requires the use of an extensive range of colourful semi-precious stones and marbles, which in turn means building up an understanding of both the stones and ancient lapidary techniques. Each stone to be used is carefully selected for its texture and colour and then sliced to a thickness of between two and four millimetres (about one-eighth of an inch), levelled, and a paper template for each individual stone is made. These templates are glued to the surface of the stone, and then slate is precisely applied to the underside before the stone is cut out using the hand-saw. Each piece is then filed by hand and fitted together like a puzzle. The area of marble into which the stones are to be inserted is then carefully cut out; the stones are inlaid with precision; and the finished work is highly polished. Polishing is done by hand, a method handed down from generation to generation over centuries, using a piece of agate and various fine grades of emery powder mixed with water.

One of the studio's most prestigious commissions was the coat of arms of Richard III for the monarch's entombment in Leicester Cathedral in 2015, which took over two months to make and was constructed from over 350 pieces of stone, many of them valuable and rare.

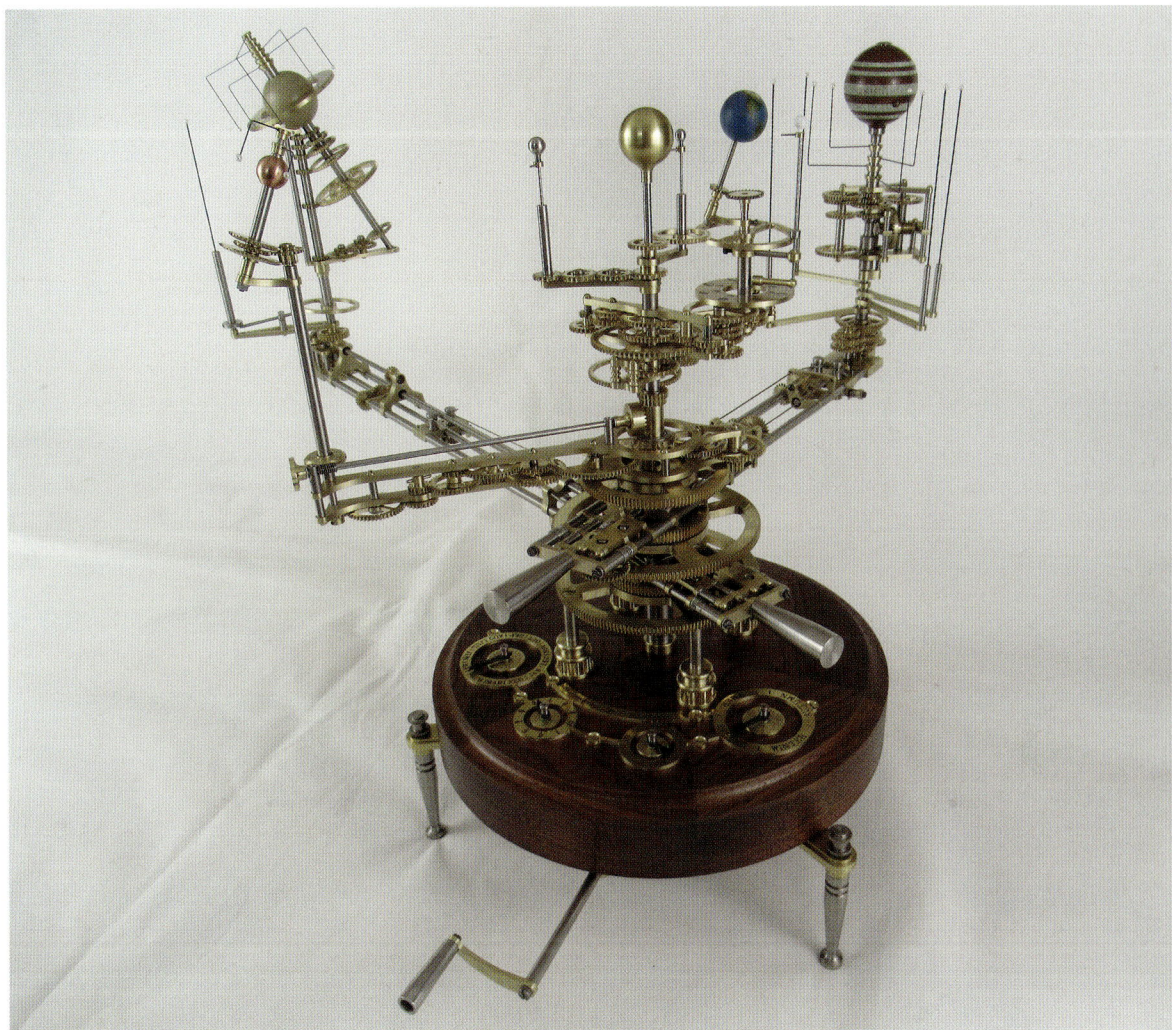

Right: The Six Planet Genesis Orrery by Staines & Son. An independent drive is supplied to each of the planets and its moons, greatly increasing the fluidity and smoothness of movement.

The Unusual and the Unexpected

Sometimes it is easy to fall into the trap of thinking of craft as something familiar and predictable. In fact, it has the power both to surprise and delight. Take orreries, for example – the making of which is on the Critically Endangered list. An orrery is a mechanical model of the solar system, illustrating and predicting the relative positions and motions of planets and their moons. In 1713, clockmaker George Graham created one of the first such models and presented it to Charles Boyle, the Fourth Earl of Orrery and Fellow of the Royal Society, naming it an orrery in his honour. In fact, the idea for an orrery goes back to ancient civilisations. According to Cicero's writing in the first century BCE, the Greek polymath Posidonius constructed a planetary model.

Derek Staines, co-founder of Staines & Son, was originally a highly trained tool maker. When he retired, he began making model steam engines as a hobby, but was inspired to make his first orrery after seeing one for the first time at Christie's in London. It was a long process of problem-solving, including the making of the high-precision tools he needed, before he perfected the art. Each orrery involves both incredible technical skill and a huge knowledge of astronomy. For example, the Inner Planet Orrery features the rotation of Mercury, Venus and Mars, each at their relative speed. A single solar day on Mercury lasts 176 Earth days. Venus turns in retrograde (the opposite direction to Earth) and is even slower, with a single solar day lasting 243 Earth days. No wonder then that these highly complex

models are not quick to create, with lead times typically between three and five years. Just as Derek passed on the love and the skill of orrery making to his engineer son, Timothy, so Timothy plans to pass it on to his nephew and other members of the family.

Within the heritage sector there are many makers who dedicate their professional lives to highly specialist skills. David Snoo Wilson, for example, is a metal caster and one of the last bell founders in the UK (a Critically Endangered craft). He established the Ore and Ingot travelling foundry in 2012, using it to cast bells in the middle of the Nevada desert for the Burning Man festival and even on site at wedding ceremonies. A QEST Scholar, he used his funding to explore the folklore of bell founding and how different alloys and casting techniques affect harmonics. The idea for the travelling foundry came about through his passion for teaching; he has run courses across the UK and Europe, sharing his knowledge of metal casting and bell founding.

Far left: A fine-tuned bell cast at the Burning Man festival in Nevada as part of the Ore and Ingot travelling foundry.

Top left: The placing of a silver ring into the mobile furnace to make a wedding bell, once a medieval ritual to create a bell with 'a silvery ring'.

Below left: Wilson taking a bell from its ceramic mould, the moment of truth for any bell founder as the bell could crack if miscast during firing.

Left: David Snoo Wilson, founder of Ore and Ingot, in his workshop close to Bristol from where he teaches hands-on foundry skills.

Greg Rowland is the second generation of Mike Rowland & Son, wheelwrights and coach builders (wheelwrighting is on the Endangered list). Mike started the business in 1964, specialising in traditional wheelwrighting of carriages and carts and gaining a Royal Warrant from HM The Queen in 2005. Part of the business today is dedicated to military wheel and cannon restorers, as well as horse-drawn vehicles. However, their family's history in the trade stretches back to the fourteenth century. Greg joined his father in the business in 1991 after a career in the armed forces and as a blacksmith. Both men are Master Wheelwrights. With over 80 years of experience between them, they and their team of two produce around 200 specialist wheels each year at the Devon workshop where Mike based the business from the start. These range from State coaches to wooden bicycles, with every wheel made bespoke and to commission. The craft demands a range of skills from wood turning and blacksmithing to engineering and joinery. Over the years, they have taught a number of apprentices a trade which takes at least three years to master. Greg's son-in-law, Sam, is the current apprentice, so it's hoped he will keep wheelwrighting in the family.

Crispinians makes lasts and trees for shoes and boots, supplying bespoke shoemakers and private clients with traditionally crafted wooden models. A last is the wooden mould on which the shoes are created, custom made to the client's foot; boot trees replicate the size and shape of the customer's leg. Last making is considered an Endangered Craft by Heritage Craft and Crispinians is the only remaining hand-crafted, non-factory commercial last maker in the UK, with owner Steven Lowe continuing the business as a team of one. The few other surviving last makers are employed full-time by companies such as John Lobb (see pages 164–165) where he himself was apprenticed forty years ago. With fewer bespoke shoemakers able to make their businesses viable, we are losing our last and tree makers. In a bid

Above: A collection of lasts and trees made by Steven Lowe of Crispinians, one of a handful of remaining independent commercial last makers and tree makers in the UK.

Opposite: A rattan weaver at Soane Britain's workshop, the last of its kind in the UK, saved from closure by Lulu Lytle, who has single-handedly revived English rattan production.

to keep the skills alive, Lowe runs introductory courses with Michael Semple (also previously a last maker for John Lobb) at Last Maker House, the Crispinians workshop in Eastbourne, Sussex.

Successfully Saved

It is always heartening to hear of crafts being saved through the passion and commitment of just one or two individuals.

Take the once-dominant Leicester rattan industry. While the product itself comes from the South East Asian jungle, it was so plentiful in the nineteenth century that it was used as a packing material for US-bound goods. In the 1840s, Cyril Wakefield saw a Boston dock nearly buried in rattan packing and recognised the potential of a material that is both solid and flexible. He established a factory in Massachusetts, making lightweight rattan furniture and baby carriages. In 1907, inspired by fine Austrian and German willow and cane work, Harry Hardy Peach and his friend Benjamin Fletcher (who was head of Leicester School of Art) formed Dryad Furniture near Leicester. By 1911, the company employed

Left and centre: Greg Rowland and Mike Rowland, Master wheelwrights and coach-builders – a craft skill now on the Endangered list according to Heritage Crafts. Photographed here with their current apprentice, Sam Phillips.

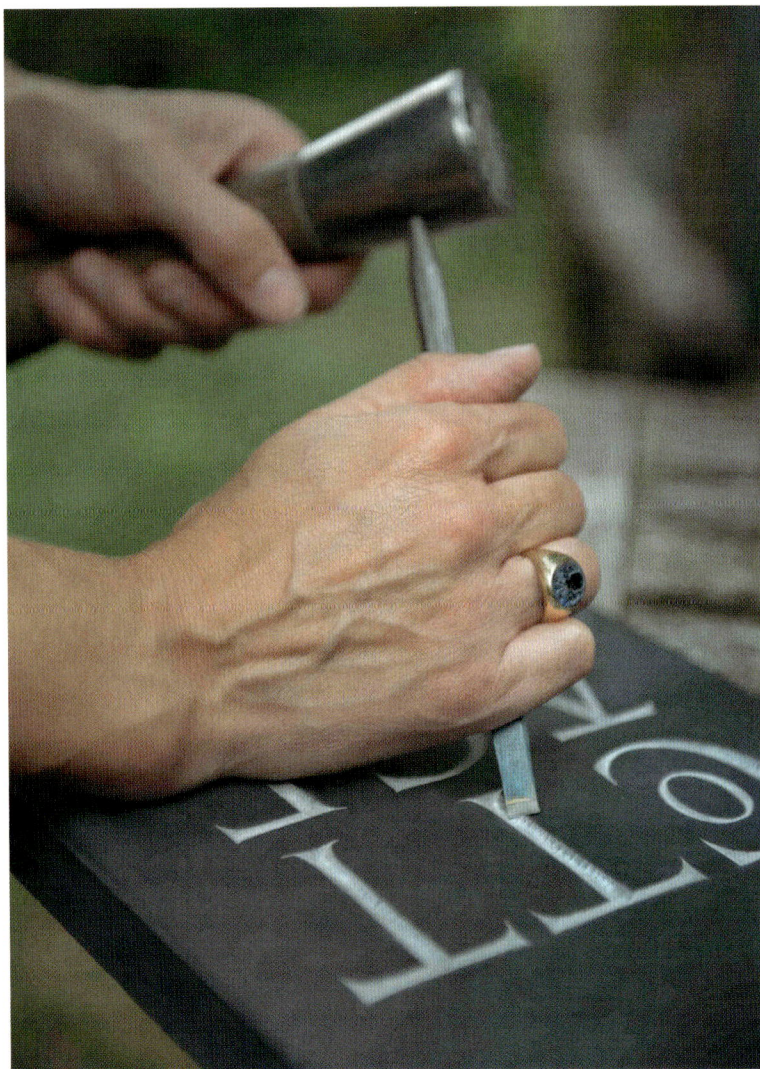

over fifty workers and its success inspired others to set up in competition, which led to about nine Midlands workshops making furnishings from rattan and willow by the outbreak of World War I. The last surviving rattan-weaving workshop, Angraves, was founded in 1912 and at its peak employed over 80 men, with projects that included the refurbishment of the QE2.

By 2010, every other rattan factory in the area had closed down because of competition from the Far East. Angraves would have suffered the same fate had it not been for the intervention of Lulu Lytle, co-founder of Soane Britain, who preserved the skills for the next generation by buying relevant machinery from the dissolved company in 2011 and re-employing their only two weavers practising traditional rattan craft skills. Soane's sculptural hanging lights, scalloped chairs and rippled tables re-energised English rattan production and introduced it to a new audience, both in the UK and internationally. Not only that, but the company has its own thriving rattan apprenticeship scheme, now in its ninth year, a determined bid to protect this almost-extinct British industry for the future.

The Lettering Arts Trust came about through personal tragedy. In 1988, founder Harriet Frazer MBE wanted to find someone to make a memorial for her step-daughter, Sophie, who had died suddenly at the age of twenty-six. Hand letter carving was then a diminishing trade and it was both hard to find a letter-carving artist to create a unique design and to navigate the many church regulations about what was acceptable on a memorial stone. Eventually, she found and commissioned artist Simon Verity, but she formed Memorials by Artists to help others in the same situation. In 2012, this evolved into the Lettering Arts Trust, with around 75 letter-carving artists on its register. While memorial stones are a big part of its output, its mission is to keep the art of hand letter carving alive in an increasingly digital and

Above: Lisi Ashbridge letter cutting into Welsh slate using dummy and chisel. The tools and methods used are largely unchanged since Roman times.

Opposite: *Walking East* by Charlotte Howarth cut in green slate to reveal the colour of the stone. It can take thirty minutes to cut just one letter.

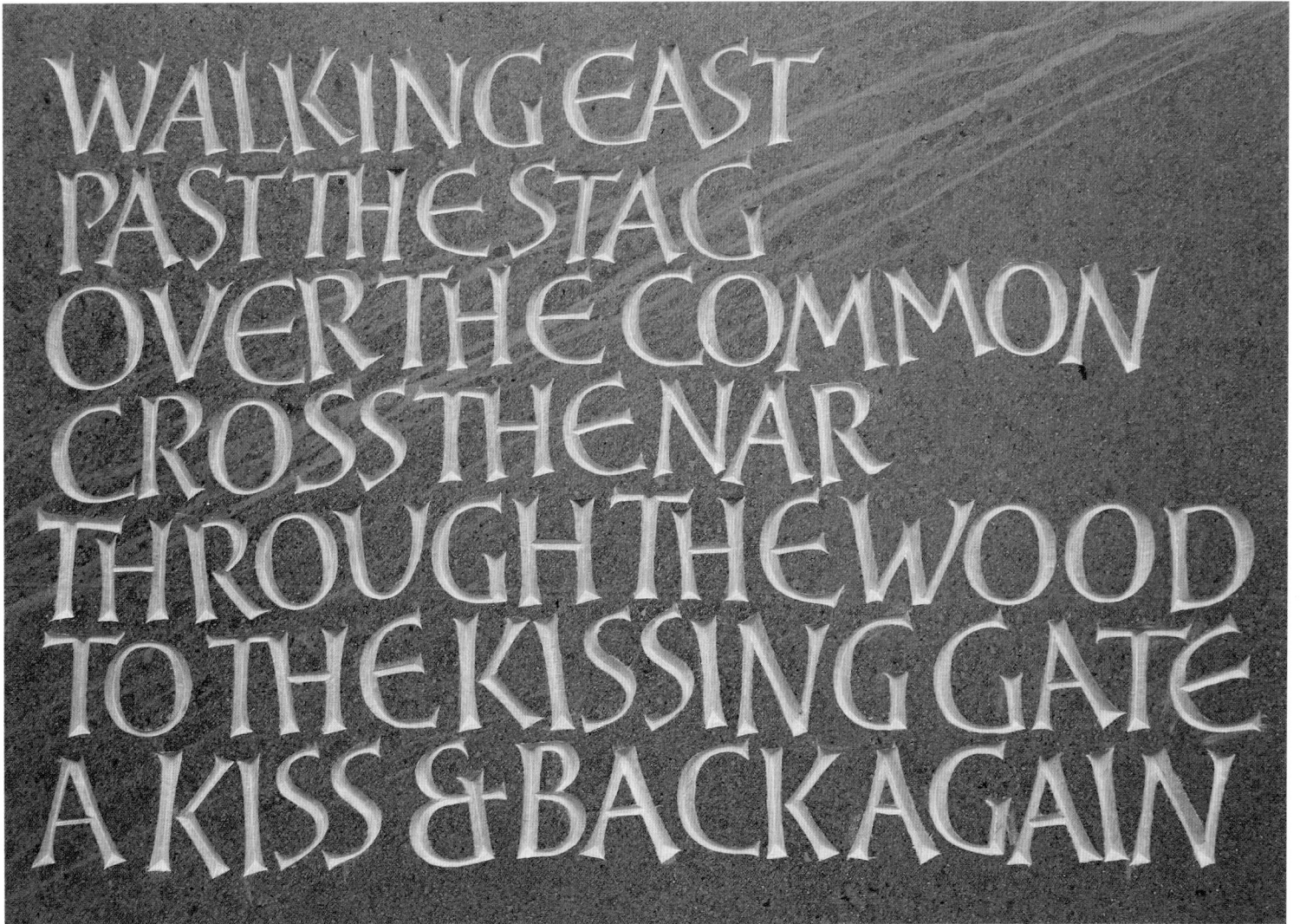

WALKING EAST
PAST THE STAG
OVER THE COMMON
CROSS THE NAR
THROUGH THE WOOD
TO THE KISSING GATE
A KISS & BACK AGAIN

mechanised world. To this end, it holds exhibitions, talks and demonstrations, and helps people through the process of commissioning a piece, be it a memorial, sundial, plaque, art work, architectural façade or unique object.

One of the beauties of the craft is that it is largely unchanged since Roman times, with letter cutters still using a chisel and dummy (a sort of mallet) to cut each letter into the stone. It can take thirty minutes to create just one letter, with the carver being calligrapher, designer and cutter. Through the generosity of its supporters, the Lettering Arts Trust has funded nine two-year apprenticeships to date. In 2014, it also launched its Journeyman scheme, providing experienced letter cutters with the chance to focus on a specific area of their craft under the guidance of a Master letter cutter. Through the Trust's efforts, hand letter carving is now safeguarded for the immediate future.

OWEN JONES:
Oak Swill Maker *Critically Endangered*

Oak swills are sturdy baskets made from young, coppiced oak. The first records of 'swill' baskets date from the fifteenth century, but of course they probably go back much further than that. Originally a cottage industry of the southern Lake District, they are part of the coppicing tradition of the oak woods of the Furness fells. However, swills proved to be so strong and durable that during the Industrial Revolution, the trade moved from cottages into swill workshops (swillshops). They had many uses, including as scuttles in the coal and iron industries; harvesting root crops on farms; collecting bracken from the fells; and by cockle pickers at Morecombe Bay – in fact the name 'swill basket' comes from swilling the cockles in water to rinse them. Domestically, they were used for laundry, logs and even as cradles. Owen Jones was taught the skill over thirty years

Opposite: Jones tears billets of oak into thin strips, having first softened the wood by boiling it for hours. As he works, he divides the billets into shorter spelks and longer taws, determining their use.

Right: Jones making swill baskets in his workshop in the Rusland Valley of the southern Lake District, where he coppices local woods to source the oak and hazel with which he works.

Above: Standing at the door of his workshop where he has kept the ancient art of swill making alive for the last thirty-five years.

ago by a retired swiller called John Barker, who in turn had learnt the craft in a swillshop back in the 1930s. He now continues the local tradition, coppicing his own wood in the Rusland valley.

To make one swill takes about four to five hours. First, slender, coppiced oak (about twenty years old) is sawn into various lengths, cleft using wedges and a lat axe into lengthwise *billets* and then boiled for several hours in a large, metal trough. Once softened, the billets are taken out one at a time and torn into thin strips. The shorter ribs (or *spelks*) are left thicker, and the longer *taws* are riven finer. It is important to work quickly during this part of the process as the material cools down when split, losing its flexibility. Spelks and taws are then smoothed and shaped with knives before being woven into the form of the swill basket. The rim – or *bool* – of the basket is a hazel rod, steamed and bent into the characteristic oval shape. It is hard, physical work that demands a great deal of knowledge and experience to do well. Apprenticeships used to take five years to master the trade at the height of swill making.

Swills are made in standardised sizes, with evocative names such as Li'le Nick. The spelks that determine the shape and size of the swill basket also have specific names, such as lapping spelk, bool spelk and kessen, allowing them to be assembled in sequence – important in the context of a swillshop.

Jones is one of only two full-time practitioners of the craft, but he is generous with his time, running workshops and short courses, including teaching Lorna Singleton (see page 110). He has lost none of his love for the craft, cutting hazels for bools in the winter and peeling oak in the spring, ready to make the swills throughout the summer. Working in the woods is something of which he never tires. 'Time has a different dimension when you are surrounded by nature. It is always an uplifting experience: every tree is different and each swill leaves me to go on its own journey.'

'Time has a different dimension when you are surrounded by nature...
Every tree is different and each swill leaves me to go on its own journey.'

Top left: Dressing spelks on the swiller's mare. Each one needs to be smoothed and dressed before being woven into the form of a basket.

Below left: As he weaves each basket, he uses the bodkin to help fit the spelks into place. Once completed, a hazel rod will be steamed and bent to form the bool or rim.

Above right: Some of the traditional oak swills made by Owen Jones. Each one is a standardised size, with its own traditional name such as Li'le Nick and Peck.

ILANA BELSKY:
Diamond Cutter *Critically Endangered*

Diamonds have been used in jewellery and decorative artefacts for thousands of years. Their popularity as the centrepiece of engagement rings began in the 1930s and continues to this day, driving a huge international trade. Diamond cutting is a highly skilled process that involves shaping a diamond from a rough stone into a faceted gem and it is now on the Heritage Crafts' Critically Endangered list.

The centres of diamond cutting and jewellery making within the UK are Hatton Garden in London and the Jewellery Quarter of Birmingham. Ilana Belsky of Belsky Diamonds trained with her father in Hatton Garden, (he was himself a Master cutter) and now bases her workshop in the Jewellery Quarter, with an office in Hatton Garden. She is one of six surviving proponents of the craft in Britain and the only woman operating in this male-dominated industry.

Right: Ilana Belsky at her bench beginning the pain-staking process of cutting a diamond – a process that can take two weeks for just one stone.

The first step for a cutter is to assess the stone, which helps determine the style and shape of the finished cut. A rough stone can be cut in any number of ways, but the skilled cutter will always try to maximise its true brilliance; size is secondary to the fire of a beautifully faceted gemstone. A stone might have to be cleaved or laser-sawn into two or more pieces and then placed on a spinning axle to be rounded off. Once the diamond is cut, it undergoes polishing – the most time-consuming and skilled part of the process. For this, it is placed on a rotating arm (the *tang*) and polished against a spinning wheel (the *scaife*) with extreme precision. The cutter also establishes symmetry and maximum light reflection through a process of faceting from blocking to brillianteering – a round, brilliant-cut diamond will have 57 facets, all in perfect proportion and symmetry. If any facets are cut too deep or too shallow, they will leak light and result in a loss of brilliance. It is not possible to correct a diamond that is already polished without recutting, so any alteration results in a loss in the diamond's weight and therefore its value.

The entire process can take up to two weeks for one stone, with no two stones ever the same. One of the biggest challenges is holding the diamond in the tools. Unlike lapidists, who glue stones to the *dop* (the cup in which the stone is held), cutters must clamp them with claws, meaning the diamond can 'jump' and fly out of the tool at high speed. For this reason, they often have to file and adjust tools to each stone's unique shape.

Belsky's craft requires dedication, attention to detail, artistic vision and an ability to unravel a complex set of decisions. Her dream is to reintroduce diamond cutting back into the UK. 'When I started diamond cutting, I didn't know it would become such a passion for me. Transforming these stones that nature produced billions of years ago, into gems that will be enjoyed beyond my lifetime, fills me with awe every day.'

'Transforming these stones that nature produced billions of years ago, into gems that will be enjoyed beyond my lifetime, fills me with awe.'

Above: Raw diamonds arrive in Belsky's studio. The entire process of cutting a stone can take a fortnight and no two stones are ever cut in the same way.

Left: Cut diamonds gleam and sparkle. The aim of a cutter is to achieve the optimal brilliance, releasing the fire within a beautifully proportioned, faceted gemstone.

4

ROOTS & REGION

Previous spread: A view
of Loch Ceos (Cheois
in Gaelic) on the Isle
of Lewis. Harris cloth
applies to the whole of
the Outer Hebrides.

One of the beauties of discovering age-old craft stories is how often they relate to the history and geography of the region in which they once flourished. Many crafts are directly related to the landscape around them through materials and resources. Coco Chanel may have made Harris Tweed famous, for example, but it has sustained its desirability as fashions have peaked and waned, in part because only cloth woven in the Outer Hebrides can be authenticated as Harris Tweed. Pure virgin wools, principally taken from flocks reared on the Scottish mainland, are first sent to one of the Hebridean mills and then delivered as beams of wool yarn to the home of the individual weaver, before being returned to the mill to be finished. Protected by an Act of Parliament, every length produced must be certified by the Harris Tweed Authority with the Harris Tweed® Orb certification mark. Weavers are all self-employed and may weave for more than one mill if they wish. By law, no weaving can take place at the mills. This unusual structure is one reason why this famous cloth is so highly valued, another, of course, being the depth and texture of the cloth, constructed of many different dyed wools spun into one yarn.

The Potteries of Staffordshire are another example of regional craft, founded on the Six Towns of Burslem, Fenton, Hanley, Longton, Stoke and Tunstall (now known collectively as Stoke-on-Trent). In the late seventeenth century – before the Industrial Revolution – pottery making was already shaping the landscape. However, it was the development of canal transport systems in the eighteenth century that allowed china clay from Cornwall to be imported, facilitating the production of creamware and bone china. Josiah Wedgwood dug out the first sod of earth for the canal in 1766, erecting his Etruria Works that same year. His many innovations included black basalt, jasperware and Queen's Ware – created for Queen Charlotte, wife of King George III – which in turn led to a 944-piece commission from Empress Catherine of Russia. Although the hand-painted decoration showed British scenes copied from prints – over 1,000 in total – at the Empress's request each piece also depicted a green frog within a shield, earning it the name of the Frog Service. Companies such as Royal Doulton, Spode and Minton – equally innovative in their time – were also founded in The Potteries, cementing the reputation of Staffordshire ceramics across the globe.

Today, Burleigh Pottery is the last pottery in the world to use the traditional skill of underglaze tissue transfer printing, an English process dating back over 200 years, creating blue-and-white ceramics that are immediately recognisable.

However, it was Ironbridge in Shropshire that was the centre of the manufacturing of ceramic floor and wall tiles in the Victorian period, likened to the Silicon Valley of the day because of its creative vision and innovation. Craven Dunnill was established here in 1872 by Henry Powell Dunnill, building its own factory at Jackfield in the Ironbridge Gorge that year. It became renowned throughout the Empire for its tiles, particularly encaustic floor tiles and highly decorative wall tiles.

Jackfield is now a World Heritage site, commemorating Britain's industrial roots, and the Craven Dunnill factory was acquired by the Ironbridge Gorge Museum Trust in the 1950s.

Above: Bobbins of spun
yarn at a mill, ready to be
sent to the Isle of Harris
weavers in their homes
to make the authentic
Harris Tweed® cloth.

Right: The Burleigh
mould archive includes
tens of thousands of
shapes dating as far
back as 1851. Known
as blocks and cases,
these original plaster
designs are used to create
working moulds.

Right: The Burleigh mould maker is highly skilled and is one of only a handful left who are masters of the craft in the pottery towns of Staffordshire.

The company moved to nearby Bridgnorth, evolving over the years into a wholesaler and retailer of tiles from around the world. However, in the year 2000, manufacturing returned to the original Ironbridge factory and Craven Dunnill Jackfield is now the oldest surviving purpose-built factory in the world, the leading manufacturer of traditionally styled decorative tiles for restoration projects internationally. It also has a second site at Burslem in The Potteries. Its team of technical experts and creative artisans enables it to take moulds of original tiles, remodel the profiles where required, and faithfully manufacture exact replicas. However, increasingly its skills are in demand not only from the heritage sector, but also for contemporary projects, including mural designs, hospitality settings and transport environments, such as the London Underground.

It has also collaborated closely with Burleigh Pottery, re-imagining its highly popular *Calico* blue-and-white pattern into pressed and cast wall tiles. *Calico* was first listed in the Burleigh pattern book in 1968 and has been in continuous production ever since but, in fact, was based originally on a nineteenth-century indigo fabric. It is encouraging to see these two heritage firms combining forces to create a collection still desirable and relevant today.

For over two millennia, Welsh slate has formed a part of local construction. In fact, records from

Opposite left: A master craftsperson at Craven Dunnill Jackfield delicately hand-carving a design onto a plaster mould ready for firing.

Opposite right: Each Craven Dunnill Jackfield tile is carefully back-stamped by hand, a sign of its provenance and authenticity.

Right: Italian lime plasterwork or stucco – such as this magnificent overmantel by Geoffrey Preston MBE (see page 228) – inspired the more rustic tradition of pargetting often seen on buildings in East Anglia.

the Roman fort of Segontium in Caernarfon show that slate was used there in 77CE. In the thirteenth century, Welsh roofing slates were shipped around Britain and into the low countries of Europe, where they were recognised as a superior material and used on high-status buildings such as cathedrals and monasteries. The beginning of the Industrial Revolution in the eighteenth century increased demand further. Many small quarries were bought up and combined into super-quarries, such as the Penrhyn Quarry, which by the 1870s was selling over 100,000 tonnes (110,000 tons) of slate per year and employed over 3,000 people. While demand dropped off substantially in the twentieth century as man-made materials dominated, in the last fifty years there has been a resurgence of demand. Today, Welsh Slate owns and operates both the Penrhyn and Cwt-y-Bugail quarries, supplying high-quality slate to projects around the world, not only for roofing and hard landscaping, but for use within interiors as fireplaces, kitchen worktops and floor tiles.

Geography and History

Interestingly, some crafts were a response to the lack of something, rather than its abundance. Pargetting (or pargeting) is the English term for *stucco*, an Italian word for ornamental lime plasterwork. The word is thought to derive from 'porgeter': to roughcast a wall. Most ancient pargetting is a mix of slaked lime, sand, hair and 'secret ingredients' known only to individual pargeters – said to include stable urine, soot, tallow, cheese, dung and even blood. In its wet state, it can be used to make a huge variety of patterns, including ribbons, chevrons, scallops, fantails, herringbones, floral motifs and coats-of-arms. As well as being decorative, lime plaster is waterproof, a way of protecting timber-framed buildings from the elements. It is especially prevalent in areas where there is little local stone with which to build, and this might explain why it is mainly associated with the counties of East Anglia, where land is marshy as opposed to rocky. The oldest surviving examples go back to the fifteenth and sixteenth centuries, with patterns often stamped, combed or drawn freehand with a stick.

Royalty and nobility prized Italian *stucco* highly: Henry VIII commissioned Italian crafts-men to model plaster figures of gods and god-desses over the outside of Nonsuch Palace (later destroyed). In the seventeenth and eighteenth centuries, wealthy young gentlemen on the Grand Tour invited Italian and Swiss plasterers to come to their imposing English country estates to decorate ceilings, overmantels and wall panels. However, this meant local pargeters found an eager client base in the wealthy yeomen classes – such as the wool merchants of Essex and Suffolk – who wished to emulate the aristocracy. As a result, some wonderful pargeting examples can still be seen today in towns such as Saffron Walden, Ipswich, Lavenham and Clare.

In contrast, the silk industry of Suffolk was shaped by politics rather than geography. In 1609, King James I had tried to establish silk making in England by encouraging the planting of mulberry trees, on which silkworms feed. However, the gov-ernment of the day supplied black mulberries for planting and not the white variety on which the silkworm relies. Over 70 years later, success in silk weaving was achieved owing to the persecution of Protestants in France, which led to many of them seeking refuge in neighbouring Britain and the Low Countries of Europe. The Huguenots were known for their many arts and craft skills, includ-ing silk weaving. A community was established in Spitalfields in London where they founded a thriving English silk industry. A hundred years later, industrial disputes led to Masters of the trade looking for new premises outside London but still within reach of the capital. Towns such as Sudbury in Suffolk already had many skilled tex-tile workers who were happy to turn their hand to silk weaving for wages far higher than they were usually paid, but far lower than London wage levels. By the mid-nineteenth century, there were about 600 silk looms in Sudbury alone.

Today, five silk companies can still be found in Sudbury. Gainsborough – formerly the Gains-borough Silk Weaving Company – holds a Royal Warrant from HM The Queen. Its fabrics have been used in the decoration of Buckingham Pal-ace, St James's Palace, Kensington Palace and Windsor Castle – including restoration work after the fire of 1992. It has also supplied fabric for the interiors of carriages at State occasions, including the weddings of HRH Prince William to Catherine Middleton and HRH Prince Harry to Meghan Markle.

As well as craft skills being transported from one region to another as a result of the politics of the day, there are other examples driven by the influence of wealthy patrons. Huguenot silk

Right: Wooden bobbins wound with silk at the Gainsborough mill in Suffolk, long the centre of the English silk industry.

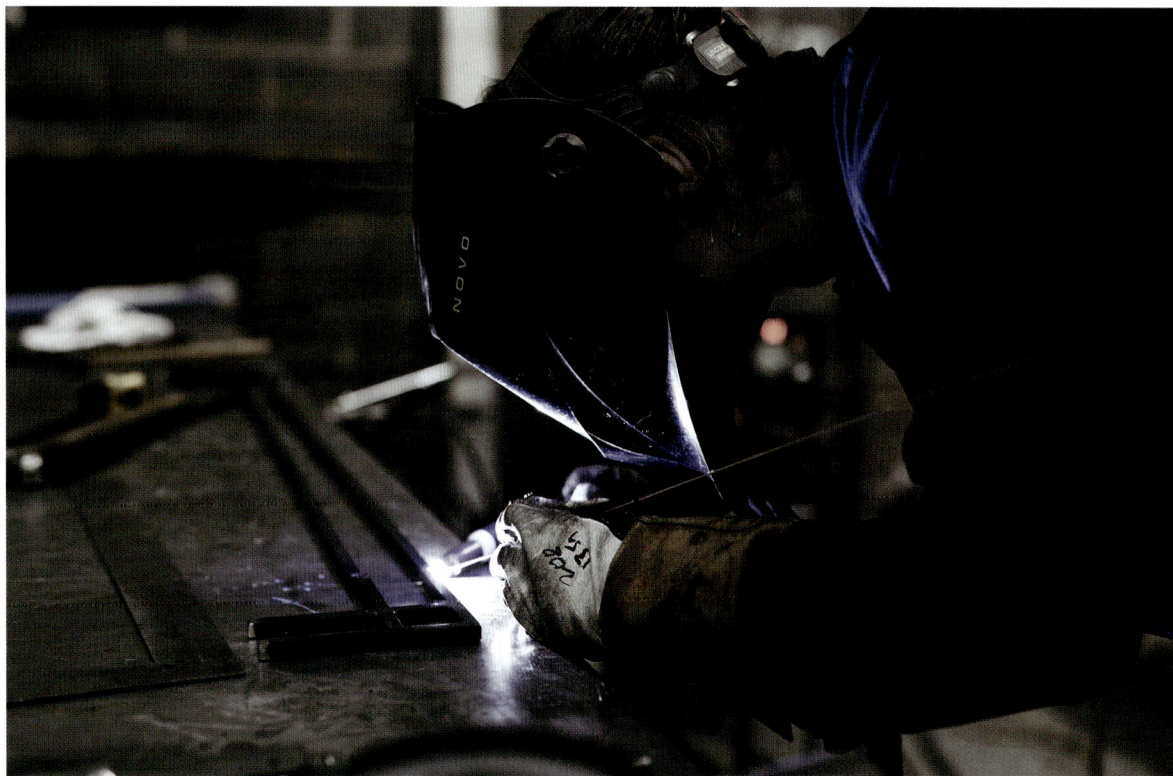

Right: **Right:** Novocastrian crafts every piece in its Tyneside workshop, using the traditional skills of welders to make these highly complex designs.

Opposite: This brass, patinated screen by Novocastrian is part of the Seven Sisters of Tyne series. This particular one is inspired by the Queen Elizabeth II bridge that links Gateshead to Newcastle-upon-Tyne.

weavers had also established their trade at Merton Abbey Mills close to London, attracted to the river Wandle not only as a source of power but because it was a chalk stream ideally suited to the washing, dyeing and printing of textiles. By 1792, it was one of the hardest-working rivers in Europe with over 1,000 people employed there. While the huge, steam-powered mills of the Midlands dominated the textile industry in terms of mass production, the Wandle Valley textile industry led the way in quality and innovation. Between 1881 and 1888, William Morris produced his textiles here. Later, in 1904, the site was purchased by Liberty – a business synonymous with the Arts and Crafts – which produced hand-blocked textiles at Merton until the 1970s.

Melding Past with Present

The North-East of England was once a centre of shipbuilding and mining. Today, the metalworking skills once so important to the region have found a new form of expression in the curated collections and bespoke commissions of Novocastrian. Founded by brothers, Richy and Paul Almond, the business pays tribute to their family's long lineage of Tyneside shipbuilders, as well as the region's once mighty industrial heritage. Metal is the speciality of the workshop, but they also combine this with Cumbrian slate and rare British marbles when required. Fiercely proud of their heritage, they produce pieces that pay homage to the area, such as the *Seven Sisters of Tyne*, a collection of patinated brass screens, each one inspired by one of the bridges that crosses the

Today, craft is a key player in the world of luxury interiors, including private residences, multi-starred hotels and superyachts. Architects and interior designers working at this level know how essential it is to find Master craftspeople and designer-artists to create work that is truly spectacular both in terms of quality and innovation. Makers working in this sphere have the unrivalled opportunity to create pieces that surpass the norm in terms of scale, material and budget.

For interiors at this elite level, paint or mass-produced wallpaper does not meet the requirements of a fully customised space. Often interior designers are searching for ways of embellishing walls, doors and panelling through the hand of the maker.

Artist Helen Amy Murray founded her studio in 2002, having evolved a way of creating three-dimensional designs from suede, leather and silk. Experimenting extensively with texture, colour, depth and light, she creates hand-sculpted works for leading interior architects, private clients and luxury brands across the globe. Over the years, she has trained a highly-skilled team of in-house artisans at her East End studio to take her hand-drawn illustrations from concept to meticulously crafted reality. Many of her designs depict flora, fauna and geometric motifs, and are used in different scales from the upholstery of individual pieces of furniture to entire wall installations. For a private residence in Houston, she composed *Distorted Star*, a panelled wall of irregular stars carved from faux leather. Working at a different scale entirely, she was invited by Rolls-Royce Motor Cars to create an artwork for its new concept, The Gallery, a

Previous spread: This spectacular installation for the swimming pool of a private client was created in lacquered birch ply by Tom Vaughan of Object Studio (see pages 132–135) and commissioned by architectural practice Rundell Associates. The undulating surface represents the flow of moving water.

Opposite: Helen Amy Murray was commissioned by 212box Architecture to create a wall of carved faux leather for a private penthouse in New York, with stars seeming to burst from the panels.

Left: *Giant White Peonies* created by Helen Amy Murray for Van Cleef & Arpel's flagship boutiques around the world as part of the company's winter 2021 scenography.

dedicated space for art integrated into the instrument panel of The Phantom (see page 155). This resulted in *Whispered Muse*, an abstract, undulating landscape of silk and suede that evokes the drapery of the Spirit of Ecstasy, the female figure which adorns the bonnet of every Rolls-Royce.

Aryma marquetry is highly regarded for its bespoke marquetry surfaces, which the studio has elevated from furniture ornamentation to site-specific installations. Founded in Wales in 2005 to keep the ancient skill of marquetry not only alive but contemporary and relevant, it has propelled a technique associated with sixteenth-century palazzos into super-prime residences, flagship retail, superyachts and private jets. The Aryma house style is a long way from common assumptions about marquetry, which is often perceived as dark-toned and classical. It has a young team of *marqueteurs*, often training students direct from art college (a process that takes three years). With a vast library of veneers at their disposal, marquetry artists can choose many different colours, grain patterns, figures and burrs, as well as incorporating other materials, such as brass, copper, mother-of-pearl and silver nickel. A single design may incorporate many thousands of pieces, each of which will have been individually cut, shaded and placed with precision into the final design. There is no distinction between designer and maker, so one person within the studio oversees a project in full, from hand-drawn artwork to the placing of the final piece of veneer.

The Bill Amberg Studio has been devoted to creating bespoke leather work for over thirty-five years. Bringing together designers and artisans from the worlds of saddlery, bookbinding, case making and other speciality leather crafts under

Above: Helen Amy Murray in her East London studio selecting silks for a special commission. Every piece she makes is site-specific and fully bespoke.

one roof, it re-interprets those traditional skills and creates bespoke furniture and interiors projects for clients around the world. The Studio is an authority on integrating leather into interior spaces, with a roster of clients that include the cream of architectural, interiors, hospitality and superyacht design practices, including a furniture collaboration with the Heatherwick Studio (see page 230) Designers and craftspeople work hand in hand to deliver commissions that range in scale from leather-clad furniture to banisters, doors, panelling and entire floors and walls. It is committed to sustainable practices, favouring traditional aniline-dyed, vegetable-tanned leathers, as opposed to modern, chrome-tanned ones.

Geoffrey Preston is one of the UK's leading architectural sculptors, specialising in the historic skill of modelled plasterwork (see page 83). He studied Sculpture at Hornsey College of Art, before training as a stonemason and carver and subsequently launching his own conservation businesses. In 2000, he moved to Devon to set up his workshop creating sculpture and decorative plasterwork. He also works in *stucco* – traditional, Italian plaster – which means working directly onto the wall or ceiling, creating wholly unique and distinctive works.

Sometimes commissioned for restoration projects – Preston was the lead conservator when Uppark House was almost destroyed by fire in 1989 – his work can be found in country houses throughout the UK and Ireland. Rather than replicating exactly what was there before, he often incorporates favourite birds, flowers or motifs of his clients in order to continue the personal narrative of the building. He also accepts contemporary architectural commissions, such as the Bar and Lounge of The Goring Hotel in

Right: The *Girih Cabinet* by Linley explores Islamic pattern through detailed marquetry of brilliant sapphire blue and rich gold tones.

London, where he and his small team created a rococo wall of high-relief, sculptural plasterwork depicting mythical sea creatures and marine life – the latter inspired by the work of nineteenth-century zoologist and artist, Ernst Haeckel. For the re-launch of Annabel's club in Mayfair in 2018, Preston created a horse-size *Flying Unicorn* that hangs over the club's stairwell.

Just as romantic and unexpected is *The Glade* in sketch restaurant, London, where artists Carolyn Quartermaine and Didier Mahieu created a fantasy, sylvan wonderland by using the seventeenth-century French skill of decoupage (which itself originated from twelfth-century China). The original antique ephemera were found in a

Left: Artists Carolyn Quartermaine and Didier Mahieu created a sylvan wonderland using the seventeenth-century art of decoupage at The Glade in sketch London.

Left below: Over 30,000 individual pieces of paper were used to cover the walls, complemented by Quartermaine's hand-painted and collaged fabrics.

Opposite: A bespoke *Ribbon* dining table by Based Upon, inspired by the tree-lined path leading to Kensington Palace that the client's home overlooks. Commissioned by Taylor Howes interior design studio, it is over six metres (twenty feet) long and sculpted from Corian, steel, bronze, timber and liquid metal.

box inherited by Mahieu from his grandmother, and each piece was enlarged, rescanned and over-painted. Having first prepared the walls, the two artists then covered them entirely with over 30,000 pieces of paper, depicting leaves, branches and trees, plus hand-painted fabrics overlaid with butterflies, collaged with Quartermaine's evocative photography – a process that took two months to complete. Quartermaine also screen-printed, hand-painted and collaged the velvets, silks and cottons used for soft furnishings, and sourced every piece of furniture.

It is an extraordinary achievement: a secret, forest garden in the heart of Mayfair created with the humblest of materials – cut paper – with the power to transport the viewer down the rabbit hole and back into joyous childhood.

Furniture

Bespoke furniture companies of a classical tradition create designs to commission that demand the highest standards of craftsmanship. Linley works with a network of specialist workshops across the UK from cabinet makers and

Earth Summer by Based Upon is made from a palette of liquid minerals and resin, with flowers, bark and leaves delicately cast and reapplied within the composition.

Left: This bronze *Fawn* dining chair is a piece in progress at the Cox London workshop, with *Oak Tree* chandelier in the foreground.

Opposite: A *Voyager* chair in polished bronze by Cox London. Its rippled surface is inspired by the swells of the ocean.

marqueteurs to silversmiths and leather workers. This is the tradition of furniture making that goes back to medieval times, with one piece visiting many different workshops, with each adding their own area of expertise.

Silverlining (see page 156) makes every piece in-house at its workshop and headquarters in Wales, using the talents of its seventy-strong team. These are trained in a diverse range of specialisations including cabinetmaking, marquetry and leatherwork. To support new talent and provide opportunities to people of diverse backgrounds, the company has launched The Silverlining Academy of Skills, a fast-track training programme designed to teach a 'PhD level' of craftsmanship over six or twelve months.

Based Upon is a London design studio and atelier that creates sculptural furniture, hand-applied surfaces and monumental artworks for elite residences, superyachts, private jets and public commissions internationally. Everything it makes comes from a fine art perspective, so all commissions begin with an exploration of person, place and purpose. The story of each project is lovingly captured through films, photographs and books, a journey of discovery that results in a true legacy piece. While it does offer its own collections of exceptional furniture, every piece is made to order and is therefore unique. The craft skills within its workshop are numerous and varied, ranging from metalwork, woodwork and engraving to model making, lacquer work and casting.

Cox London (see back cover image) was founded by sculptor makers, Christopher and Nicola Cox, and has established its reputation for creating distinctive furniture, lighting, mirrors and decorative objects. Inspired by the natural world, they use form, patina and palette to echo the flow and structure of leaves, branches, shells, flowers, rock strata and other influences, infusing every design with a joyous appreciation of the organic world. Every piece is made in-house at the company's North London workshops,

with a team of over thirty specialist artists, artisans and technicians working collaboratively to create exceptional collections and bespoke commissions. The combined craft palette includes sculpting, bronze casting, iron forging, traditional patination techniques, metal fabrication, gilding, lacquer work, plaster work, stonemasonry, glassblowing, embroidery and traditional upholstery.

The company also has a Belgravia showroom where it sells the 200 or so pieces that comprise its own collection. The majority of commissions are customised versions of this, made for a wide range of private and professional clients, including interior architects, interior designers and private collectors worldwide.

Lighting

This is the area where craft rubs up against engineering, with technology of equal weight to aesthetics. Atelier 001 was founded by renowned illumination artist and sculptor, Eva Menz, with the aim of making beautiful lighting objects more accessible to a wider audience, while also supporting a network of artisans in often endangered trades. She runs a small capsule studio, but each design benefits from many different creative collaborators, including specialist glassblowers, metalworkers, ceramicists, patina artists, silk weavers and brass spinners. The collections of floor, ceiling, wall and table lights are quietly elegant and deceptively simple, reminiscent of Art Deco forms and mid-century modern Scandinavian designs. They are designed to be used singly or in bespoke assemblages. While the studio uses LED elements, the light source is always hidden from the eye, avoiding glare and providing a warm, calming ambience.

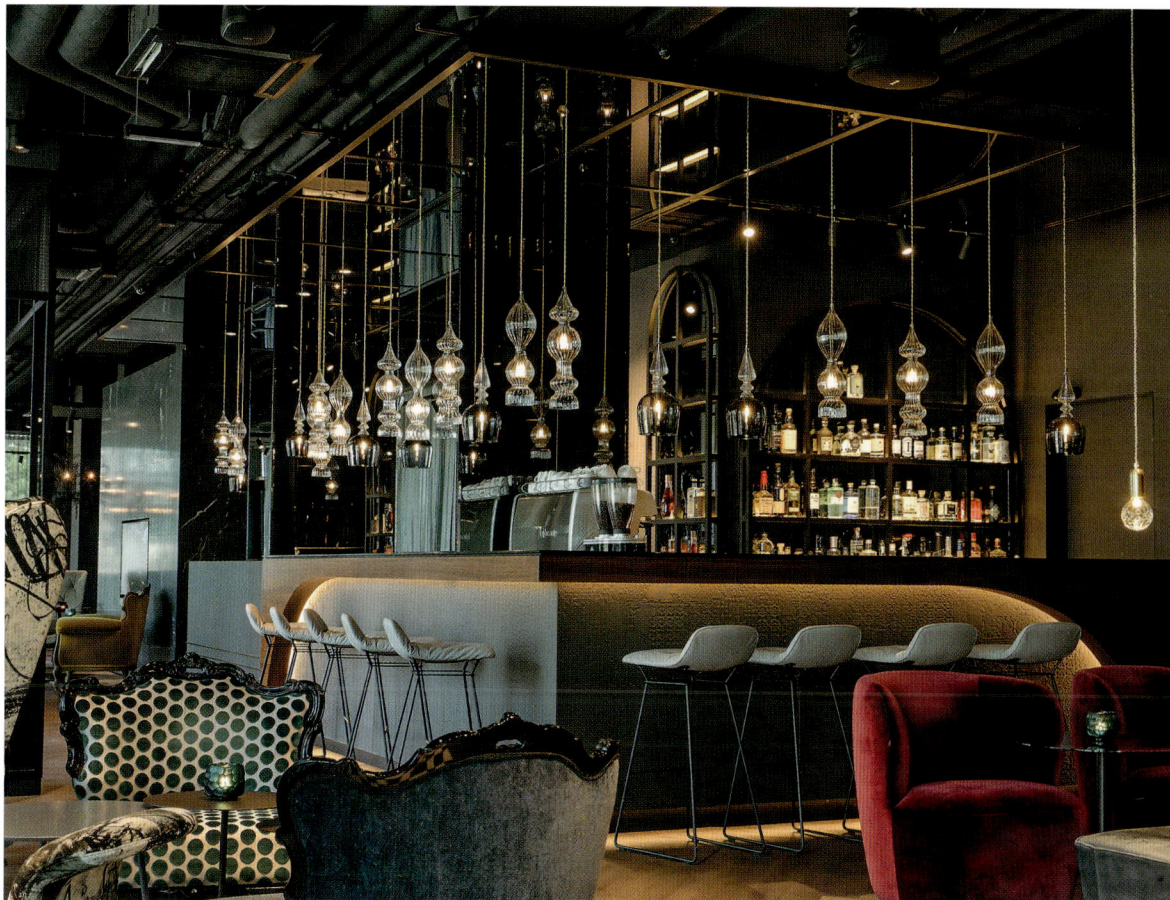

Opposite top: A highly skilled glassblower in the process of making a handblown light for one of the collections of Atelier 001.

Opposite below: An installation of *Liquid Vortex Quin* ceiling pendants by Atelier 001. Each one is hand made by a London-based Master glassblower.

Above: A group of handblown glass *Spindle* pendants by Rothschild & Bickers grouped over the foyer bar in Motel One of the Salzburg Mirabell.

Atelier 001 also offers a fully bespoke service. Menz has spent twenty years creating theatrical lighting installations across the world with international clients that include hotels, restaurants, corporate headquarters, flagship retail stores and the private owners of superyachts and elite residences.

Victoria Rothschild and Mark Bickers founded Rothschild & Bickers, determined to create a sustainable production of contemporary glass lighting in the UK. Both are glassblowers who graduated from the Royal College of Art with a shared admiration of heritage craft and the decorative detailing found in antique pieces by

Whitefriars Glass and Morris & Co., but with a determination to translate these ideas into an elegant and timeless aesthetic. Today, they have assembled a skilled team, all of whom are passionate about glass and its ability to transform an everyday object into a piece of art. It takes up to seven years to train as a Master glassblower and the company is dedicated to a structured teaching programme. Every light is custom-made to order, allowing the client to choose from a wide variety of forms, scales, colours and flex. As well as creating its own collections of pendants, clusters and wall lights, the studio offers bespoke solutions for every scenario, both domestic and commercial.

VALÉRIA NASCIMENTO:
Installation Artist

Below: Each installation that Valéria Nascimento created is made from thousands of individually-made porcelain pieces, like the blossoms of *White Flora* shown here.

Having grown up in Brazil where she studied Architecture, Valéria Nascimento cites landscape architect Roberto Burle Marx and architect Oscar Niemeyer as important, cultural influences. When she was first introduced to clay, she became fascinated by its multiple possibilities for expression and the development of spatial ideas. Her inspiration is drawn mostly from the natural world, and she chooses to work with porcelain because it has the smoothness and the malleability that she needs to create new shapes, manipulating it to appear virtually weightless. Her work focuses on repetitive sequencing, where separate elements form a cohesive, sculptural group. Site-specific commissions include

sculptural assemblages for private clients, public art and hospitality environments. She has also created work for global luxury brands, including Chanel, Escada, Tiffany, Christian Liaigre and Wedgwood.

With her own architectural background, it is natural she should consider the space in which her installations are to be housed before proposing possible compositions, whether for walls or suspended from ceilings. Her work is poetic and sensitive, based on the patterns and rhythms of nature, including spirals, waves, petals, leaves and the undulating forms of birds in flight. Every piece of porcelain she uses – although seemingly a duplicate – is in fact unique. When repeated over many metres, they are reminiscent of coral reefs or blossoms flying in the wind, each small form engaging in dialogue with the others to dynamic effect.

Nascimento's artistic reputation has continued to rise year on year with her work shown at many international art fairs, including Collect, Art Miami/Basel and Salon (NYC). Since her first solo exhibition in 2009 at Woolff Gallery in London, she has had many more shows internationally with multiple galleries.

When asked about her work, she responds with a quote from French designer Andrée Putman, 'To not dare is to have already lost. We should seek out ambitious, even unrealistic projects, because things only happen when we dream'.

'We should seek out ambitious, even unrealistic projects, because things only happen when we dream.'

Right: Nascimento in her West London studio. She is shown working on a piece called *Organism*, combining spirals and ovals into one cohesive group.

Far right: *Black Botanica* is a work she created as a response to the destruction of the Amazonian rainforest in her native Brazil, with the charred oak base referencing deforestation.

Right below: A detail from *Rainforest*, which she created for the Christian Liaigre flagship store in Mayfair. It comprises over ten thousand individual porcelain elements.

HEATHERWICK STUDIO:
Designers and Architects

The team at Heatherwick Studio have long assimilated traditional craft skills into their extraordinary buildings. It brings the right and left sides of the brain together, combining high-performing and rational thinking with human, emotional responses to materials and hand craft. In a similar vein, they have also collaborated with craft ateliers on concepts for furniture.

The *Friction* table was originally inspired by a commission to design a carpet in 2004. This prompted the studio to look for ways of going beyond a two-dimensional design woven into the surface and instead explore whether the carpet could be designed to change shape – from circular to oval, for example, or rectangular to square through the use of a pivot mechanism. Seeing the prototype then sparked the idea of a table top that could also change shape as it expanded. It took sixteen years of research and development to perfect the concept. Combining robotics with traditional hand-crafting processes, *Friction* can transform from a smooth circle eighteen metres (sixteen feet) in diameter to an ellipse of over four metres (thirteen feet) long.

The finished design is a collaboration with the Bill Amberg Studio (see pages 217–218) and multi-award-winning maker-designers, millimetre. Comprised of forty-five slats of aerospace-grade polished aluminium, each slat hand-clad in leather, it marries precision manufacturing with soulful materiality. The hand process was the integral counterpoint needed to its high-tech ingenuity. Not surprisingly, *Friction*'s ability to radically and magically transform shape immediately captured press attention and public imagination on its launch in 2021.

The working-from-home necessity caused by the COVID pandemic inspired another design, the *Stem* desk. This took its inspiration from the proven benefits of greenery in the home – known as biophilia – resulting in a desk comprised of American maple legs clamped to a glass top, with each leg also doubling as a ridged plant holder. Developed in partnership with the American Hardwood Export Council, Benchmark furniture (see pages 118–119 and 127), and the Design Museum, *Stem* is ideally suited for home living and working. By creating a desk that borrows from the complexity and beneficial effect of nature, Heatherwick Studio has brought balance to the WFH experience.

Of this balance between engineering, design and craft, Thomas Heatherwick says, 'Furniture is a miniature version of architecture, which allows us to play with craft at different scales. It is easy to forget that emotion is itself a function. If someone doesn't care about what you have created – whether a building or a table – it will ultimately be knocked down or thrown away, and that is a catastrophe for the planet. It is all to do with emotion. We want people to feel love for what we do, not just admiration.'

'It is easy to forget that emotion is itself a function ... We want people to feel love for what we do, not just admiration.'

Right: Thomas Heatherwick surrounded by maquettes of Heatherwick Studio's world-famous projects and a diverse collection of objects that inspire him and his team.

Below: The *Stem* desk that the Studio conceived as an ideal working-from-home solution, with legs of ridged wood that double as plant holders.

Below left: The *Friction* table top was originally made of polished aluminium slats, but cladding them in leather gave the design warmth and soul.

Right: The success of the concept is down to the precision engineering that allows each slat to reposition smoothly and flawlessly as the mechanism is activated.

Right: At first glance, *Friction* is a leather-clad table of 1.8 metres (six feet) in diameter, with little to suggest how radically it can change shape.

Opposite: The fully extended table is an elegant ellipse that measures four metres (thirteen feet) lengthways, allowing a variety of uses.

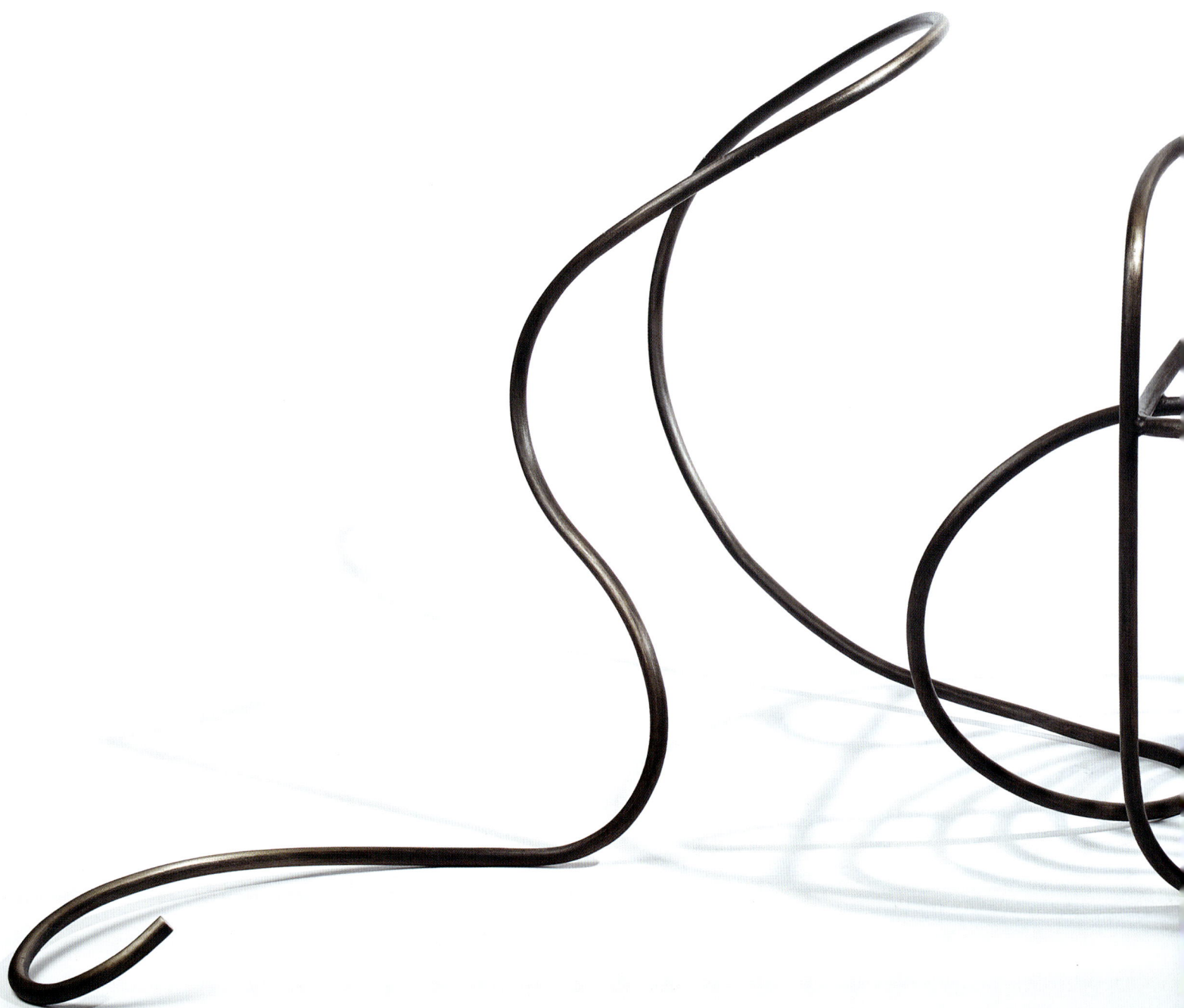

12

People often assume that however beautiful and desirable craft objects may be, they are not reflective of the twenty-first century. This is far from true. Many makers are embracing new technologies within their work, including 3D printing, 3D modelling, digital fabrication and advancements of materials.

Hull Studio specialises in the design, prototyping, manufacture and installation of bespoke furniture and unique decorative finishes for superyachts and elite residential projects. Central to its ethos is the relationship between traditional craftsmanship and modern technology. Founder and Creative Director, Alex Hull, studied Product and Furniture design at Nottingham Trent University, having been fascinated by architecture and car design since childhood. As well as his work heading up the studio, he creates limited-edition and one-off art pieces, likening 3D prototyping to digital craftsmanship, but with the Apple Pencil as his chisel. However, he always begins with hand-drawn sketches before experimenting with 3D digital renderings, then collaborates with expert cabinet makers and leather workers who transform his ideas into physical reality. In this way he creates pieces such as *Line Bench*, created from a single line of hand-forged bronze; *Blaze Cabinet*, with its marquetry surface of tulip wood and brass; and the *Split Armchair* of hand-stitched suede and leather.

Michael Eden is an artist-maker whose work sits at the intersection of craft, design and art. Having originally trained as a potter, he used an MPhil research project at the Royal College of Art to explore how digital technology could be developed and combined with traditional hand skills. This resulted in the *Wedgwoodn't Tureen*, where he utilised Rapid Manufacture (RM) and Rapid Prototyping (RP) – methods of 3D printing – to create a ceramic object that could not have been made through conventional means. Eden enjoys the limitless possibilities of customisation that results and the fact that working in this way gives him the creative freedom to do things that would be impossible with the wheel and clay.

Potter-artist Jonathan Keep, has also developed a system whereby the shapes of his forms are created in computer code. This digital information is passed to a studio-based 3D printer that prints out the form layer by layer. These coiled forms are then fired and glazed in the usual way. At the core of his work is his love for, and fascination with, the numerical code that underpins all nature. Pottery draws on the elemental forces of earth, fire and water. By using computer code, Keep adds a further layer of elemental and natural mathematical patterns and structures.

Material World

As the climate emergency deepens, scientists and designers are increasingly joining forces to find ways to tackle the many challenges it presents.

Saltyco is a materials science company that makes planet-positive textiles. Its aim is to actively heal damaged eco systems through the innovative use of processes and plants by building a supply chain based on regenerative agriculture and involving a community of farmers and conservation groups. Its agricultural ethos focuses on three areas: restoring natural eco systems by removing invasive species; introducing paludiculture (the practice of farming on wetlands, such as rewetted peatlands, bogs and fens); and fostering steady growth. Peatlands sequester and store

three to five percent more carbon than any other terrestrial land or forest but have been turned into carbon emitters through industrial farming. By cultivating thousands of native plants on these precious wetlands instead, Saltyco hopes to reverse the damage and return eco systems to their natural, healing state. In order to make use of these plants, it has a manufacturing facility located in Scotland, the Halolab, where it develops ground-breaking textiles. This includes the BioPuff, a plant-based fibre fill material designed to keep people warm without harming the environment. An alternative to animal and petroleum-based products, it is created by growing plants using regenerative, wetland agriculture.

Osmose Studio is a research-and-development project focused on organic and bio-fabricated textiles as a cruelty-free and sustainable alternative to cow leather. Founded in 2019 by bio-designers, Aurélie Fontan and Ashley Granter, it has created a vegan and bio-based leather based on mycelium (fungi). Mykkö does not impact the environment, but rather contributes to solving the recurrent problem of biodegradability in the fashion industry by providing a material that is suitable for luxury leather goods. The Studio also supplies the raw material to be used by other designers and artists. This has resulted in a diverse range of products including mycelium lights, insulation and bowls.

The two founders have different backgrounds, but are driven by common purpose. After graduating from Edinburgh College of Art where she studied Fashion, Fontan went on to collaborate with the ASCUS Lab of Art and Science in Edinburgh. There, she pioneered the integration of Kombucha, slime mould, mycelium (fungi) and other living systems as part of her ongoing research into more sustainable practices. She now runs her own fashion label, focused on 'techno craft', creating womenswear from the latest technologies and unconventional materials. Granter, who studied Product Design at Sheffield

Opposite top: *Spiralis* by Michael Eden was inspired by the Neo-Renaissance details of Waddesdon Manor and created using 3D printing methods, allowing the artist to create "impossible" objects for the first time. (Courtesy of Adrian Sassoon.)

Opposite below: *After Saly* by Michael Eden was inspired by the "fantasy vases" of eighteenth-century sculptor, Jacques Saly. Based on engravings in the Waddesdon Manor collection, it was created using 3D CAD software and incorporated 3D scans of Sèvres ceramics. (Courtesy of Adrian Sassoon.)

Right: *Mandelburb Urn II* by Jonathan Keep in stoneware was made by the artist using a computer-guided coil digitally linked to a coded 3D drawing. (Courtesy of the Sarah Myerscough Gallery.)

Hallam University, specialises in the process of growing materials with mycelium in his design studio, Natura.

Modern Synthesis comprises a multidisciplinary team of scientists, designers, makers and researchers. Co-founder and bio-designer, Jen Keane, is a graduate of the MA Materials Futures programme at Central Saint Martins and holds a BSc in Fibre Science and Apparel from Cornell University in NYC. She worked previously for Adidas exploring materials, design development and innovation strategy. Today, she and the team at Modern Synthesis are exploring how to partner with biology to design a new generation of hybrid materials. This includes studying nature to explore how bio-materials and emerg-

ing bio-fabrication techniques could influence everyday products. Its patent-pending microbial weaving process uses bacteria to 'grow' bio-textiles and composites. Just as traditional weaving uses the warp and the weft, here the 'warp' is a scaffold made of robotic yarn and the 'weft' are the bacteria that grow around this to create a material with limitless customisation potential. Microbial weaving harnesses the natural growing behaviour of a bacteria called *K.rhaeticus*, found in kombucha tea, which naturally produces a material called nanocellulose. Cellulose is the most abundant polymer on earth, the building block for plant-based materials, such as cotton and linen. The fibre that the bacteria produce is a particularly strong and fine form of cellu-

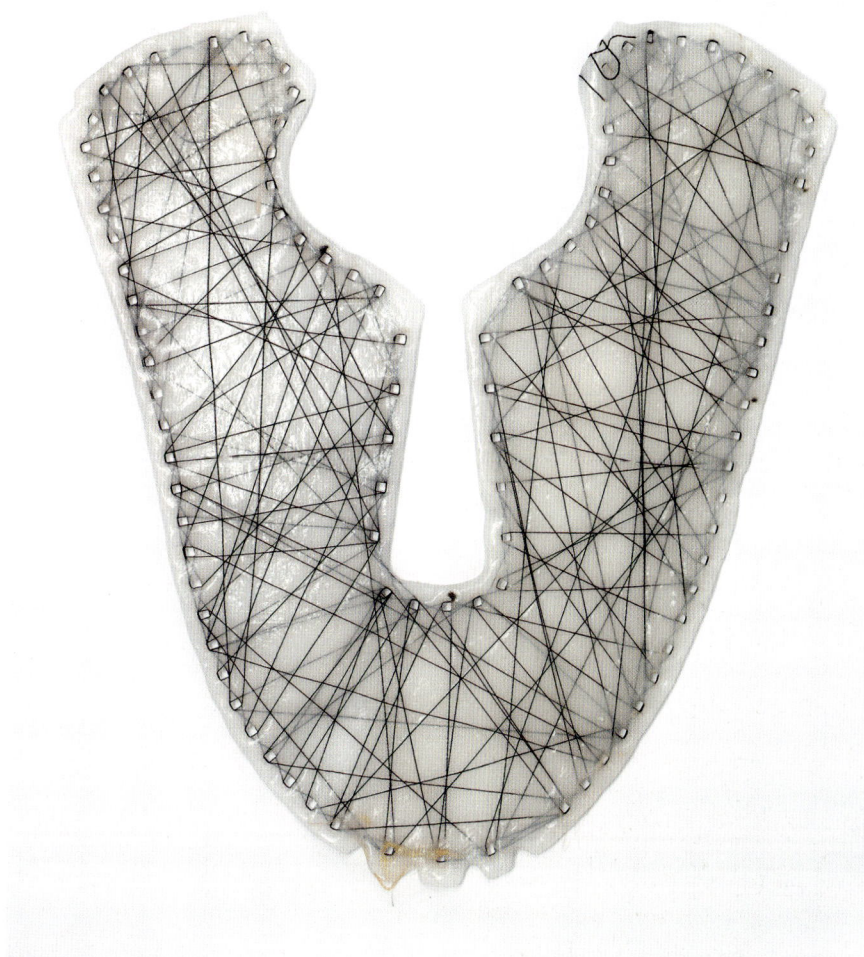

Opposite: The paludiculture landscape of the Great Fen in Cambridgeshire where Saltyco aims to protect and regenerate peatland to make planet-positive textiles.

Right: A microbial-woven upper part of a shoe, grown by Jen Keane of Modern Synthesis, showing the potential of the material and process.

lose, which is eight times stronger than steel and stiffer than Kevlar but inherently low cost and bio-degradable. Grown at nanoscale, the mesh of fibres are packed so tightly they appear like semi-transparent film or gel. When studied under the microscope, they look like tiny, weaving shuttles, leaving a trail of fibres in their wake.

In 2018, Keane unveiled *This Is Grown*, a microbial-woven upper part of a shoe to show the potential of the material and the process. In 2019, she joined forces with synthetic biologist, Marcus Walker, to show the next step of the project, using genetically engineered bacteria to grow both the colour and structure of the upper part of a trainer.

As Keane explains, 'Nature doesn't make materials in sheets and cut them down for assembly as we manufacture today. One of the biggest advantages of microbial weaving is its versatility. Just like 3D printing or knitting, you can design a piece entirely bespoke and in so doing eliminate waste.'

She also considers craft to be an important, but often overlooked, aspect of innovation, 'The textile industry we know today only exists upon the cumulative knowledge of craft built up over thousands of years. One of the reasons we are in such a consumer conundrum today is that we have lost sight of how things are made. We need to focus on making better things and making them well. That is why the involvement of designers and artisans is so critical in the context of Modern Synthesis.'

Spotlight on

SCIENTIFIC GLASS:

In some scenarios, the future is embedded firmly in the past. Glassmaking is an ancient process, but the material itself has some extraordinary properties, being non-reactive, resilient and pure. For this reason, it is still used in medical environments, including scientific glassblowing. This is the highly specialised process of creating glass apparatus and systems used in government, educational and industrial laboratories. It is also important in fields such as advanced fibre optics, electrochemical cells and semiconductors. Heritage Crafts estimates there are now fewer than fifty scientific glassblowers employed in the UK, so has classed it as an Endangered Craft.

Some of the projects are extraordinary. In 2013, Lee Mulholland, Head of the Glassblowing Workshop at the University of Southampton, was commissioned to make a hollow glass baby. This was to replace a previous glass model used by Professor David Phillips of Imperial College in lectures to illustrate the treatment of neonatal jaundice with blue light. It was a challenge to make as limbs, head and trunk had to be created separately before being joined together, requiring a mixture of scientific and artistic flame-working techniques.

Terri Adams, Design and Fabrication Facility Manager of the University of Oxford, is the University's only scientific glassblower. A Fellow of the British Society of Scientific Glassblowers, she has been working in the field for over thirty years. The piece she is most proud of is a perfusion apparatus, used to keep human organs functioning outside of the human body.

However, one of the most remarkable projects to date using glass in a surgical setting has been the collaboration between glass artist, Matt Durran (not himself a scientific glassblower) and Doctor Lola Osceni at the Royal Free Hospital,

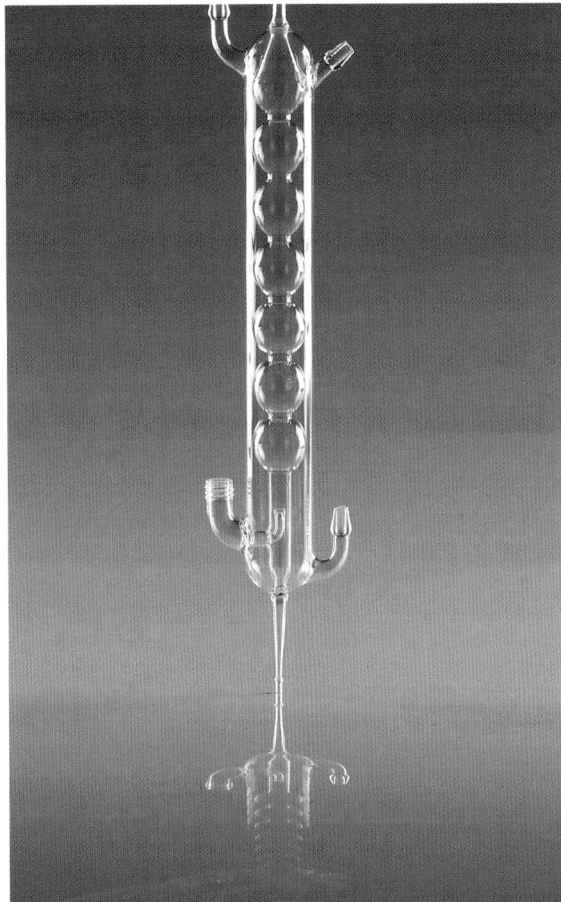

'The Royal Free research was an exchange of skills that contributed in a wider way to society.'

London. Her PhD research project – led by Professor Alexander Seifalian – was to tissue-engineer a human nose for patients recovering from facial cancer. The wider project was a collaboration between clinicians, cell biologists, material scientists and engineers, whose joint work continues to be critical to the rapid progress of this type of surgery.

The project aimed to make a synthetic material that could form and host cell growth for human-tissue transplants. However, the team needed someone who could create bespoke, highly accurate, non-reactive moulds for tissue-engineered cartilage to create a nose. The more accurate these would be, the less chance of the body rejecting the transplant.

Durran began by experimenting with a number of different moulds of his own nose, beginning with a plaster cast and then slumping warm glass over the mould with painstaking care. Once he had perfected the technique, he worked with 3D-printed models of a section of the patient's face, making each mould entirely bespoke.

As part of the research, he went on to subsequently create glass moulds for ears and even trachea. For the wider medical team at the Royal Free, it was a revelation on what was possible. Once he had presented the blueprint of how to make the moulds, the hospital could commission external glass technologists to take over the process.

The project won many accolades and awards,

among them a Design and Innovation award from the Associate and Parliamentary Group. For Durran, it is this real-world application of a traditional craft practice that gives him most satisfaction. 'The Royal Free research was an exchange of skills that contributed in a wider way to society. I was also keen to show other artists who work with glass, the type of projects that could benefit from their expertise.'

GARETH NEAL:
Designer-maker

Gareth Neal established his design and craft studio in 2002, six years after graduating with a degree in Design and Craftsmanship at Buckinghamshire University. His father was an archaeologist and Neal spent many childhood summers working as a volunteer on various digs, often finding shards of Roman pottery that the professionals had missed. It was this opportunity to look back in time through objects that gave him his respect for history and for ancient forms of craft.

He and his small team are hands-on makers, working with both traditional tools and the latest computer-controlled routers. Two of his pieces are in the permanent collection of the V&A Museum London: the *Brodgar Occasional Chair* (2012), which he created with Kevin Gauld, the Orkney Furniture Maker (see pages 105–106); and the *George* chest-of-drawers (2009) created using traditional cabinetry and CNC routing. His studio practice is a continuous dialogue between historical and contemporary design.

His mastery of technical skill and knowledge, combined with openness to digital technologies, has resulted in some intriguing collaborations in this arena, including fluid, sculptural vessels conceived with the late legendary architect Zaha Hadid and originally made by Benchmark in 2014, as part of *The Wish List* project with the American Hardwoods Export Council (AHEC).

More recently, Neal has explored digital crafting techniques through works such as his *Hack Chair* series, combining progressive digital craftsmanship and traditional handiwork. *Hack Chair I*, for example, involves the use of a robotic, six-axis CNC arm, which becomes an extension of the craftsman's hand. The arm is programmed to hack a block of green oak, which is itself a process of exploring the glitches, fractures, splits and rings stored within the timber. The result is a distorted Georgian archetype, which would never have existed had it not been for the use of the robotic technology. Neal then subjects these pieces to traditional *Shou Sugi Ban* charring, preserving them for future centuries.

In 2020, he created the *Sio2* series of limited-edition vessels 3D-printed in black silicate (and made solid with binder). These exaggerated forms range in size from the miniature to the monumental. The ability to finely control singular particles of sand within the printing process, alongside advanced 3D modelling, enables him to create fluid forms that would be unobtainable in wood. An example of this work is on display at the Toyama Prefectural Museum of Art and Design in Japan.

For Neal, the ethos within his practice is best described as, 'One of respect and honesty for the origins of traditional craft techniques, while exploring and experimenting with forms, tools and processes. In this way I strive to create new designs and timeless collectibles for the future.'

'While exploring and experimenting with forms, tools and processes, I strive to create new designs and timeless collectibles for the future.'

Right: Gareth Neal in his studio with *Twisted Pair* 900 and *Mirror Pair* 650 (in foreground) from the *Sio2* series of vessels that have been 3D printed in sand, creating exceptionally fluid shapes.

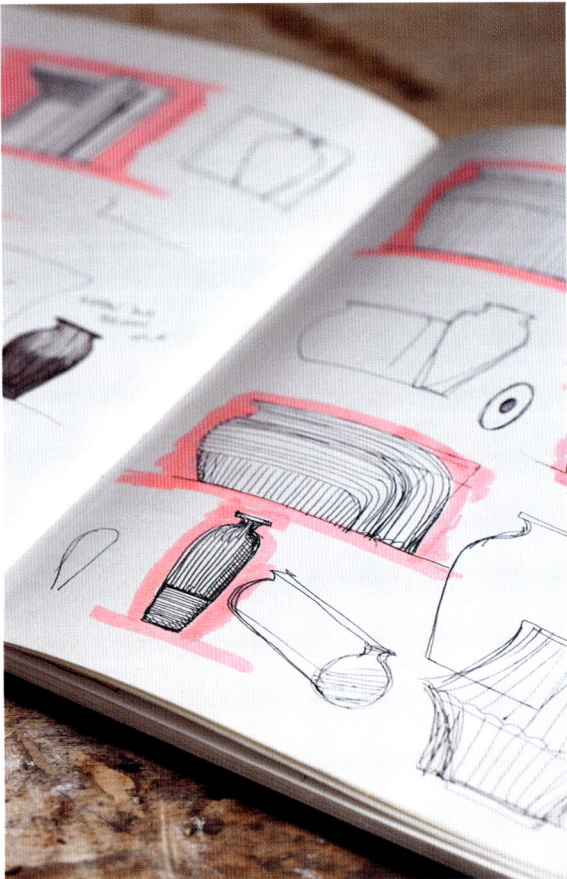

Opposite top left: Having utilised robotic technology to make pieces such as *Hack Chair 1*, Neal then used the hand process of Shou Sugi Ban to preserve them.

Opposite top right: *Hack Chair 1* is hacked from a block of green oak using a robotic arm, which produces a raw, Georgian-style form.

Opposite bottom left: Neal's sketch book with early drawings for the *Sio2* series of vessels, exploring the forms that 3D printing in sand could achieve.

Opposite bottom right: Oak vessels, named *VES-EL*, created in collaboration with the late architect, Zaha Hadid, combining hand process with digital technology.

Right: *Twisted Pair 1/55* (see front cover) from the *Sio2* series of 3D forms, which illustrates Neal's continuous dialogue between hand craftsmanship and radical technologies and materials.

About the Authors

HELEN CHISLETT @helenchislett

Helen Chislett is a journalist and author who specialises in design and decoration of the finest level, encompassing everything from interiors, art, antiques and architecture to craft, gardens and decoration. She has contributed to numerous national newspapers and magazines over the last thirty years, and is the author of twenty books to date. Having forged strong relationships with artists and makers whose work she has passionately championed within her features, she founded her own arts agency in 2013 to connect superb artisanship with those seeking exceptional pieces.

DAVID LINLEY

David Linley has been passionate about the arts for as long as he can remember, choosing to study furniture making at the Parnham House School for Craftsman in Wood in Dorset on leaving Bedales School. In 1985, he founded his own business focusing on the production of bespoke furniture for individual commissions. Forty years later, this has established an international reputation for hand-made furniture, interior design and home accessories of the highest quality.

David Linley was appointed Chairman of Christie's UK in December 2006 and was promoted to Honorary Chairman with responsibility for Europe, the Middle East and Africa (EMEA) in June 2015. In 2018, he was appointed Vice President of The Prince's Foundation, which reflects HRH The Prince of Wales's commitment to championing holistic and sustainable solutions to the challenges the world faces today. Most recently, he founded the Snowdon Summer School in cabinet-making at Highgrove as part of the work of the Foundation. He is also Vice Patron of the Queen Elizabeth Scholarship Trust (QEST), founded by the Royal Warrant Holders Association in 1990 to support education and excellence in craft.

We would like to thank the following individuals and organistions who have made such a difference in their generous contributions to the success of this book:

Matthew Rice.
Simon Sadinsky from The Prince's Foundation.
Scott Simpson.
The Crafts Council.
QEST and its Scholars.
Heritage Crafts.
Hugo Burge of Marchmont.
Clive Beecham of Grandey's Place.
Andrew Winch.
Philippa Hobson.
Naomi Davenport.

In addition, we would like to thank:

Stephen Bayley for writing the splendid Foreword.

Caroline Michel of PFD for believing in the book with such passion from the first.

Kate Pollard, our book editor at Welbeck, for her enthusiasm, dedication, patience and good humour.

David Rowley for marrying text with images so beautifully, while working against the clock!

Helen Chislett would like to say a sincere thank you to her husband, John, for his constant support and encouragement.

David Linley would like to thank his esteemed colleagues and friends at Christie's who have taught him so much and inspire him daily. He would also like to thank Linley for forty years of design and craftmanship of the highest possible standard.

We also would like to thank the professional photographers who so generously waived their fees in order to support the craftspeople within these pages, including:

Thierry Bal, Sam Barker, Simon Bevan, Marcos Bevilacqua, Joakim Blockstrom, Matthew Booth, Max Brockman-More, Iain Brown, Simon Brown, Edward Bryan, Tom Bunning, Ellie Burd, Alun Callender, Liz Calvi, Simon Camper, Nick Caro, James Champion, Arran Cross, Jake Curtis, Susan Davis, Tiree Dawson, Jon Day, Sylvain Deleu, Jan Faukner, Tara Fisher, Kasia Fiszer, Tom Foxall, Kenneth Gray, Camilla Greenwell, Michael Harvey, Steve Hickey, Guy Hinks, Jack Hobhouse, Hot Icarus, Jo Hounsome, Deborah Husk, Richard Jackson, Betty Jaresova, Jerrie Jarmeh, Richard Kalina, Will Killen, Petr Krejci, Edward Lakeman, Leslie Lau, David Lindsay, Julian Love, Dan Lowe, Matilda Lowther, Rebecca Marr, Andy Mather, James Merrell, James T Millar, Rowan Morgan, Martin Morrell, James Munson, Reuben Paris, Agata Pec, Christopher Pillitz, Michael Pollard, Benjamin Pryor, Mark Reeves, Nick Rochowski, Liz Seabrook, Jake Seal, Jo Sealy, Sarah Sheldrake, Susana Silver, Christian, Maier Smith, Dan Stevens, Marc Swadel, Anna Vlasyuk, Dan Walsh, Dave Watts, Asia Werbel, Brianna Wild, Andrew F Wood, Peter Wood, Thomas Joseph Wright.

Acknowledgements

We would like to thank the many craftspeople, ateliers, small manufacturers, interior designers, craft organisations, charities and galleries who have helped us put together the content of this book. We would also like to acknowledge those who may have been disappointed not to be included. We hope by raising the subject of craft so widely, everyone involved will ultimately benefit.

1882 Ltd: www.1882ltd.com
212box: www.212box.com

Saelia Aparicio: www.saelito.com
  (see Gallery FUMI)
Artwise: www.artwisecurators.com
Aryma: www.aryma.co.uk
Lisi Ashbridge:
  www.itswritteninstone.co.uk
  (see The Lettering Arts Trust)
Atelier 001: www.atelier001.com
Lora Avedian:
  www.loraavedian.com
  (courses available)

Laura Ellen Bacon:
  www.lauraellenbacon.com
  (see Hignell gallery)
Tristram Bainbridge
  (Bainbridge Conservation):
  www.bainbridgeconservation.com
Bamford Watch Department:
  www.bamfordwatchdepartment.com
Barnaby Barford:
  www.barnabybarford.co.uk
Based Upon: www.basedupon.com
Ilana Belsky (Belsky Diamonds):
  www.belskydiamonds.com
Benchmark:
  www.benchmarkfurniture.com
Aimee Betts: www.aimeebetts.com
Bibbings & Hensby:
  www.bibbings-hensby.co.uk
  (online courses available)
Bill Amberg Studio:
  www.billamberg.com
Blowfish Glass:
  www.blowfish-glass.widget.obby.co.uk
  (courses available – see Vessel
  Gallery)
Chris Bramble:
  www.chrisbrambleceramics.com
  (courses available)
Neil Bromley:
  www.calligraphyandheraldry.com
Burleigh Pottery:
  www.burleigh.co.uk

Sarah Burns:
  www.sarahburnspatterns.com
  (courses available)

Candida Stevens Gallery:
  www.candidastevens.com
Helen Carnac: www.helencarnac.co.uk
  (courses available)
Carréducker: www.carreducker.com
  (courses available)
Clay College:
  www.claycollegestoke.co.uk(
  (courses available)
Cox London: www.coxlondon.com
Craft Design House:
  www.craftdesignhouse.com
Craft NI: www.craftni.org
Craft Scotland: www.craftscotland.org
Craftmasters:
  www.craftmastersgallery.co.uk
  (courses available)
Crafts Council:
  www.craftscouncil.org.uk
Crafty Fox Market:
  www.craftyfoxmarket.co.uk
Craven Dunnill Jackfield:
  www.cdjackfield.com
Crispinians: www.crispinians.com
  (courses available)
Alison Crowther:
  www.alisoncrowther.com

Pedro da Costa Felgueiras (Lacquer
  Studios): www.lacquerstudios.com
Aiveen Daly: www.aiveendaly.com
Michelle de Bruin: www.artist.org.uk
Rebecca de Quin:
  www.rebeccadequin.co.uk
  (see Craftmasters gallery)
Samantha Donaldson:
  www.samanthadonaldsonglass.com
  (see Vessel gallery)
James Dougall:
  www.jamesdougall.com
  (see Craftmasters gallery)
Dovecot: www.dovecotstudios.com
  (courses available)
Hugh Dunford Wood:
  www.dunfordwood.com
  (courses available)
Matt Durran: www.mattdurran.com

Michael Eden:
  www.michael-eden.com
  (see Adrian Sassoon)
Ndidi Ekubia: www.ndidiekubia.com
  (see Adrian Sassoon)
Fenella Elms: www.fenellaelms.com
Ettinger: www.ettinger.co.uk

Garry Fabian Miller:
  www.garryfabianmiller.com
  (see Dovecot)
Lucas Ferreira:
  www.ferreiravisuals.com
  (see jaggedart)
Firmdale Hotels:
  www.firmdalehotels.com
Forest + Found:
  www.forest-and-found.com
Martha Freud: www.marthafreud.com
  (see Nonemore Gallery)

Gainsborough:
  www.gainsborough.co.uk
Gallery FUMI: www.galleryfumi.com
David Gates:
  www.davidgatesstudioworkshop.co.uk
Kevin Gauld
  (The Orkney Furniture Maker):
  www.orkneyfurniture.co.uk
Grandey's Place:
  www.grandeysplace.co.uk
  (courses available in range of crafts)
Great Northern Contemporary
  Craft Fair (GNCFF):
  www.greatnorthernevents.co.uk
Thomas Greenaway
  (Greenaway Mosaics):
  www.greenawaymosaics.com
  (courses available)
Caroline Groves:
  www.carolinegroves.com

Lisa Hammond MBE:
  www.lisahammond-pottery.co.uk
Hand & Lock:
  www.handemboidery.com
  (courses available)
Harris Tweed Authority:
  www.harristweed.org
Stewart Hearn:
  www.stewarthearn-shop.com
Heatherwick Studio:
  www.heatherwick.com
Heritage Crafts:
  www.heritagecrafts.org.uk
Hignell Gallery:
  www.hignellgallery.com
Jochen Holz: www.jochenholz.com
Homo Faber: www.homofaber.com
Hitomi Hosono:
  www.hitomihosono.com
  (see Adrian Sassoon)
Charlotte Howarth:
  www.making-marks.com
  (see The Lettering Arts Trust)
Hull Studio: www.hullstudio.com
  (see Gallery FUMI)

Felicity Irons (Rush Matters):
  www.rushmatters.co.uk
  (courses available)
Isle of Auskerry:
  www.isleofauskerry.com

jaggedart: www.jaggedart.com
Edward Johnson:
  www.edwardjohnsonstudio.com
  (courses available)
Owen Jones: www.oakswills.co.uk
  (courses available)
Jessica Jue: www.jessicajue.com
  (see Craftmasters gallery)

Jonathan Keep: www.keep-art.co.uk
  (see Sarah Myerscough Gallery)
Seth Kennedy: www.sethkennedy.co.uk
Thomas Kennedy:
  www.kennedy-scagliola.co.uk
Alice Kettle: www.alicekettle.co.uk
  (see Candida Stevens gallery)
Daisy Knatchbull (The Deck):
  www.thedecklondon.com
Knit For Peace:
  www.knitforpeace.org.uk
  (courses available)
Knithub24: www.knithub24.com
  (courses available)
Anja Kuch: www.kastanjaviolins.com

Nikki Laird (The Kiltmakery):
  www.kiltmakery.com
  (courses available)
Eleanor Lakelin:
  www.eleanorlakelin.com
  (see Sarah Myerscough Gallery)
Max Lamb: www.maxlamb.org
Danny Lane: www.dannylane.co.uk
Linley: www.davidlinley.com
John Lobb: www.johnlobb.com
Lock & Co: www.lockhatters.com
London Cloth Company:
  www.london-cloth.com
London Craft Week:
  www.londoncraftweek.com
Alexandra Llewellyn:
  www.alexandrallewellyn.com

Emily Mackey:
  www.emilymackey.com
  (courses available)
Make Hauser & Wirth:
  www.hauserwirth.com
John Makepeace:
  www.johnmakepeacefurniture.com
Marchmont:
  www.marchmonthouse.com

Peter Marigold:
 www.petermarigold.com
 (see Sarah Myerscough Gallery)
Ian McChesney:
 www.mcchesney.co.uk
Allyson McDermott:
 www.allysonmcdermott.com
 (courses available)
Nina Casson McGarva:
 www.ninacassonmcgarvaglass.com
 (see Vessel gallery)
Lucy McGrath (Marmor Paperie):
 www.marmorpaperie.co.uk
 (courses available)
Rowan Mersh: www.rowanmersh.com
 (see Gallery FUMI)
Hal Messel: www.halmessel.com
Messums Creative:
 www.messumswiltshire.com
 (courses available)
Messums London:
 www.messumslondon.com
Michelangelo Foundation:
 www.michelangelofoundation.org
millimetre: www.millimetre.uk.net
Modern Synthesis:
 www.modern-synthesis.com
Jason Mosseri (Hopespring Chairs):
 www.hopespringchairs.com
 (courses available)
Mourne Textiles:
 www.mournetextiles.com
Helen Amy Murray:
 www.helenamymurray.com
Sarah Myerscough Gallery:
 www.sarahmyerscough.com
Mykkö: www.mykko.co.uk
 (see Osmose Studio)

Nafisi Studio: www.nafisi.design
 (courses available)
Valéria Nascimento:
 www.valerianascimento.com
National Centre for Craft and Design:
 www.nationalcraftanddesign.org.uk
Gareth Neal: www.garethneal.co.uk
 (see Sarah Myerscough Gallery)
Lawrence Neal:
 www.lawrencenealchairs.co.uk
Neon Workshops:
 www.neonworkshops.com
 (courses available)
Nonemore Gallery, 12a Rathbone
 Place, London, W1T 1HU
Novocastrian: www.novocastrian.co

Object Studio (see Tom Vaughan):
 www.objectstudio.co.uk

Alex O'Connor:
 www.alexoconnorsilver.co.uk
 (see Craftmasters gallery)
Dame Magdalene Odundo –
 please see Salon 94
 and Anthony Slayter-Ralph
Osmose Studio:
 www.osmosestudio.co.uk
 (see Mykkö)
Annemarie O'Sullivan:
 www.annemarieosullivan.co.uk
 (courses available)
OTZI London: www.otzilondon.com

Parabola: www.parabola.com
Parndon Mill:
 www.parndonmill.co.uk
 (courses available see Vessel Gallery)
Elizabeth Auriol Peers:
 www.artistsilversmith.com
 (see Craftmasters gallery)
Geoffrey Preston:
 www.geoffreypreston.co.uk
Jacky Puzey: www.jackypuzey.com

QEST: www.qest.org.uk
Carolyn Quartermaine:
 www.carolynquartermaine.com

Tom Raffield: www.tomraffield.com
Helen Reader www.hrsaddlery.com
Angus Ross: www.angusross.co.uk
Rothschild & Bickers:
 www.rothschildbickers.com
Mike Rowland & Son:
 www.wheelwright.org.uk
Sophie Rowley:
 www.sophierowley.com
Michael Ruh: www.michaelruh.com
Rundell Associates:
 www.rundellassociates.com

Salon 94: www.salon94.com
Saltyco: www.saltyco.co.uk
Tom Sands: www.tomsandsguitars.com
Kathryn Sargent:
 www.kathrynsargent.com
Adrian Sassoon:
 www.adriansassoon.com
Royal School of Needlework:
 www.royal-needlework.org.uk
 (courses available)
Silverlining Furniture:
 www.silverliningfurniture.com
Lorna Singleton:
 www.lornasingleton.co.uk
 (courses available)
Anthony Slayter-Ralph:
 www.anthonyslayter-ralph.com

Soane Britain: www.soane.co.uk
Staines & Son: www.orrerydesign.com
Swaine Adeney Brigg:
 www.swaineadeneybrigg.com

Kazuhito Takadoi:
 www.kazuhitotakadoi.com
 (see jaggedart)
Taylor Howes: www.taylorhowes.co.uk
The Artworker's Guild:
 www.artworkersguild.org
The Bowes Museum:
 www.thebowesmuseum.org.uk
The Black Artisans:
 www.theblackartisans.org
The Cornish Bed Company:
 www.cornishbeds.co.uk
The Creative Dimension Trust:
 www.thecreativedimension.org
The Glass Hub: www.theglasshub.com
 (courses available – see Vessel
Gallery)
The Lettering Arts Trust:
 www.letteringartstrust.org.uk
 (courses available)
The Marchmont Workshop:
 www.themarchmontworkshop.com
The New Craftsmen:
 www.thenewcraftsmen.com
The Prince's Foundation:
 www.princes-foundation.org
 (courses including the
 Snowdon Summer School)
The Royal Collection Trust:
 www.rct.uk
The Society for the Protection of
 Ancient Buildings
 (SPAB): www.spab.org.uk
Peter Ting: www.peterting.com
Toye, Kenning & Spencer:
 www.toye.com
Carolyn Truss:
 www.bespoke-bridlework.co.uk
 (courses available)

UK Mens' Sheds Association
 (UKMSA):
 www.menssheds.org.uk
Under Winch's Wing:
 www.winchdesign.com

Tom Vaughan (Object Studio):
 www.objectstudio.co.uk
Vessel Gallery:
 www.vesselgallery.com
 (several of its artists run courses –
 see The Glass Hub, Blowfish Glass
 and Parndon Mill)

Vezzini & Chen:
 www.vezziniandchen.com
 (see Adrian Sassoon)
Victoria & Albert Museum:
 www.vam.ac.uk

Katie Walker:
 www.katiewalkerfurniture.com
Olivia Walker:
 www.oliviawalker.co.uk
Rob Walker (Signs by Umberto):
 www.signsbyumberto.co.uk
 (courses available)
Nic Webb: www.nicwebb.com
 (see Sarah Myerscough Gallery)
Welsh Slate: www.welshslate.com
West Dean College of Arts and
 Conservation: www.westdean.org.uk
William Cowley:
 www.williamcowley.co.uk
David Snoo Wilson (Ore and Ingot):
 www.oreandingot.com
 (courses available)
Mary Wing To: www.marywingto.com
Woolff Gallery:
 www.woolffgallery.co.uk
Thurle Wright: See jaggedart
Wyvern Bindery:
 www.wyvernbindery.com

Photographic acknowledgements

Front Cover: Courtesy of Gareth Neal (see pages 244–247), the Sarah Myerscough Gallery and photographer Jan Faukner.

Back Cover: Courtesy of Cox London (see pages 224–225) and photographer Alun Callender.

Endpapers: Courtesy of Lucy McGrath of Marmoir Paperie.

Title page: Courtesy of Kazuhito Takadoi and jaggedart.

Contents page: Courtesy of Christopher Riggio, jaggedart and photographer Betty Jaresova.

Page 6 – Foreword: Courtesy of Owen Jones (see pages 70–73) and photographer Jerri Jarmeh, with thanks to Heritage Crafts.

Pages 8–9: Courtesy of Caroline Groves (see pages 161–162) and photographer Dan Lowe.

PAST & PRESENT

Pages 12–13: Courtesy of Jason Mosseri (see page 103); taken by James Winspear.

Pages 15–16: Courtesy of Bibbings & Hensby, with thanks to the Michelangelo Foundation.

Page 17: Courtesy of Eleanor Lakelin, the Sarah Myerscough Gallery, the Michelangelo Foundation and photographer Alun Callender.

Page 19: Courtesy of Rob Walker and photographer Arran Cross of Department Two. The project is a collaboration with Michael C Place and Nicola Place of Studio Build. With thanks to QEST, Under Winch's Wing and Fortnum & Mason.

Page 20: Above: Courtesy of Emily Mackey and photographer Alun Callender.

Above right: Courtesy of The Prince's Foundation and Iain Brown.

Page 21: Courtesy of Seth Kennedy, with thanks to Grandey's Place.

Pages 22–23: Courtesy of Michelle de Bruin, with thanks to Marchmont House.

Pages 24–25: Courtesy of The Marchmont Workshop.

Page 27: Right: Courtesy of Nikki Laird. Far right: Courtesy of Chris Bramble and photographer Jo Sealy.

Pages 28–29: Photographs courtesy of Mary Wing To and photographer Marc Swadel.

Page 30: Portrait of Lucy McGrath courtesy of Liz Calvi.

Page 31: Courtesy of Lucy McGrath; taken by James Winspear.

HERITAGE & HISTORY

Pages 32–33: Courtesy of Pedro da Costa Felgueiras/The Lacquer Studios.

Page 35: Courtesy of Gainsborough and photographer Alun Callender.

Page 36: Courtesy of Hugh Dunford Wood.

Page 37: Courtesy of Allyson McDermott.

Page 38: Courtesy of Tristram and Abigail Bainbridge.

Page 39: Courtesy of the Royal School of Needlework.

Pages 40–41: Courtesy of Hand & Lock.

Page 42: Courtesy of William Cowley Ltd and Neil Bromley. Heraldic panel detailing the Royal Arms of Scotland designed and created for Brian Williamson and the Barony of Craigmillar. Photographs courtesy of Neil Bromley.

Page 43: Courtesy of Lock & Co. and photographer Edward Lakeman.

Pages 44–45: Courtesy of Lock & Co. and photographer Edward Lakeman.

Page 46: Courtesy of Lock & Co. and photographer Edward Lakeman.
Page 47: Courtesy of Swaine Adeney Brigg.

Pages 48–49: Courtesy of Ettinger.

Page 50: Portrait of Pedro da Costa Felgueiras courtesy of Camilla Greenwell.

Page 51: Courtesy of Pedro da Costa Felgueiras/The Lacquer Studios.

Pages 52–53: All images courtesy of Toye, Kenning & Spencer. Photographs top right and top left courtesy of photographer Anna Vlasyuk.

RARE & ENDANGERED

Pages 54–55 and page 57 Courtesy of Thomas Kennedy and photographer Tom Foxall.

Pages 58–59: Courtesy of Thomas Greenaway, photographer Mark Williamson and Country Life/Future Publishing Ltd.

Page 61: Courtesy of Staines & Son.

Pages 62–63: Courtesy of David Snoo Wilson. Photographs on page 62 far left and on page 63 courtesy of John Smedley Ltd and photographer Asia Werbel. Photographs on page 62 of bell casting courtesy of Nick Caro.

Page 64: Courtesy of Crispinians.

Page 65: Courtesy of Soane Britain.

Pages 66–67: Courtesy of Mike Rowland & Son. Photograph taken by Robert Hesketh.

Page 68: Courtesy of Lisi Ashbridge, The Lettering Arts Trust and photographer Max Brockman-More.

Page 69: Courtesy of Charlotte Howarth and The Lettering Arts Trust.

Pages 70–73: All photographs courtesy of Owen Jones and photographer Jerri Jarmeh, with thanks to Heritage Crafts.

Pages 74–75: Courtesy of Ilana Belsky and photographer Brianna Wild (B.Wild).

ROOTS & REGION

Pages 76–77 and page 79 Courtesy of the Harris Tweed Authority.

Pages 80–81: Courtesy of Burleigh Pottery and photographer Jake Seal.

Page 82: Courtesy of Craven Dunnill Jackfield.

Page 83: Courtesy of Geoffrey Preston and Jennifer Lawrence.

Page 85: Courtesy of Gainsborough and photographer Alun Callender.

Pages 86–87: Courtesy of Novocastrian.

Pages 88–89: Courtesy of Neon Workshops and photographer David Lindsay (www.photosbydavid.com).

Pages 90–91: Courtesy of the London Cloth Company and photographer Kasia Fiszer.

Pages 92–93: Courtesy of Isle of Auskerry.

Pages 94–95: Courtesy of 1882 Ltd, Barnaby Barford and photographer Thierry Bal.

Pages 96–97: Courtesy of 1882Ltd, Max Lamb, Linley and photographer Andrew F Wood.

KIND & SUSTAINABLE

Pages 98–99: Portrait of Felicity Irons by Andrew Montgomery.

Page 100: Courtesy of Angus Ross and photographer James T. Millar.

Page 102: Courtesy of Angus Ross.

Page 103: Top: Courtesy of Nafisi Studio and stylist Serena Lake. Bottom: Courtesy of Jason Mosseri; photograph Jonathan Bassett.

Pages 104 and 105 (top left): Courtesy of Lawrence Neal and photographer Benjamin Pryor.

Page 105 (top right): Courtesy of The Marchmont Workshop with photograph by Sam Cooper.

Page 106: Portrait of Kevin Gauld courtesy of Rebecca Marr. Orkney chair courtesy of Kevin Gauld.

Pages 107–109: Courtesy of Annemarie O'Sullivan and photographer Alun Callender.

Page 110: Courtesy of Lorna Singleton and photographer Tiree Dawson/Random Chair.

Page 111: Courtesy of Sarah Burns.

Pages 112–113: Courtesy of Felicity Irons, Country Living magazine, the Hearst Corporation and photographer Andrew Montgomery.

Pages 114, 115, 116 and bottom left of page 117: Photographs courtesy of Tom Raffield and photographer Alun Callender.
Page 117 top right and bottom right: Courtesy of Tom Raffield Ltd.

USEFUL & BEAUTIFUL

Pages 118–119: Courtesy of Benchmark, architect Ian McChesney and photographer Jack Hobhouse.

Page 121: Courtesy of Carolyn Truss.

Page 122: Courtesy of Tom Sands and photographer Dan Walsh.

Page 123: Courtesy of Tom Sands, Evoke Studios, performer Nii and photographer Will Killen.

Pages 124–125: Courtesy of Otis Ingrams.

Page 126: Courtesy of Lora Avedian and photographer Liz Seabrook.

Page 127: Top: Courtesy of The Cornish Bed Company and The Really Good Media Company. Bottom: Courtesy of The Cornish Bed Company and Jon Day.

Page 128: Top left: Courtesy of Aimee Betts and photographer Alun Callender. Top right: Courtesy of Stewart Hearn and photographer Simon Camper/Lumen Photography.

Page 129: Top: Courtesy of Katie Walker. Below: Courtesy of Edward Johnson, photographer Edward Bryan and with thanks to Under Winch's Wing.

Pages 130–131: Courtesy of Mourne Textiles and photographer Tara Fisher.

Pages 132–135: All images courtesy of Tom Vaughan of Object Studio.

Pages 132–133: Photographs courtesy of Sam Barker.

Page 134 top: Photograph courtesy of Christian Maier Smith; bottom: Photograph courtesy of Sam Barker.

Page 135 top left and top right: Photographs courtesy of Sam Barker; bottom: courtesy of James Champion.

HEALTH & WELLBEING

Pages 136–137: Courtesy of Alice Kettle, the Candida Stevens Gallery and photographer Michael Pollard. Ground (2018) includes contributions from Pipka/Lesvos Solidarity, Ahmad Ali, Somaya Hossaini, Yakob and many other residents at Calais refugee camp working with Suzanne Partridge; Nahomie Bukasa, Sahira Khan and Ai Ling with Linda Leroy at the Helen Bamber Foundation; Nisrin Albyrouty, Khouloud Alkurd, Heba Almnini, Heidi Ambruster, Marwa Ammar, Amal Ayoubi, Stella Charman, Susan Colverson, Jenny Cuffe, Lama Hamami, Miriam Jones, Asmaa, Ruth le Mesurier, Vanessa Rolf, Samar Sobeih, Chaymae Yousfi and many children from English Chat Winchester; Farhia Ahmed Ali, Nawad Hersi Duale, Amran Mohamud Ismail with Refugee Action working with artists Jenny Eden and Richard Harris;

Julie Firman, Victoria Hartley, Louise Jung, Susan Kamara, Sam. Stitch and life jacket material on printed canvas, 3m x 8m.

Page 139: Courtesy of the UK Men's Sheds Association.

Page 140: Courtesy of Knit For Peace.

Page 141: Courtesy of The Prince's Foundation and photographer Guy Hinks.

Page 142: Courtesy of Hugh Dunford Wood.

Page 143: Courtesy of West Dean College of Arts and Conservation.

Page 145: Courtesy of Jason Mosseri and photographer Alun Callender.

Pages 146–147: Courtesy of Knithub 24.

Pages 148–149: Courtesy of Alice Kettle, the Candida Stevens Gallery and photographer Michael Pollard. Sky includes contributions from Amran Abdi Mohamed, Iqra Abdi Mohamed, Idil Abdi Mohamud, Ayantu Abdii, Abdirahman, Abdi Muse, Farhia Ahmed Ali, Bile Ali Aden, Alias Aliye Musa Aliye, Gutu Habib, Monica Hamakami, Isha Hassan Bare, Nawad Hersi Duale, Muno Idiris Mohamed, Mohamed Ahmed Mezan Ismail, Tajura Lamiso Gatiso, Khadar Mohamud Ismail, Sahra Mohamud Ismail, Amran Mohamud Ismail, Fartun Umar Jimale – All with Refugee Action and working with artists Jenny Eden and Richard Harris – Julie Firman, Victoria Hartley, Louise Jung and Sam. Interpreters: Ramadan Ahmed, Abas El Janabi and Mohamed Hirey. Stitch on printed canvas, 3m x 8m.

Page 145: Both images courtesy of Alice Kettle, the Candida Stevens Gallery and Dan Stevens.

UNIQUE & PERSONAL

Pages 150–151: Courtesy of Caroline Groves and photographer Dan Lowe.

Page 153: Courtesy of Jacky Puzey and photographer Jo Hounsome.

Page 154 (Wyvern): Courtesy of Wyvern Bindery and photograph Julian Love.

Page 155: Courtesy of Helen Amy Murray, Rolls-Royce and photographer Jake Curtis.

Page 156: Courtesy of Silverlining and Mark Reeves Photography.

Page 157: Courtesy of Aiveen Daly and photographer Simon Bevan.

Pages 158–159: Suit image – courtesy of Kathryn Sargent and photographer Dish Creative James Munson. Portrait image courtesy of Reuben Paris.

Page 160: Courtesy of Daisy Knatchbull and photographer Matilda Lowther.

Page 161: Courtesy of Caroline Groves and photographer Rowan Morgan.

Page 162: Courtesy of Caroline Groves and photographer Dan Lowe.

Page 163: Courtesy of Carréducker and photographer Alun Callender.

Pages 164–165: All courtesy of John Lobb Ltd and for top left and top right photographer Tom Bunning.

Pages 166–169: all images courtesy of Alexandra Llewellyn.

Page 166: portrait of Alexandra courtesy of Hot Icarus.

Page 167: top left: Courtesy of Hot Icarus; top right: courtesy of Susana Silver.

Pages 168–169: courtesy of Susana Silver.

MASTERFUL & MAGICAL

Pages 170–171: Courtesy of Olivia Walker and photographer Sylvain Deleu.

Page 173: Courtesy of Vezzini & Chen, Adrian Sassoon London, and photographer Sylvain Deleu.

Page 174: Courtesy of Samantha Donaldson, Vessel Gallery and photographer Agata Pec.

Page 175: Courtesy of Nina Casson MGarva, Vessel gallery and photographer Agata Pec.

Page 176: Courtesy of Olivia Walker and photographer Sylvain Deleu.

Page 177: Courtesy of Hitomi Hosono, Adrian Sassoon London, and photographer Sylvain Deleu.

Page 178: Courtesy of Fenella Elms, photographer Deborah Husk and with thanks to Under Winch's Wing.

Page 179: Courtesy of Lucas Ferreira and jaggedart.

Page 180: Top: Courtesy of Eleanor Lakelin, the Sarah Myerscough gallery and photographer Michael Harvey. Bottom: Courtesy of John Makepeace, the Sarah Myerscough gallery and photographer Michael Harvey.

Page 181: Courtesy of Alison Crowther and photographer Sarah Sheldrake.

Pages 182–183: Courtesy of Nic Webb, the Sarah Myerscough gallery and photographer Alun Callender.

Page 184: Courtesy of the artists, Craftmasters Gallery and Richard Kalina Photography.

Page 185: Top: Courtesy of Ndidi Ekubia, Adrian Sassoon London, and photographer Alun Callender. Bottom: Courtesy of Hal Messel and photographer Richard Jackson.

Pages 186–187: Courtesy of Dame Magdalene Odundo and photographer Alun Callender.

Page 188: Courtesy of Danny Lane and photographer Peter Wood.

COLLECTED & CURATED

Pages 190–191: Courtesy of Thurle Wright and jaggedart.

Page 193: Courtesy of Kazuhito Takadoi, jaggedart and photographer Alun Callender.

Page 194: Courtesy of the artists, Make Hauser & Wirth and photographer Dave Watts.

Page 195: Courtesy of Saelia Aparicio, Gallery FUMI and photographer Thomas Joseph Wright of Penguins Egg.

Page 196: Courtesy of Martha Freud, the Nonemore Gaallery and photographer Joakim Blockstrom.

Page 197: Courtesy of Martha Freud, Firmdale hotels and photographer Simon Brown.

Pages 198–199: Courtesy of Rowan Mersh, Gallery FUMI and photographer Leslie Lau.

Pages 200–201: Courtesy of Kazuhito Takadoi and jaggedart.

Page 202: Courtesy of the Ting Ying Gallery.

Page 203: Courtesy of Peter Ting and photographer Alun Callender.

Page 204: Left: Courtesy of Forest + Found and the New Art Centre. Right: Courtesy of Dr David Gates.

Page 205: Courtesy of the artists, the Sarah Myerscough Gallery and photographer Michael Harvey.

Page 207: Top and below left: Courtesy of Laura Ellen Bacon and Alun Callender. Below right: Courtesy of Laura Ellen Bacon and Steve Hickey.

Pages 208–209: Courtesy of Garry Fabian Miller, Dovecot Studios and photographer Kenneth Gray.

Pages 210–211: Courtesy of Dovecot Studios, the estate of Leon Kossoff, Parabola for Edinburgh Park and photographer Andy Mather.

INSPIRATIONAL & ASPIRATIONAL

Pages 212–213: Courtesy of Tom Vaughan, Rundell Assocs and photographer Sam Barker.

Pages 214–215: Courtesy of Helen Amy Murray, architects 212box and photographer Nick Rochowski.

Page 216: Courtesy of Helen Amy Murray, Van Cleef & Arpels and photographer Marcos Bevilacqua.

Page 217: Courtesy of Helen Amy Murray, Rolls-Royce and photographer Jake Curtis.

Page 218: Courtesy of Aryma and photographer Ellie Burd.

Page 219: Courtesy of Linley and Mark Reeves photography.

Page 220: Courtesy of Carolyn Quartermaine, sketch London and photographer James Merrell.

Page 221: Courtesy of Taylor Howes, Based Upon and photographer Martin Morrell.

Pages 222–223: Courtesy of Based Upon.

Pages 224–225: Courtesy of Cox London and photographer Alun Callender.

Page 226: Courtesy of Atelier 001.

Page 227: Courtesy of Rothschild & Bickers and Motel One, Salzburg Mirabell.

Page 228: Courtesy of Valéria Nascimento and photographer Lucas Ferreira.

Page 229: Courtesy of Valéria Nascimento and photographer Christopher Pillitz.

Pages 230–231: Top: Portrait of Thomas Heatherwick: Photography by Andy Parsons / Time Out, Camera Press London. Bottom: Stem desk: Courtesy of the American Hardwood Export Council.

Pages 232–233: Friction Table: Photography by Raquel Diniz / Heatherwick Studio.

INNOVATIVE & COLLABORATIVE

Pages 234–235: Courtesy of Hull Studio, Gallery FUMI and Mark Reeves Photography.

Page 237: Courtesy of Michael Eden, Adrian Sassoon London and photographer Sylvain Deleu.

Page 238: Courtesy of Michael Eden, Adrian Sassoon London and photographer Sylvain Deleu.

Page 239: Courtesy of Jonathan Keep, Sarah Myerscough Gallery and photographer Michael Harvey.

Page 240: Courtesy of Saltyco.

Page 241: Courtesy of Jen Keane, Modern Synthesis.

Page 242: Courtesy of Terri Adams and photographer Susan Davis.

Page 243: Courtesy of Matt Durran and photographer Matthew Booth.

Page 245: Courtesy of Gareth Neal, the Sarah Myerscough Gallery and photographer Alun Callender.

Page 246: Hack Chair images: Courtesy of Gareth Neal, Sarah Myerscough Gallery and photographer Petr Krejci. Sketch book image: courtesy of Alun Callender. VES-EL image: Courtesy of Gareth Neal, Zaha Hadid Architects, Sarah Myerscough Gallery and photographer Petr Krejci.

Page 247: Sio2 vessel courtesy of Gareth Neal, Sarah Myerscough Gallery and photographer Jan Faukner.

Index

Page references in *italics* are illustrations

1882 LTD 94–7, *94–7*

A
Adams, Terri 242, *242*
Aparicio, Saelia *195*
architectural sculpture 218–20
art galleries and crafts 194–9
artists utilising crafts 192–4
Arts and Crafts movement 14–16
Artworkers' Guild 14–16
Aryma marquetry 217, *218*
Ashbridge, Lisi *68*
Atelier 001 226–7, *227*
Avedian, Lora 124, *126*

B
Bacon, Laura Ellen 194, 206–7, *207*
Bainbridge, Abigail *37*
Bainbridge, Max 204, *205*
Bainbridge, Tristram 37–9, *38*
Based Upon 223, *225*
basket weaving 70–3, 107–11
Beecham, Clive 21–3
bell founding 62
Belsky, Ilana 74, 74–5, *75*
Benchmark 127
bespoke crafts 152–4
Betts, Aimee 124, *128*
Bibbings & Hensby *14*, 16
Bill Amberg Studio 217–18
bookbinding 31, *154*
Booth, Abigail 204, *205*
Bramble, Chris *27*
Brexit 26
Bromley, Neil *43*
bronze foundries 192
built heritage/buildings 34–9, 43
Burge, Hugo 21
Burleigh Pottery 78, *80–1*, 82
Burns, Sarah *111*, 111

C
Carré, Deborah 162–3
Carréducker 162–3, *163*
ceramic tiles 78–82
ceramics 94–7, 176–80, 186–7
Chanel Le 19M 26
Clarke, Brian 192
Clay College 23
clothing 157–62
coach building 64
Collect Fair 14
Cologni, Franco 21
concept and craft 199–205
conservation 34–9

Cornish Bed Company 125–7, *126*
Costa Felgueiras, Pedro da *34*, *50*, 50–1
courses 144
Covid, impact of 16, 26, 138
Cowley, William 40, *42*
Cox London *224*, 226
Craft Design House 23–6
crafts
  and art 192–9
  and concept 199–205
  diversity of craft makers 26–7
  endangered 56–9, 61, 62, 64–5
  market for 26
  organisations supporting 14–20
  philanthropists 21–6
  rare 59–60
  revival of 58–9
  tactility of 172
  unusual 61–5
  and wellbeing 138–44
The Crafts Council 14, 26–7, 143–4
Crafty Fox Market 18
Create Day 18
Creative Dimension Trust (TCDT) 16–18
cricket bats 56
Crispinians 64–5
Crowther, Alison *182*

D
Daly, Aiveen *157*, 157
Day, Chris 176
De Bruin, Michelle *22*
De Waal, Edmund 194
decoupage 221–5
Dhanani, Asif 146–7
diamond cutting 74–5
diversity of craft makers 26–7
Donaldson, Samantha *174*, 176
Dougall, James *184*
Dovecot Studios 208–11, *209*, *211*
Ducker, James 163, *163*
Durran, Matt *242*, 242–3

E
Eden, Michael 236, *236*, *239*
Elms, Fenella *178*
embroidery 148–9
Emin, Tracey 192
endangered crafts 56–9, 61, 62, 64–5
equestrian leatherwork 120, *121*
Ettinger 49, *49*

F
Ferreira, Lucas *179*
Fontan, Aurélie 238–40
footwear *9*, 162–5

Freud, Martha *197*, 202–4
furniture 125–9
  bespoke 225–6
  conservation 37–9
  couture furniture 154–7
  decoupage 221–5
  Object Studio 132–5
  steam-bent furniture 114–17
  sustainability 101–7, 114–17, 127

G
Gainsborough Mill *35*, 85
galleries and crafts 194–9
games makers 166–7
Gates, David 204–5, *205*
Gauld, Kevin 105–7, *106*
glassware 125, 174–6, 188–9
  scientific glassblowing 242–3
Govani, Farah 146–7
Grandey's Place 21–3
Granter, Ashley 238–40
Great Northern Contemporary Craft Fair (GNCCF) 18
Greenaway, Thomas *58*, *59*, 60
Groves, Caroline *152*, *161*, 162, *163*

H
Hammond, Lisa 23
Hand & Lock 39–40, *40*
Harris, Daniel 91
Harris Tweed 78
hats 42, *44–6*
Hay-Edie, Karen 130–1
Hearn, Stewart *128*
Heatherwick Studio 230, *231–2*
Heatherwick, Thomas 230, *231*
Hensby, Matthew 16, *16*
Heritage Crafts 16, 27, 56, 58
Holz, Jochen 194
home accessories 122–5
Hood, Helen 184–5
Hope Spring Chairs 103
Hosono, Hitomi 176
Howarth, Charlotte *68*
Hull, Alex 236, *236*
Hull Studios 236

I
Ingrams, Otis 124
insignia 52–3
interior design 215–25
Ironbridge 78
Irons, Felicity *100*, 112–13, *113*
Isle of Auskerry *92–3*, 92–3

J
Jack, Robina 194
Johnson Brothers 94–7
Johnson, Edward 128, *129*

Johnson, Emily 94–7
Jones, Owen 70–3, *71*, *72*
Jue, Jessica *184*

K
Keane, Jen 240–1, *241*
Keep, Jonathan 236, *239*
Kennedy, Seth *21*
Kennedy, Thomas *54*, *57*, 59–60
Kettle, Alice *138*, *148–9*, 148–9
The Kiltmakery *27*
Knatchbull, Daisy 158–60, *161*
Kneebone, Rachel 194
Knit for Peace 138–42
KNITHUB 24, 146–7
knitting 138–43, 146–7
Knitwise 142–3
Kuch, Anja *122*

L
Laird, Nikki *27*
Lakelin, Eleanor *16*, *180*
land art 206
Landseer, Sir Edwin 192
Lane, Danny *188*, 188–9
laquering *38*, 50–1
last making 64–5, *152*
leather work 47, 49, 217–18
  equestrian 120, *121*
  Mary Wing To 28–9
lettering 68–9
Lettering Arts Trust 68–9
lighting 226–7
Linley, David *218*, 225
Llewellyn, Alexandra 166–7, *166–9*
Lobb, John *164*, 164–5
Lock & Co. 42, *43*, *44–6*
London Cloth Company 91
London Craft Week (LCW) 18
looms *91*
Lowe, Steven *64*, 64–5
Lytle, Lulu *64*, *68*

M
Mackey, Emily *20*
Mahieu, Didier *220*, 221–5
Make Hauser & Wirth 194, *194–8*
Makepeace, John *181*
marbling 30–1
Marchmont House 21
Marigold, Peter 205, *205*
Marmor Paperie 30–1
marquetry 217
materials 172, 236–41
McChesney, Ian *120*
McDermott, Allyson *36*, 37
McFadyen, Jock 211
McGarva, Nina Casson *174*, 176
McGrath, Lucy *30*, 30–1, *31*

Men's Sheds' *139*, 144
Menz, Eva 226–7
Mersh, Rowan *198*, 199
Messel, Hal *184*
Messum, Johnny 198
metalworking 86–7
  bronze foundries 192
  metal casting 62
Michelangelo Foundation for
  Creativity and Craftsmanship 21
Miller, Garry Fabian *209*, 211
Monzon, Angel 174–6
Morris, Annie 194
Morris, William 14
mosaics 60
Mosseri, Jason *102*, 103, *145*
Mourne Textiles 130–1, *130–1*
Mulholland, Lee 242
Murray, Helen Amy *154*, *215*, 215–17,
  216, *217*
musical instruments 56–8, 120–2
Myerscough, Sarah 180–4

N
Nafisi Studio *102*, 103
Nascimento, Valéria 228, *228*, *229*
Neal, Gareth 244, *245–7*
Neal, Lawrence 103–5, *104–5*
neon bending 87–91, *89*
North Ronaldsay sheep 92–3
Novocastrian *86*, 86–7

O
oak swills 70–3
Object Studio 132–5
O'Connor, Alex *184*
Odundo, Magdalene Dame *186–7*,
  186–7
Ore & Ingot Foundry 62, *63*
  orreries 61–2
Osmose Studio 238–40
O'Sullivan, Annemarie *106*, 107–11,
  109
OTZI London 124, *124–5*

P
paper 30–1, 56
parchment 40–1
pargetting *83*, 83–4
Patel, Karen 27
pattern cutting 158–60
Peers, Elizabeth Oriel *184*
Perry, Grayson 192–4
philanthropists 21–6
pietra dura 60
plasterwork 59–60, 83–4
Platt, Richard *24*
The Potteries 78
pottery 78, 236

Preston, Geoffrey 218–21
The Prince's Foundation 18–20
Probert, Teresa 92–3
Puzey, Jacky *153*, 156–7

Q
Quartermaine, Carolyn *220*, 221–5
The Queen Elizabeth Scholarship
Trust (QEST) 14
Quin, Rebecca de *184*

R
Raffield, Tom 114–17, *114–17*
rattan weaving *64*, 65–8
Reader, Helen 120
regalia 52–3
Reyntiens, Patrick 192
Ross, Angus *101*, 101–2, *102*
Rothschild & Bickers *227*, 227
Rowland, Mike 64, 67
Rowley, Sophie *194*
The Royal Drawing School 20
The Royal School of Needlework
(RSN) 39
Rupert, Johann 21
Rush Matters *100*, 112–13

S
Saltyco 236–8, *241*
Sands, Tom 120–2, *122*
Sargent, Kathryn 158, *159*
Sassoon, Adrian 176–80
Savile Row *158* 60
scagliola 59–60
Scott, Gillian 23
sculpture 192, 206, 218–20
Sealy, Jo 27
shoemakers 9, 162–5 see also last
making
Sierra, Mario 130–1
silk weaving 84–6
silver 184–5
Silverlining furniture 157
Singleton, Lorna *110*, 110–11
slate 82–3
Soane Britain 64, 68
Society for the Protection of Ancient
Buildings (SPAB) 14
sports equipment 56 see also
equestrian leatherwork
stained-glass 192
Staines & Son 61, 61–2
statues 192
steam-bent furniture making 114–17
Stoke-on-Trent 78, 94–7
stucco 83–4
Suffolk 84
sustainability 101, 236–41
Swaine Adeney Brigg 46, 47–9

T
tailoring 158–60
Takadoi, Kazuhito 192, 201
tapestries 192–4, 208–11
Taplin, Guy 194
technology 236
textile art 148–9
textiles 39–40, 111, 130–1, 236
Thread Bearing Witness 148–9
tiles 78–82
Ting, Peter 202, *202*
Toye, Kenning & Spencer 52, 52–3
Tozawa, Tadanori 205
Truss, Carolyn *120*, 121

U
umbrellas 47
UNESCO Convention for the
Safeguarding of Intangible Cultural
Heritage 16

V
Vaughan, Tom 132–5, *132–5*, 215
vellum 40–1
Vessel Gallery 174
Vezzini & Chen 173

W
Walker, Eliot 176
Walker, Katie *128*, 129
Walker, Olivia *172*, 176
Walker, Rob 19
wallpapers 37
Walmsley, Dennis 28–9
Watts, George Frederic 192
weaving 90–1 see also textiles
  basket weaving 70–3, 107–11
  rattan weaving *64*, 65–8
  sculptures 206, *207*
  silk weaving 84–6
Webb, Nic 182
Wedgwood, Josiah 78
wellbeing and crafts 138–44
West Dean College 144
Whalen, Tracey 20
wheelwrighting 64, 67
whip making 28–9
Whittle, Alberta 210
Wilson, David Snoo 62, *63*
Under Winch's Wing 26
Wing To, Mary *28*, 28–9
Wood, Hugh Dunford 36
woodland management 101–3
woodworking 101–3, 180–4
wool industry 90–3
Wright, Thurle 192
Wyvern Bindery 154

Published in 2022 by OH Editions
Part of Welbeck Publishing Group.
Based in London and Sydney.
www.welbeckpublishing.com

Design © 2022 OH Editions

Text © 2022 Helen Chislett and David Linley
Photography © see pages 251—253

A CIP catalogue record for this book is available from the British Library.

ISBN 978-1-91431-786-6

Publisher: Kate Pollard
Editor: Wendy Hobson
Designer: David Rowley www.davidrowleydesign.com
Index: Cathy Heath
Production controller: Arlene Alexander
Colour reproduction: p2D

Printed and bound by RR Donnelley in China

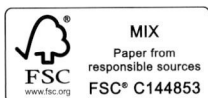

FSC
www.fsc.org
MIX
Paper from
responsible sources
FSC® C144853

10 9 8 7 6 5 4 3 2 1

Front Cover: *Twisted Pair 1755* from the *Sio2* series of vessels cast in sand by Gareth Neal (see pages 244–247).

Back Cover: Three bronze founders by the furnace in the Cox London foundry (see pages 225–226).

Title page: *Morning Dew* by Kazuhito Takadoi (courtesy of jaggedart).

Contents page: *Acqua Alta* group by Christopher Riggio (courtesy of jaggedart).

Tyne between central Newcastle and Gateshead; or the *Otterburn* chess set, named after an ancient Northumbrian village, the scene of the 1388 Battle of Otterburn.

Neon was discovered in 1898 by two British scientists, William Ramsay and Morris W Travers. They had been experimenting with krypton and argon, allowing solid argon to evaporate and collecting the gas it gave off under reduced pressure. When they put this new gas into their atomic spectrometer, they were startled by its brilliant red glow. Ramsay named this new gas, neon, based on *neos*, the Greek word for new. While red is the colour of pure neon, other colours can be created through the addition of various gases.

The French engineer and inventor, Georges Claude, popularised its use in the early twentieth century and by the 1920s, it had been introduced into the American market. By the 1930s, it was part of the landscape of America, immortalised by the paintings of Edward Hopper and others. In fact, few materials have infiltrated our culture so successfully through art, architecture, film, music, fashion, theatre and retail.

What is often overlooked is that every neon sign, past and present, has been hand bent by a skilled maker. These glass tubes are shaped using only heat and expert manipulation. While the craft of neon bending may be on Heritage Crafts' Endangered list, neon itself is plentiful – the fifth most abundant element in the Earth's atmosphere. Neon is comparable in its efficiency with LEDs, but with the advantage of being 100 per cent recyclable. After all, neon is simply inert

Sphere, a remaking
and scaling up of Fred
Tschida's work of the
same name from 2000,
was installed at the
Neon Workshops project
space in Wakefield in
2021. Neon production
in the UK was once
concentrated in West
Yorkshire.

Opposite: 2.3-metre (90-inch) wide Dobcross loom made in the mid 1950s. Slow by modern standards, these can weave practically anything once set up correctly from suiting to carpet.

Right: A wall of spare parts stripped from other looms, including fresh shuttles ready for use and 1970's punch cards that controlled the early rapier models.

gas, harnessed from the air, injected inside a vacuumed glass tube and charged with electricity.

British neon production was traditionally centred on West Yorkshire, where there were at least two dozen workshops in the first half of the twentieth century. Oldham Signs in Leeds was the largest neon fabricator in Europe until it closed its doors in 2003. Artist Richard Wheater studied Glass at Edinburgh college of Art before discovering the possibilities of neon at Alfred University in New York under the tutorage of artist, Fred Tschida. In 2010, he opened Neon Workshops in Wakefield, specialising in the design, fabrication and installation of neon projects across the globe through a talented team of makers and installers. In 2021, Neon Workshops produced Fred Tschida's work in the UK for the first time. It has also facilitated work by other artists, including Alfredo Jaar, Tim Etchells, Jochen Holz, Mary McCartney and Martin Creed, as well as producing Wheater's own work.

The wool industry once thrived in South-West England and Wales, owing to the topography of rolling hills and winding rivers that created the perfect pasture for the breeding of sheep. In 2010, Daniel Harris decided on a whim to go into weaving, with no training or experience whatsoever (although he knew how to sew). He rescued a rusting loom dating from the 1920s from an old barn in rural Wales, took it apart and put it back together, and then realised it was missing various parts – such as a winder to wind the bobbins. All in all, it took a year before he had tracked down all the missing pieces and had a fully working loom. He then taught himself to use it, eventually establishing a successful micro-mill on the outskirts of London. The London Cloth Company now produces over 60 types of indigo cloth and an extensive range of wool tweeds. Harris has managed to buy more original looms over the years, including four from the 1880s, that he still uses to weave linen. His most recent looms come from the 1970s to 1990s, the last era of the mechanical mill before computerised models became ubiquitous. He may be a long way from Wales, but the looms he uses pay testament to that heritage.

ISLE OF AUSKERRY:
Fleece Producer

Right: Dyed yarn drying in the wind at the family home in Auskerry. The yarn is dyed in small batches to reflect the island colours.

Isle of Auskerry is a family business based on the remote Orkney island of the same name. Simon Brogan moved there from London in 1975 and in 1983 married Teresa Probert, with the couple subsequently giving their three sons – Rory, Owen and Hamish – the surname Auskerry. The family breed North Ronaldsay sheep that thrive not on pasture but on seaweed, which they graze along the numerous pebble beaches, living in perfect harmony with the thousands of seabirds that nest there each year, including puffins, stormy petrels and black guillemots. In summer, they also feast on a variety of wild flowers and grasses that grow inland. North Ronaldsay, Orkney's native sheep, is a rare breed and the family's flock is one of only two surviving. Their unique fleeces are symmetrically marked with a range of colours from camel and black to creamy silver and dark grey, and the yarn is renowned for its lustre and softness. The family hand-clip the fleeces, making

'Our business grew from our determination to preserve the North Ronaldsay sheep genes for future generations, and our delight in working with their beautiful wool.'

shearing a calm procedure for both humans and sheep. Because the sheep lead such a natural life, the wool produced is 100 per cent organic and environmentally friendly.

Fleeces are sent to mainland Scotland for spinning and weaving by a cottage industry of small co-workers. Every skein of wool yarn bought helps conserve these seaweed-eating sheep for future generations. Isle of Auskerry sells a variety of products from its online shop, including sheepskin rugs and cushions, lambskin rugs, handwoven blankets (which can be personalised), knitting kits for hats, scarves, mittens and cushions, horn buttons, raw fleece for spinners, felt table accessories and, of course, balls of wool yarn. In addition, it offers free online tutorials and welcomes visitors who make it to their remote and beautiful part of the British Isles.

Teresa Probert says, 'When we first started farming these sheep, there was only one flock left in Orkney and a very real danger of their becoming extinct in their natural habitat. Our business grew from our determination to preserve their genes for future generations, and our delight in working with their wool. Every fleece I clip is different and full of so many beautiful shades of colour that I never get bored with looking at them.

'I love watching the ewes grazing on the living weed as the tide recedes. They are so well camouflaged amongst the rocks by their fleeces, even with their tiny lambs jumping over the rock pools behind them. Developing the business in this remote, and at times harsh, landscape has not been easy, but we love being intimately involved with every part of the making of our products, from the rearing of the lambs to the selling of the knitting kits.'

Left: Finished yarns showing the range of natural colours produced from the fleeces of North Ronaldsay sheep from creamy silver to chocolate brown.

Below: A seaweed-loving North Ronaldsay sheep on the shore in Auskerry. This is a rare breed native to the islands of Orkney, which produces fleeces renowned for their soft texture.

1882 LTD:
Ceramic Studio

1882 Ltd is a design-led ceramics studio in Stoke-on-Trent established by the fourth and fifth generations of the Johnson Brothers family. It is named after the year in which Alfred and Frederick Johnson founded their eponymous company, having bought up a bankrupt pottery called JW Pankhurst. Their factory was situated in Hanley, the largest of the Six Towns of The Potteries. Johnson Brothers produced mainly White Ware but became famous for their underglaze printed ware, exporting it not only around Britain but to the USA. Over the years, the company prospered and expanded, opening the Hanley Pottery, Imperial Pottery, Alexandra Pottery and Trent Sanitary Works by the turn of the twentieth century. By the 1950s, it was producing an extraordinary one million pieces of pottery each week.

Johnson Brothers became part of the Wedgwood Group in 1968, but Christopher Johnson – the last of the family to be connected to the business – retired in 2002, having held the role of Production Director. In 2011, he formed 1882

Opposite: In 2015, 1882 collaborated with artist, Barnaby Barford, to create *The Tower of Babel* for the V&A Museum in London, comprising 3,000 individual, bone china shops and standing six metres (twenty feet) high. It took the studio two years to complete.

Right: Each building depicted a real London shop, with the artist cycling over 1,000 miles to visit every postcode in the city – a monument to the British pastime of shopping.

'Having started off in television advertising, I couldn't now imagine doing anything else. Bone china is the most fantastic medium with which to work.'

with his daughter, Emily Johnson, who had previously been working in television advertising in Los Angeles for eight years. She returned home and studied a Masters in Architectural Interior Design at the Inchbald School of Design, choosing fine bone china for her research project and realising how undervalued it was as a vehicle for innovative design. With her creative eye and her father's wealth of experience, it seemed a good moment to combine their talents and in so doing support the traditional ceramics industry of Stoke-on-Trent.

In the ten years since they began, the company has produced wonderfully innovative collections of lighting, tableware and candles. Its own collections are sold all over the world, from Europe and the USA to Japan and China. It has also initiated exciting collaborations with many architects and designers, including Barnaby Barford, John Pawson, Max Lamb, Faye Toogood and Paul Smith. Pawson's *Cast Bowl* is conceived as a quiet landscape made in the palest of hues – an essay in simplicity and geometry. Lamb's *Big Vase 1 and 2* began as a solid block of plaster that has been hand-carved by hammer and chisel into the raw shape of a vase, with a hollow mould then created from which multiple vases could be slip-cast. Toogood's *Indigo Rain* puts a fresh spin on the forms and traditions of English creamware – a contemporary interpretation of the familiar blue-and-white striped crockery. Smith's *Stack* is a series of vessels that at first glance seem to be a stack of plates; each 'plate' hand-glazed in colours inspired by Paul Smith's iconic stripes. However, the studio's most ambitious project to date was the spectacular six-metre (twenty-foot) high *Tower of Babel* with Barnaby Barford, comprising three thousand uniquely decorated fine bone china mini shops, which was displayed at the V&A Museum in London.

Of her change of career direction and love of bone china, Emily Johnson says, 'I couldn't now imagine doing anything else – the industry is full of amazing people and bone china is the most fantastic medium.'

Opposite top: Crockery Black, a collaboration with Max Lamb, is an interpretation of the black basalt first developed by Josiah Wedgwood in 1766. Seen here with Crockery White also by Max Lamb.

Opposite below: Big Vase 1 is also a collaboration with Max Lamb. It began as a solid block of plaster, which Lamb hand-carved with hammer and chisel into a raw form and had slip-cast in fine bone china.

Left: The first fire of porcelain Linley candle holders. It is during the firing process that clay transforms into ceramic, making it stronger and more durable.

Below: Each candle is stamped with the Linley name to show its authenticity and provenance. The vessels are inspired by iconic Doric columns of antiquity.

5

Previous spread: Felicity
Irons in her fourteenth-
century Bedfordshire
barn from where she
runs Rush Matters (see
pages 112–113).

A lot is written and said about the need for a kinder and more sustainable future, but crafts have been championing these principles for centuries. Indeed, they would never have survived without naturally adhering to a 'green' ethos. Historically, they reflected the materials abundant within the local landscape; wasted little in terms of resource; found their market within a small radius; and recycled any by-products. Anyone who commissions or buys a hand-crafted object can be sure that it has left little in the way of a carbon footprint. Not only that, but the chances are he or she will treasure that object in a way they might not a mass-produced item, meaning it is less likely to be discarded to landfill.

One of the most encouraging aspects of craft in Britain today has been how makers are highlighting sustainable practices from which we can all learn. Today, their low-carbon way of working is applauded, but those who have been following their craft profession all their working lives have never deviated from these eco-friendly principles.

Designer and furniture maker, Angus Ross, moved to the Highlands of Perthshire in 2002 with his wife, Lorna, with whom he owns an ancient and beautifully diverse local bluebell wood of about twenty hectares (fifty acres). This includes timbers such as veteran, native oak trees (*Quercus robur*), as well as birch, hazel and alder. Traditionally, oaks were coppiced here so that tannin could be extracted for use by the local leather industry, but the move to chemical processing was well under way by World War I, meaning that the woodland was largely abandoned. Some of the Rosses' oaks have root systems that are 200 years old or more.

Left: A memorial bench by Angus Ross is placed to enjoy the view over the Schiehallion Mountain in Perthshire, Scotland.

Opposite top: A brightly-coloured reinterpretation of the iconic *Sussex Chair* by Nafisi Studio, using timber sourced close to their Sussex studio.

Opposite below: *Shaker Bench* by Jason Mosseri of Hopespring Chairs with dark 'milk' paint contrasting against the natural wood grain.

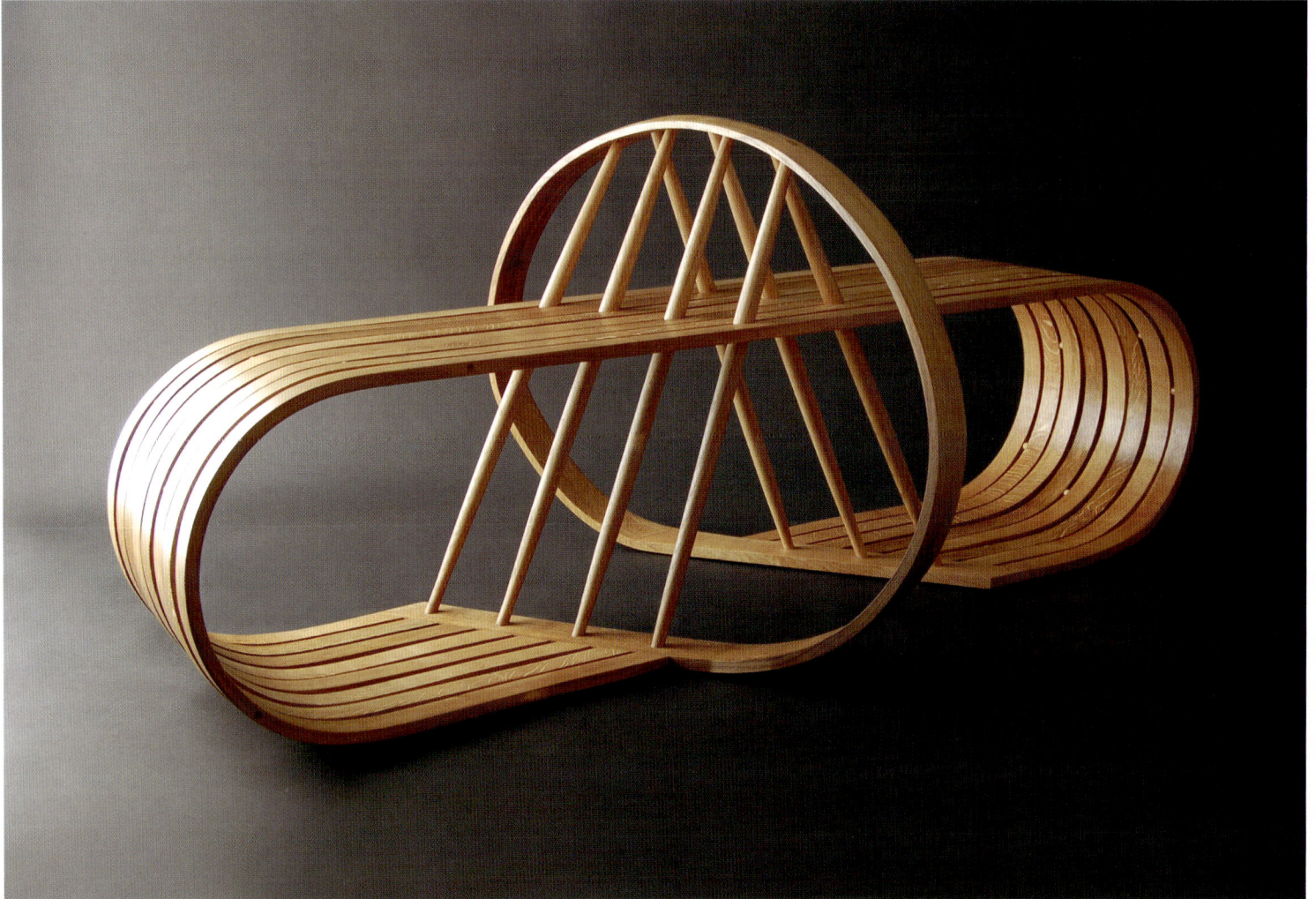

Above: *Forth Bench* is one of a series of sculptural, steam-bent, 'river' benches by Angus Ross. He describes the process of making pieces such as this as 'sketching with wood'.

It may seem counter-intuitive, but one of the best ways of improving a neglected native woodland is to fell trees, because if a wood is overcrowded it prevents new trees from growing. Selective felling brings light to the woodland floor and results in greater biodiversity of plants, fungi, insects, birds, bats and other creatures. The trees selected for coppicing are by their nature often ones that are spindly, bent and gnarled. As well as sourcing good timber from small-scale timber yards that specialise in Scottish hardwoods,

Ross has experimented over time with ways to use this imperfect coppiced wood within his designs, perfecting innovative methods of steam-bending, twisting, slicing and sculpting it into characterful forms. Coppicing is more akin to foraging and very different from imported, industrial-scale 'clear fell', the method used for so much mass-produced oak furniture. Ross believes and hopes his furniture will last decades, maybe even centuries, but is also comforted by the fact it can be repaired, recycled and will eventually biodegrade.

It is a similar story at the other end of the country in West Sussex. Here, Abdollah and Kate Nafisi founded Nafisi Studio in 2019. Originally from Iran – where he ran his own woodworking workshop and spent six years travelling with nomads and tribes in order to study their craftsmanship and skill of improvisation – Abdollah is a designer-craftsman with over fifteen years' experience. Kate is both a designer and a curator, with a particular interest in provenance of materials and sustainability. Together, they create furniture that is both beautifully made and has a playful spirit – such as the iconic *Sussex Chair* by William Morris & Co. that they have re-imagined in bold colours. Wood is locally sourced from carefully managed Sussex woodland, with any sawdust waste composted.

In neighbouring East Sussex, QEST Scholar Jason Mosseri founded Hopespring Chairs in 2017, having become hooked on the skill of green woodworking after taking a chairmaking course with Paul Hayden at Westonbirt Arboretum. Mosseri had previously enjoyed great success as a professional, custom tattooist, but in chairs he found a new way to express his artistic vision. As with the Nafisis, each chair he makes begins with a day in local, sustainably-managed woods, selecting freshly felled ash, oak, beech or cherry. Seats are carved from a single, seasoned board of timber. Once the chair is complete, he adds a modern flavour and bold silhouette by finishing it with a dark 'milk paint' that contrasts boldly with the wood's natural grain. He also runs highly successful, six-day chairmaking courses where attendees leave with a Windsor chair of their own making (see page 145).

Weaving the Landscape

Lawrence Neal spends two weeks each year harvesting rush on the river Avon near his Warwickshire workshop, as he has done for over fifty years. Neal makes traditional ladderback chairs, which are characterised by their rush seats and the

Left: Lawrence Neal weaving a rush seat on the traditional ladderback chairs first made popular by Philip Clissett, who in turn influenced the Arts & Crafts designer Ernest Gimson.

Opposite left: Neal harvests rushes from the river Avon and soaks them in water before beginning the careful and time-consuming process of weaving each chair seat by hand.

horizontal pieces of wood that form the chair's back. He learnt the craft from his father, Neville Neal, when he joined his workshop as an apprentice in 1966. Today, he makes two to three chairs a week, in eleven styles that range from side chairs to rocking chairs. All are based on those first made by the Arts and Crafts designer, Ernest Gimson. His own father was apprenticed to Gimson's collaborator, Edward Gardiner, in 1939, so it is a very direct line from Gimson down to Neal. He continues to use the tools and techniques employed over 100 years ago, with a small nod to the modern world in the shape of a handful of mechanical saws and a sander. The ash and oak he uses to make the chairs are sourced from local woodlands and sawmills, with green wood (not yet dried) used to make the back of the chair and the front of the legs, because green wood shrinks and in doing so holds the frame together. A bundle of rushes is dunked in water and then Neal

begins weaving the seat; this is the most time-consuming part of the process.

When his father died in 2000, he became the sole custodian of this historic craft. With the help and support of Hugo Burge of Marchmont House in Scotland and of Heritage Crafts, he has now passed a lifetime of skill and knowledge to two apprentices, Richard Platt and Sam Cooper, who have now finished their training and opened their own workshop at Marchmont (see pages 21, 24–25). Happily, his son, Daniel, also intends to continue the family tradition when Neal eventually retires.

Kevin Gauld – aka The Orkney Furniture Maker – has lived and worked on Orkney for all his life. His great-grandfather was a furniture maker in Kirkwall and his grandfather was a boat builder on the island of Westray, so the desire to make was in his genes. At the age of sixteen, he became apprentice to a local maker, Traditional

Above: Neal has passed on his skills to Richard Platt and Sam Cooper of The Marchmont Workshop, who have set up a rush-seated chair atelier following his principles.

Left: Kevin Gauld weaving the straw back of a traditional Orkney chair, using oats grown on his family's farm. It is a skilled process as there is no internal structure to provide support.

Below left: A 'Gentleman's Fan-backed Chair' by Gauld featuring a scalloped back. With no uprights or arms involved, it was an ideal chair to make in a place where wood was scarce.

Opposite left: Willow rods drying in the garden of Annemarie O'Sullivan's East Sussex garden. She grows about twenty types of willow, with her favourite being Dicky Meadows.

Opposite right: Once dried, she soaks them to increase their malleability before weaving, knotting and binding them into all manner of elegant, woven objects.

Orkney Crafts, before setting up his own studio in 2007. His work brings together his passion for the islands, traditional techniques and local materials, and an innovative eye for design.

Orkney chairs have been at the heart of the islanders' homes for centuries. Few trees grow on Orkney, so crofters traditionally made these chairs from reclaimed wood, often gathered on the shoreline. They have distinctive woven oat straw backs, designed to provide shelter from the chilly winds blowing through old stone croft houses. Many also had a drawer in which the man of the house might keep a Bible – or a warming bottle of whisky. Gauld grows his own oats to create these straw backs on the farm that has been in his family for four generations, now run by his uncle. The process of making the straw back is a slow and careful one, as there is no internal structure to provide support. Straw is built up row by row, each bound by sisal string and sewn to the row below. Over time, the solid straw back will meld to that of the sitter.

Gauld is not afraid to break with tradition, re-interpreting age-old designs in his own style. Importantly, he endeavours to run a zero-waste business. Sawdust leftovers are passed on to local butchers and fishmongers to smoke their produce, while smaller offcuts fuel his workshop wood burner. The oats are used as feed for his chickens, while any leftover oat straw is used as their bedding. Not only is he training others to continue the tradition of Orkney chairs, but he is also recognised as a design champion by the V&A Dundee.

Basket maker Annemarie O'Sullivan also gathers materials local to her home and workshop in East Sussex. She and her husband, Tom McWalter, grow around twenty types of willow on their one-fifth hectare (half acre) osier bed. Each year, the willow rods are cut right back, regrowing in full the following year. After harvesting, the rods must be sorted and then dried for several months. Later they are soaked and mellowed to prepare them for use. Willow has a wonderful variation of colour, often fluctuating in tone along its length. This means that no two items will ever be the same, something O'Sullivan loves and respects. Her personal favourite is called Dicky Meadows, a slender rod with a grey-green hue.

Working from a wooden studio in her garden, she harnesses ancient weaving, knotting

O'Sullivan's Sussex studio is filled with her beautifully, sculptural designs – people often comment on how much they love the earthy scent of freshly woven baskets.

and binding techniques to make contemporary and elegant objects including lighting, furniture, log baskets, laundry baskets, paper baskets and statement, sculptural pieces. She also makes special objects to commission and welcomes collaborations with designers and other makers. While she is the Master weaver, McWalter plays an important supporting role helping to resolve the technical challenges of one-off commissions (he was previously a product designer), steam-bending frames and preparing leather for handles. Everything she creates shows her connection not just to this ancient craft but to the land which nurtures the raw materials: willow, coppiced chestnut, straw and hay. A QEST Scholar, she herself was mentored by Master basket maker, Mary Butcher. Now she passes on her skill and knowledge: as well as currently training a QEST apprentice, she runs day and week-long courses to inspire others.

Passing It On

Inspired by the work of makers such as these, new generations of craftspeople are springing up who want passionately to find a way of making a living that is sustainable, satisfying and joyous.

Lorna Singleton is one of the UK's last remaining swillers, a maker of traditional baskets, called *swills* or *spelks*, made in coppiced oak and hazel. She was trained in the art of oak swills by Owen Jones (see pages 70–73) and is one of the last people practising this ancient skill and keeping the knowledge of it alive. It was another apprentice of Jones, Ruth Pybus, who taught her to weave hazel baskets (spelks). These are found all over Europe, with basketry patterns changing from region to region. Being so much softer than oak, hazel can be worked with far more ease. Singleton can sit by the side of the road and create a spelk basket using nothing more than a pocket knife.

Trained in coppice management by the Bill Hogarth MBE Memorial Apprenticeship Trust, she works from a workshop tucked away in the ancient Cumbrian woods between Coniston Water and Windermere that she maintains in a responsible and renewable way. Coppicing begins in January and by the end of winter,

Left: A traditional oak spelk basket by Lorna Singleton. This craft stems from the Furness Fells region of Cumbria and is now considered to be Critically Endangered.

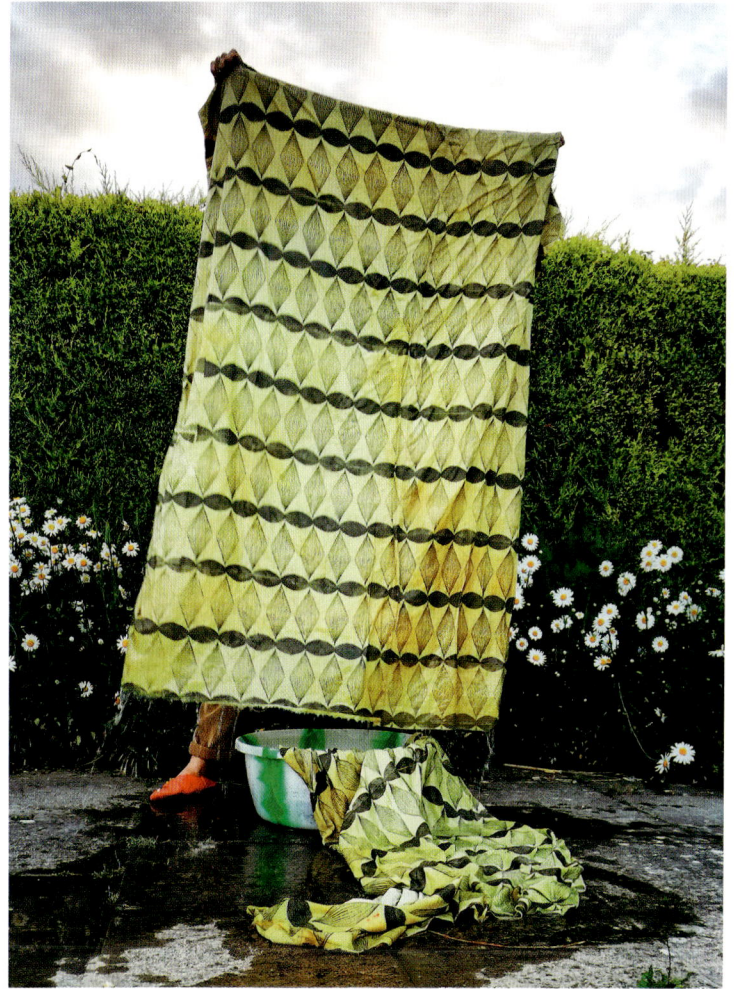

the only trees standing are those destined to become baskets or peeled for their bark. Before the following winter, the whole area will have been cleared ready for new life to spring up. All the bark is sold to the last remaining oak bark tannery in the country, J & FJ Baker & Co., while peeled poles are sold to other craftspeople and artists.

As well as coppicing and making her swills and spelks, she shares her knowledge through workshops at woodland venues in the Rusland Valley, Cumbria, aware how precious it is to pass on a skill that connects to the many generations of basket makers and woodland workers before her.

Sarah Burns is a pattern maker and textile artist who is committed to revitalising ancient techniques such as natural dyeing and block printing that don't rely on harsh chemicals and

that are zero-waste processes. She uses only water-based inks, and organic hemps and linens that are regenerative to the soil. Seasonal dyes are harvested from plants of the woodlands and open downlands, and from the fields around her home on the South Downs in Sussex, such as cow parsley in the spring, St John's wort in the summer and walnuts in the autumn and winter. The colours and patterns within her work are inspired by the Downs, the water meadows and ancient tracks and villages where she lives. She has a natural affinity with early twentieth-century textile artists, such as Peggy Angus, Phyllis Barron and Dorothy Larcher (and has written a book on Barron & Larcher) and is also inspired by the beautifully decorated churches of the region. Burns also teaches her own dyeing and printing workshops.

Above left: Sarah Burns hand block-printing fabric using a design that she carved from Sussex oak galls foraged from the woods on the South Downs.

Above right: Burns dipping the fabric into dyes she has made herself from plants gathered locally. She has rediscovered the traditional use of weld to create this vibrant yellow.

FELICITY IRONS:
Rush Weaver

Felicity Irons BEM is custodian of the rush weaving craft that can trace its roots back to the Anglo-Saxons. Having taught herself to weave the seats of rush chairs by following a book on the subject thirty years ago, she founded Rush Matters in 1992, helped by a grant and a loan from The Prince's Trust. She bought the raw materials from Tom Arnold, whose family had been cutting rushes in the Cambridgeshire area since the 1700s. When he died, he left no children to pass the skill onto, so the tradition of rush cutting looked likely to die out. Irons decided to buy the business herself in order to save it, which in turn meant learning to navigate the river on a punt with enough confidence to safely cut the rush using the traditional one-metre (three-foot) scythe blade mounted on a pole. Now she and her team of three cut rushes each year non-stop for six weeks from mid-June to late July on the river Nene, Ivel and the Great Ouse, leaving areas of the rivers untouched for two to three years afterwards so that the rushes can regenerate. Between them, they can harvest about 1.8 tonnes (two tons) of rush per day. Rushes are then left to dry standing against a hedge outside the barn.

Although English freshwater bulrush, *Scirpus lacustris schoeneplectus*, is all one plant, it grows differently according to location – some thick and tall, others delicate and fine. The different textures are good for different objects: for example, fat rushes for log baskets; finer bolts for table mats. In Irons' Bedfordshire barn (see pages 98–99), where she employs three other craftspeople, dried rushes are woven into all manner of objects from table mats and furniture seating to baskets, bags and hats.

However, the core of the business is rush matting – also known as medieval or apple matting. For this, the rush is plaited by hand and woven into lengths 7.6 centimetres (three inches) wide that are then hand-sewn with jute twine. Each mat is made bespoke to the client's requirements, with size no object. Once laid, it benefits from regular watering using an atomiser. One of the most beautiful aspects of true rush matting is that its colour mellows over time from fresh green to golden honey tones. Edges are typically bound in a narrow rush plait or linen tape, with plaiting interwoven with herbs, such as lavender, southernwood, wormwood and camomile.

Irons loves to pass on her knowledge and skills with hugely popular weekend courses that teach the basic techniques of weaving, twining, coiling, plaiting, knotting, sewing, roping and chair seating. She is as passionate about her craft as she has been from the first. 'The cutting season is relentless, but I love the peace and quiet of being out on the river in a punt from dawn to dusk. I'm always sad when it ends, but excited to plan what we are going to make once the bolts of rush are dry.'

'The rush-cutting season is relentless, but I love the peace and quiet of being out on the punt from dawn to dusk.'

Right: Felicity Irons cutting rushes at Oakley Bridge on the Great River Ouse. When Tom Arnold, the last cutter on the river died, she had to learn the skill herself.

Below left: She can cut more than half a tonne of rush per day using the traditional method of a one-metre (three-foot) scythe blade mounted on a pole.

Below right: A Rush Matters shopping basket, woven in rushes with a leather handle. This is just one of the many items made and sold by Irons and her team.

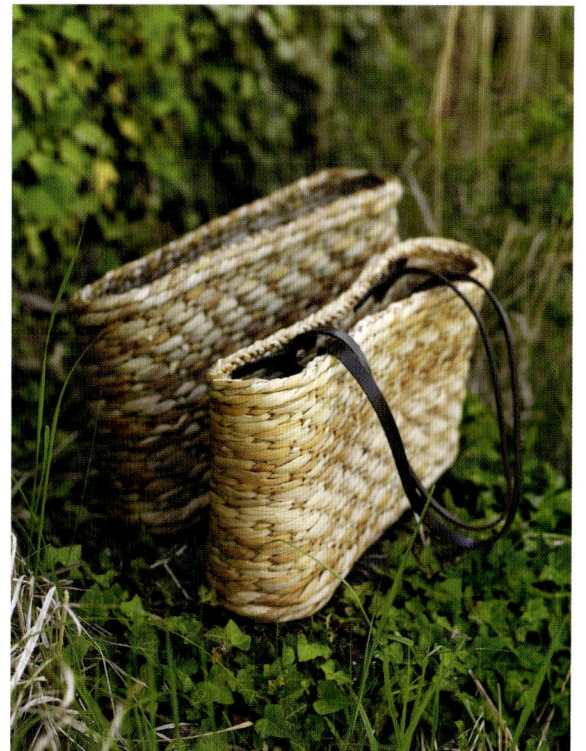

Spotlight on

TOM RAFFIELD:
Steam-Bent Furniture Maker

Right: Tom and Danielle Raffield designed and built their own low-impact home in Cornwall, which is a feat of steam-bending craftsmanship both inside and out.

Designer Tom Raffield discovered the age-old technique of steam-bending wood while studying 3D Sustainability and Design at Falmouth Art College. Having taught himself to understand and develop the skill, he became fascinated with the intricate curves and twists that it allowed him to create. His goal is to create new ways of living by producing unique, quality homewares that are inspired by nature and handmade to last a lifetime, using traditional craft practices in sustainable and innovative ways.

He launched his eponymous business in 2008, centred at his BREEAM workshop in Cornwall, where he has trained a dedicated team of makers in the art of steam-bending and where his signature collections of furniture, lighting and home accessories are created. Leading the charge in sustainable design from when he founded the business, he has made it part of his mission that his designs result in as little environmental impact as possible.

Timber is air-dried naturally. This means

Right: His studio is also the place where Raffield experiments with steam-bending techniques, using his craft in innovative and contemporary ways.

'For us, sustainability is a calling not a business. We put our heart and soul into it, determined always to put people and planet first.'

Above: Raffield in his workshop surrounded by steam-bent prototypes. Every design is intended to have as little impact on the environment as possible.

little waste is produced, but any waste wood is donated to small enterprises. Renewable energy is sourced from solar panels on the workshop, with any additional energy coming from a 100 per cent renewable supplier. Wood is sourced from sustainably managed forests, while fabric comes from Abraham Moon & Sons, one of the last woollen mills in the UK. The wool is derived from pasture-fed, ethically reared sheep, helping to support independent farms who follow the best farming practices. All packaging is proudly plastic-free, using FCS cardboard and bespoke recyclable and compostable solutions made by local company, Flexi-Hex. The Tom Raffield business is a member of the WWF 2030 Circle, which is dedicated to restoring natural habitats and ecosystems that have been lost to human intrusion and destruction.

He strives to inspire a like-minded community and have a positive impact helping to create a world where people and nature thrive for future generations to enjoy. 'Our team of talented craftspeople is driven by a shared passion for design, long-lasting quality and the knowledge that sustainable practices once rooted in tradition are in fact the key to a new way of doing things. For us sustainability is a calling, not just a business. We put our heart and soul into it, determined always to put people and planet first.'

Left: The *Amble Hanging Seat* is one of his statement pieces. It is formed from two lengths of sustainably-sourced ash that are joined by hand, giving the illusion of a perfect circle.

Below left: Raffield's hands-on 'design-through-making' approach is at the root of the confidence with which he transforms the straight into the curved.

Above: The *Verso Pendant* light is cleverly crafted from one continuous length of timber, looped to create a sense of eye-catching asymmetry.

6

USEFUL & BEAUTIFUL

Previous spread: Bench
designed by architect
Ian McChesney and
made by Benchmark.

'Have nothing in your house that you do not know to be useful, or believe to be beautiful' wrote William Morris. Happily, many craft objects tick both boxes perfectly. These are the crafts that people barely perceive as such, driven as they are by their practical use. Of course, a hand-thrown teapot or hand-woven basket are also functional, but very often people buy them to display rather than to use. Craft objects bought primarily to be used are different: it is the intrinsic beauty of their function that sets them apart.

The equestrian world is a good place to start. Few people would go to the expense of ordering a handmade saddle simply to hang it on their wall. A bespoke piece of bridle work or saddlery is designed for the comfort and wellbeing of both rider and horse. A well-fitting bridle will reduce uncomfortable pressure on the horse's face, just as a well-fitting saddle will allow it freedom of movement, meaning it will perform better.

Master saddlers, such as Helen Reader, often have riding in their blood. Aged five, Reader began riding, saw a Master saddler at work and decided that was what she wanted to do. In 2004, she founded HR Saddlery in Carmarthenshire, offering a full range of services from bespoke bridle work to saddle fitting. A QEST Scholar of 2015, she used her funding to study side-saddle manufacture and refurbishment (and is herself a keen side-saddle rider). In 2018, Reader became the only member of the Society of Master Saddlers to hold the four titles of Master saddler, Master bridle maker, Master harness maker and Master saddle fitter. She is now President of the Society.

Hooked on horses from her first riding lesson at seven years old, Carolyn Truss grew up near Newmarket, the horse capital of England, giving her the opportunity of weekend jobs in many different yards, including the chance to work with racehorses, polo ponies, show ponies, eventers and breeding stock. Truss recently became a QEST Scholar, which allowed her to learn the skills and techniques for making a traditional straw-filled collar for heavy horses, a craft listed as Critically Endangered by Heritage Crafts. She is also in demand for the making of re-enactment items such as stitched, laced, riveted and buckled Vambraces (forearm guards), and leather skulls for the Dragoon helmets of the Napoleonic era.

The Music Makers

As we noted in chapter 3, there has been a sad decline in recent years of those making musical instruments in the UK. Happily, there are some luthiers still able to make a viable living – a luthier being a maker or restorer of stringed musical instruments, such as violins, cellos and guitars.

One such is Tom Sands. He originally studied Industrial Design at the Glasgow School of Art, before training as a cabinet maker at Rupert McBain Furniture in Durham. Having forged a successful career in the making of fine furniture, a chance meeting with leading British luthier, Jim Fleeting, sparked his interest in acoustic guitars. A QEST Scholarship enabled him to be accepted as the first British apprentice to world-renowned luthier, Ervin Somogyi, in Oakland, California. Somogyi is considered to be the re-inventor of the modern, steel-string guitar – with his work sought by many musicians and collectors and typically selling for around £30,000 ($40,000). On his return in 2017, Sands opened his eponymous studio in North Yorkshire where he makes custom

Above left: This in-hand bridle for a shire horse was hand-stitched by Carolyn Truss using English leather with purple patent leather inlays to match the owner's ribbon colours.

Above right: This brown bridle was also made by Carolyn Truss, using Light Havana Sedgwick English leather with solid, British-made brass crown buckles.

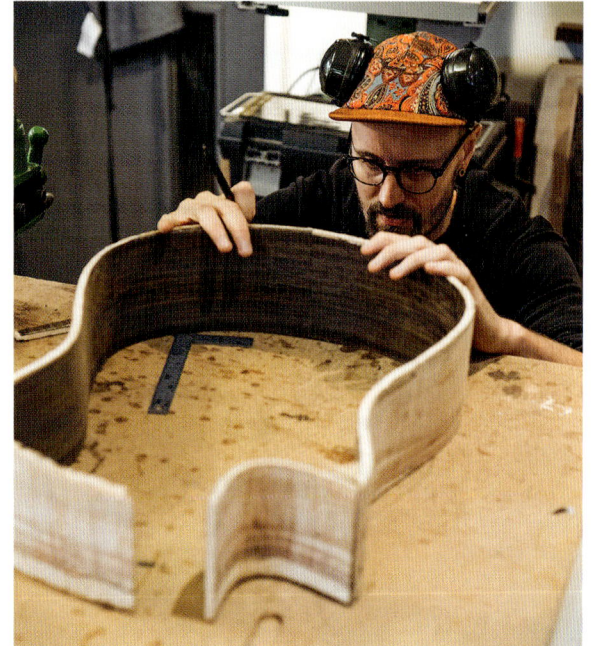

Above left: Tom Sands
carefully positioning a
rosewood fingerboard
on a Cuban mahogany
neck. The making of one
instrument takes about
200 hours on average.

Above right: Guitar
making is an art form,
which involves working
wood to an exceptionally
high standard. Here Sands
is assembling the bent
wooden sides to form the
rim of the guitar.

Opposite: The moment
of truth is when the
strings go on for the first
time and the guitar comes
alive. One of Sands'
guitars is played here by
Nii at Evoke Studios.

guitars that are highly regarded for their beauty
and responsiveness.

Sands works hard to support young, emerging music artists from the North, recognising
that instruments such as these are out of reach
for many young musicians. In collaboration with
Evoke Studios in Leeds, he invites an artist for
a recording session with each new instrument
made, giving up-and-coming artists the chance to
make their mark. Sands and Evoke are also working on plans to offer an artist bursary scheme to
further support the wealth of local talent in the
region. In addition, he is currently mentoring
apprentice, Ted Smith, who at only eighteen is
already excelling in the craft.

Other luthiers, such as Anja Kuch, specialise
in the repair and restoration of violins, violas and
cellos. Kuch began to learn the violin at the age
of seven and is herself an enthusiastic chamber
and orchestral musician. In 2003, following work

experience with violin maker, Michiel de Hoog
in Dublin, she was awarded a place at the New-
ark School of Violin Making in the East Midlands. Since graduating in 2006, she has both
taught violin and worked for professional workshops and private clients as a freelance repairer
and restorer, including for the Royal Academy of
Music. She now has her own workshop at Grandey's Place in Hertfordshire (see page 21).

The Home Lovers

For those searching for hand-made alternatives
to ubiquitous, mass-manufactured furniture and
home accessories, the choice has never been
better. The UK is liberally sprinkled with small
workshops and artisan businesses that make both
their own collections of beautifully designed
objects and are happy to take on special commissions. Many of them are featured in this book,
but organisations such as the Crafts Council,

QEST and the Homo Faber guide published by the Michelangelo Foundation (see page 21) publish lists of professional makers covering every craft imaginable.

Otis Ingrams founded OTZI London in 2013, producing his own pieces but also working closely with designers, artists and brands to create unique and functional leather pieces. The studio only uses leather that is predominantly oak bark and vegetable tanned from the UK, Italy and Spain. Ingrams pairs this with a variety of native hardwood timbers to create practical, durable and timeless pieces. His work is based on a belief that natural and sustainable materials offer intrinsic value and idiosyncratic character-

istics that synthetic materials do not have.

Having graduated in Mixed Media Textiles from the Royal College of Art, multidisciplinary artist Lora Avedian began to create couture textiles for interiors and fashion, including lampshades, cushions and table cloths. These often combine traditional and machine embroidery, with hand embellishments. Her work is grounded in history, inspired by antique textiles and folk costume. Often she assimilates scraps of antique or vintage fabric within her compositions, preserving their narrative through her process.

Aimee Betts is also a talented mixed-media textile artist. These skills run in her DNA, given the fact she can trace her ancestors back

Right: Leather is also the ideal material for seat upholstery. These oak-framed *Cinch* chairs by OTZI London are upholstered in undyed oak-bark-tanned leather.

to the framework knitters and stocking makers of nineteenth-century Leicestershire. Having graduated in Mixed Media Textiles from the Royal College of Art, she now specialises in stitching, knotting, braiding and the manipulation of different materials. In this way, she creates contemporary and highly tactile designs for textiles, lighting, cabinetry ornamentation and architectural installations, including door handles and lamp bases. She has also collaborated with other makers, including Gareth Neal (see pages 244–247) with whom she created *The Stitched Sideboard*, featuring hand-braided front and side panels, for The New Craftsmen.

Glassmakers such as Michael Ruh, Rothschild & Bickers, Atelier 001 and Stewart Hearn also create wonderful collections and one-off pieces for the home, including hand-blown lighting and artisan glassware. Founder of the London Glassworks (established in 2002), Hearn is an award-winning, Master glass artist, designer and creator of bespoke hand-blown glass objects and collections for elite, international clients. His own works often explore the hues, patterns and textures found in the English landscape, such as the Ely chandelier, Fenland bowl, Westmorland lamp and Thames river vases.

Hand-made furniture is a particularly fertile and diverse sector. The Cornish Bed Company was established a quarter of a century ago and

Right: Lora Avedian at work in her studio, meticulously hand-embroidering a napkin, part of a limited-collection of table linen.

Opposite top: One of the metal workers in the foundry of The Cornish Bed Company, hand-pouring molten metal into the cast of a traditional locking knuckle joint.

Opposite below: The *Beckett* bed by The Cornish Bed Company. Metal beds grew in popularity during the Victorian era when they were associated with better hygiene in hospitals.

is the last foundry in the UK to hand cast iron, brass and nickel beds using traditional methods. Metal beds first began to be made in Britain at the beginning of the nineteenth century. The traditional manufacturing process used in Victorian times – including hand pouring of metal, and intricate polishing and lacquering methods – are still used by The Cornish Bed Company today. All beds are made with hand-cast knuckle fixings, as used on original Victorian beds. These self-locking joints attach the side rails to the head and foot of the bed, a far cry from the flimsy bolts that hold many modern beds together. Every bed made is unique, individually numbered and custom made.

Benchmark (see opener on page 118) was founded in 1984 by furniture maker, Sean Sutcliffe, and Sir Terence Conran and is still located in the grounds of Conran's home in Berkshire. Their friendship was founded on a shared interest in making, design, wood and sustainability, an ethos that has remained unchanged. From a staff of just three, it has evolved into a highly skilled team of around 70 people, with every craftsperson involved caring deeply about the making process. There are now dedicated workshops for milling, cabinet making, veneering, metalworking, upholstery and finishing. As well as designing its own furniture collections, Benchmark has created work for many great British institutions, such as museums, Oxbridge colleges and Westminster Abbey.

From the first, sustainability has been at the heart of the company, which has twice been awarded The Queen's Award for Enterprise in Sustainable Development. It was the first furniture maker in the UK to be awarded Chain of Custody certification from the Forest Stewardship Council (FSC), guaranteeing all its timbers come from well-managed forests. It also made the world's first cradle-to-grave furniture, recording the impact on the environment through the product's entire life cycle. Benchmark offers an excellent apprenticeship scheme, which has now

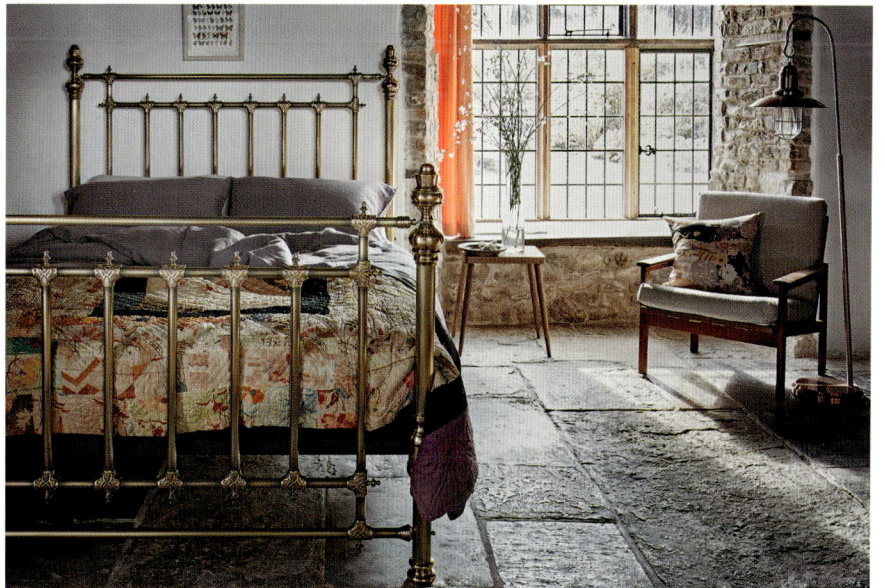

Right: Braided and knotted *Ricasso* pull handles by Aimee Betts, inspired by the decoration of European sword handles on display at The Wallace Collection in London.

Far right: *Westmorland* lamp by Stewart Hearn, which is inspired by the colours, hues, patterns and textures found in the dramatic landscapes of the southern Lake District.

been running for over thirty years and has trained around 60 apprentices to date.

Designer-maker Edward Johnson makes furniture that is both functional and beautiful, using the finest, sustainably-sourced materials – primarily timber. He founded the business in 2009, moving to his current studio and workshop in West Sussex in 2014. He and his team produce both in-house 'Made and Ready' collections (for immediate delivery) and 'Made to Order' versions in a range of materials and finishes. The latter includes designs such as A*sh & Oak Arc Cabinet*, with free-flowing veneers that are reminiscent of Venetian glass.

Originally torn between studying sculpture or architecture, Katie Walker chose Furniture &

Product Design, before graduating with a MA in Furniture Design from the Royal College of Art. Since then she has established her name with a number of elegant designs that draw on traditional styles, while coaxing them firmly into the twenty-first century. Her pieces are made through a network of UK workshops, each individually commissioned from her own collection of constantly evolving designs. The award-winning *Ribbon Rocking Chair*, for example, is inspired by the sculptures of Naum Gabo, with backrest, armrests and runner created from one continuous line. Walker has long been committed to sustainable practices, being careful to source timber from responsibly-managed woodland.

Left: The award-winning *Ribbon Rocking Chair* in ash by Katie Walker is based on the sculptures of Naum Gabo and is created from one continuous line of timber.

Below: The *Ash, Olive Ash & Fumed Oak Arc Cabinet* from Edward Johnson's *Murano* collection features hundreds of strips of wood that create the sweeping lines and curves of the veneer.

MOURNE TEXTILES:
Textile Weavers

Mourne Textiles was founded in 1954 by Norwegian textile designer, Gerd Hay-Edie, taking its name from the Mourne Mountains in County Down, Northern Ireland, close to Rostrevor where she settled after the War. Gerd's iconic weaves are part of the rich legacy of mid-twentieth century design in Britain, including her collaborations with icons such as Robin Day and Sir Terence Conran. Today, the studio is run by her grandson, Mario Sierra, alongside his mother and Master weaver, Karen Hay-Edie. The weavers still work from the studio that was purpose-built for Gerd, with many of the looms they use now six decades old. However, the company is as forward-looking as it was in her day, including recent partnerships with modern greats such as Margaret Howell and Carl Hansen.

Sierra and Hay-Edie's combined technical expertise and passion for weaving has been instrumental in breathing new life into Gerd's

'At a time when Irish mills are decreasing in numbers, the importance of continuing my grandmother's legacy has never been so clear to me.'

original designs. Today, the company produces a wide range of collections, including furnishing fabrics, blankets, rugs, wall-hangings and scarves that are sold worldwide. They have also launched Mourne Weavers, producing upholstery fabrics, cushions and throws for the interior design sector. This is based in nearby Warrenpoint and brings together innovative manufacturing techniques with impeccable craftsmanship. Lovingly woven on vintage Dornier looms, the Mourne Weavers' collection pays homage to Gerd's early designs, including Mourne Check and Mourne Mist, both of which were used by Robin Day in the 1950s.

The studio takes its commitment to sustainable and responsible practices seriously, determined that the company has a positive impact on the local community. They source their fleece for rugs and wall-hangings from Freda Magill, a rare-breed sheep farmer based in the Mourne Mountains, whose flocks of Soay, Hebridean, Balwen, Manx Loaghton and others create a spectacular variety of tones and textures within the wool. Hay-Edie and Sierra are proud to surround themselves with a dedicated team of skilled workers and are committed to handing down the technique of hand-weaving to the next generation, working alongside QEST to offer apprenticeships in the craft.

For Sierra, Mourne Textiles has been a part of his life for as long as he can remember. 'At a time when Irish mills are sadly decreasing in numbers, the importance of continuing my grandmother's legacy has never been so clear to me. I am in awe of all that was achieved in the years gone by and filled with pride and excitement at the prospect of what lies ahead. It makes me immensely proud to be entrusted with its future.'

Left above: The mill is full of objects that relate directly back to Gerd Hay-Edie, such as this beautiful collection of vintage bobbins, some still entwined with thread.

Left: The textile development process at Mourne combines ongoing yarn research with archival elements to create designs in touch with their heritage roots.

Above: The soft pinks and greys of throws and cushions are ideally suited to contemporary interiors, while staying true to the original ethos and vision of Mourne.

TOM VAUGHAN OF OBJECT STUDIO:
Designer-Maker

Right: The *Scarpa* desk in ebonised ash is part of Vaughan's *Nodum* series, which draws inspiration from the orthogonal work of architect Carlo Scarpa.

Opposite: Tom Vaughan, founder of Object Studio, working on *Homage To Bernini*. This sculptural piece of outdoor seating was commissioned for a private collection in Zurich.

Object Studio is a design practice, a workshop for making, a laboratory for experimentation, and the meeting point of traditional craft with modern manufacturing. It was founded by Tom Vaughan in 2010, a designer and maker who trained in Cabinet Making at London Guildhall University and in Three-dimensional Design at Brighton University, before taking a Masters in Contemporary Product Design at the Royal College of Art under the tutelage of Ron Arad (he himself is now a visiting lecturer at the RCA). Vaughan runs a small team of specialist craftspeople based in east London and at Grandey's Place in Hertfordshire (see page 21). Object Studio takes on ambitious commissions for galleries, public institutions and private clients, including the fabrication of complex three-dimensional structures in woods, metals and synthetics.

Vaughan is best known for the way in which he manipulates timber and metals into sculptural

'My furniture pieces, however sculptural, are functional objects
that are made to be used and enjoyed - beautiful to the eye
and pleasing to the touch.'

organic forms, such as the perpetual, looped tim-ber of *Ribbon Chair*, the *Ripple* table of American black walnut and Arctic white maple, and the mid-century-modern inspired *Manta* dining set. He is a QEST Scholar, who used the experience to investigate the casting of metals and associated crafts such as welding, chasing, figuring and patinating. This resulted, among other things, in a reworking of his *Goldsmiths Chair*, originally commissioned by The Worshipful Company of Goldsmiths and made in black ash as a foil to exquisite British silverware. The newer version is hand-crafted in mirror-polished bronze with bridle leather seat. QEST marked the turning-point from Vaughan being a designer focused solely on wood, to one who now embraces many more choices of material within his work.

The *S Chair* was one of his earliest designs, an exploration into flow inspired by the movement of the paintbrush, with the chair's profile

arising directly from the two-dimensional lines of calligraphy into a functional, three-dimensional form. This piece demonstrates the inspiration he takes from artists such as Barbara Hepworth and Henry Moore. Similarly, the privately commissioned *Scarpa Desk* is heavily influenced by the designs of architect Carlos Scarpa, and is the natural companion to *Ribbon* chair.

A great believer in giving back, over the last ten years he has run his own training programme for design and craft students, working closely with universities in the UK and Europe. Three students each year spend time working in the studio, learning both craft techniques and how to run a small business. In addition, he supports them through their final year, offering consultation advice and access to the workshop. The proof of his success is that his own studio comprises craftspeople who have all successfully completed this programme.

Of his passion for what he does, he says, 'My furniture pieces, however sculptural, are functional objects that are made to be used and enjoyed – beautiful to the eye and pleasing to the touch. Behind the organic forms is the constant development of my fabricating processes, which is a convergence of traditional crafts combined with modern cutting-edge digital design and production techniques. I aim to produce quality pieces that will last many lifetimes, growing in character as they are used over time.'

Above top: The *Ribbon* chair features a perpetual, looped timber ribbon that forms a generous seat. Shown here in ebonised ash, it can be commissioned in a variety of timbers and finishes.

Above: The *Manta* dining set in fumed European oak is inspired by mid-century modern Scandinavian furniture, which has long been an important influence on Vaughan's work.

Left: The *Goldsmiths Chair* in mirror-polished cast bronze. This was the first in a series of pieces produced for QEST.

Above: The highly tactile *Ripple* desk with its softly undulating surface takes its name from the rippled surface of sand on the beach when the wind and waves retreat.

Left: Part of a set of thirty S *Chairs* in fifteen shades commissioned for a private residence in Dubai. The form arises directly from the flowing curves of a hand-drawn S.

7

HEALTH & WELLBEING

It was heartening when the COVID pandemic took root to see how projects such as For the Love of Scrubs, the Big Community Sew and many regional sewing groups rose to the challenge of making garments for NHS workers, giving those who contributed a very real sense of purpose. However, many people have been left traumatised by the effects of the pandemic, not only in relation to sickness and bereavement but also the loneliness and uncertainty caused by successive lockdowns and their economic aftermath. There is hard evidence to show that engaging directly with craft could help.

In November 2019, the World Health Organisation (WHO) published a report on *What Is the Evidence on the Role of the Arts in Improving Health?* by Professor Daisy Fancourt and Saoirse Finn. It provided compelling evidence on the health benefits of making, and being actively creative overall, among children and adults. The report focused primarily on Europe but also referenced positive participation outcomes from countries such as China. For example, children who survived the 2008 China earthquakes and were given thirty days of calligraphy training had greater decreases in hyperarousal symptoms and stress hormones. In Boston, USA, folk-art exhibitions have been used to bring together Jewish and Palestinian communities. Refugees and asylum seekers have also found that engagement with the arts has both supported them in creating new support networks and helped them develop practical skills that have helped them find work.

This research complements the results of the Great British Creativity Test released in May 2019, also led by Dr Fancourt. The largest study of its kind, run in conjunction with the BBC's annual Get Creative campaign, this explored how being creative can help us manage our mood and boost wellbeing. Making emerged as the most popular category of creative practice, with nearly twenty-four per cent of respondents naming it as one of their favourite pastimes. Inspired by this research, the Crafts Council decided to take part in the MARCH mental health network of 2021, also led by Dr Fancourt, which further examined and galvanised evidence on how the creative arts are good for us.

A January 2021 study on coping and wellbeing strategies during the pandemic by What Works Wellbeing (which aims to improve wellbeing across the UK) showed that time spent engaging with home-based arts and crafts resulted in a decrease in depressive symptoms, a decrease in anxiety and an increase in life satisfaction. The study also noted that there was a rapid increase in the sale of paints, wool and other craft materials during the first lockdown. Twenty-two per cent of respondents said they had increased their engagement with arts and crafts during this time, including many young adults, aged eighteen and nineteen, encouraged by virtual activities offered by museums, galleries and other arts venues.

This was important work in 2019, but in late 2022 – nearly three years after COVID reared its ugly head – it has taken on a whole new level of relevance. If creativity can alleviate stress, no wonder we are finding such comfort in making skills once again.

The Magic of Knitting

Knit for Peace was founded twenty years ago by Dame Hilary Blume of the Charities Advisory Trust, as an income-generating project for Hutu

Above: A Shedfest event organised by the UK Men's Sheds Association (UKMSA), which encourages men to connect to their communities through a number of craft activities.

and Tutsi widows, victims of the Rwandan genocide and civil war. In return for knitting jumpers for the many orphans, the women were paid by the Trust, through money raised by its Good Gifts Catalogue. Hearing of the project, the Trust's colleagues in India set up a similar scheme with Hindu and Muslim women in the slums of Delhi. The idea began to spread with Knit for Peace women's groups established in Pakistan, Bangladesh, Nepal and Afghanistan. When knitters in the UK heard of the project, many of them also began sending hand-knitted clothing to the charity. These were distributed through troubled and war-torn regions, and to those in need in the UK. Knit for Peace now has around 40,000 volunteer knitters in the UK – and more in groups around the world including South Africa and the Middle East – the majority of them of post-retirement age. Today, the charity distributes knitted items to hospitals, women's refuges, prisons, community groups in low-income areas, hospices and refugee groups. It also passes on donations of yarn and needles to those on low incomes to enable them to knit.

Knit For Peace estimates that 67 per cent of its knitters are over the age of 60, with many in their 70s, 80s, 90s and a few who have even passed the 100 milestone. In 2016, it conducted a survey on the health benefits of knitting, particularly in relation to the elderly. With the help of academics, Professor Muki Haklay and Professor David Metz, and a grant from the Big Lottery Accelerating Ideas Fund, Knit for Peace began to look both at the effect of knitting (and crochet) in the elderly population, and its benefits to the population as a whole.

The research, comprising evidence-based research and a survey of 1,000 knitters in its UK network, produced some striking results. The positive effects of knitting for the elderly, both physical and mental, were clear: it was found to lower blood pressure; reduce depression and anxiety; slow the onset of dementia; distract from chronic pain; reduce loneliness and isolation; increase a sense of wellbeing, and increase the sense of being useful in society – particularly when used as a volunteering activity. Importantly, it can still be

enjoyed by those whose sight, hearing and mobility are severely affected.

In fact, as Knit for Peace references in its own research, there have been other studies predating this one that show the clear health benefits of knitting. In 2013, a survey [1] published in the *British Journal of Occupational Therapy* of 3,545 knitters worldwide indicated a relationship between knitting frequency and feeling calm and happy, with respondents citing knitting for relaxation, stress relief and creativity. More frequent knitters also reported higher cognitive functioning. In 2020, the Royal Society for Public Health published a report [2] in *Perspectives in Public Health* that explored the relationship between crochet and wellbeing. A total of 8,391 individuals responded to the survey, with 89.5 per cent reporting that crocheting made them feel calmer; 82 per cent saying it made them feel happier; and 74.7 per cent that it made them feel more useful. Many respondents said they used crochet to manage mental health conditions and life events, such as grief, chronic illness and pain.

There are neurological reasons for this. Knitting and crochet require pattern recognition, fine motor control and maths – all of which contribute to keeping the mind sharp. In Steiner Waldorf schools, knitting is often taught at kindergarten level because the skills it teaches are deemed so important for future learning. Supporting this notion is the fact that knitting groups are increasingly being established for adults with dementia who learned to knit early in life. Many people with conditions such as

Above: HRH The Prince of Wales and HRH The Duchess of Cornwall with an installation artwork of three huge knitted panels, highlighting the wellbeing benefits of the craft.

Above: A student enjoys foot-printing wallpaper on a course in traditional, lino-block techniques run by Hugh Dunford Wood (see page 36).

Opposite: West Dean College of Arts and Conservation offers a programme of over 300 art and craft subjects, including blacksmithing as shown here.

Alzheimer's struggle with short-term-memory loss but retain memories from earlier in their lives. The repetitive motion of knitting engages the cerebellum – what is known as 'muscle memory' – making skills such as knitting and crochet easier to retain.

According to a recent report [3] from Age UK, around 1.4 million older people 'often feel lonely' in the UK. The Knit for Peace report suggests that knitting – particularly as a volunteering activity – could help reduce loneliness by making people feel more useful and connected. Too often dismissed as a 'grandmotherly' occupation, knitting should be embraced by the NHS as a potentially important tool in combating the effects of old age.

The Prince's Foundation and the Joseph Ettedgui Charitable Foundation have led the way through the Knitwise initiative, led by Ashleigh Douglas, Future Textiles Manager for The Prince's Foundation. It was originally established to train a group of knitters local to Dumfries House, giving them enough skills to potentially turn an enjoyable hobby into a viable business proposition. When the COVID pandemic prevented the group meeting in person, The Prince of Wales had the idea for a remote project: a patchwork mosaic of over 9,000 knitted squares to celebrate knitting as a craft form and highlight its associated mental health benefits. Using WhatsApp, Zoom and social media channels to spread the word, Knitwise appealed to volunteers to contribute squares that could be included. Soon, people all over the world were involved – the youngest contributor was nine years old and the oldest was 101.

The next step was to find a way of sewing them all together. For this, the Foundation partnered with Cornton Vale Prison – a facility for female offenders near Stirling in Scotland – and developed an outreach workshop for volunteer inmates, teaching them the techniques required for stitching the knitted squares together. In this way, the group created a vast number of blankets.

The final task was attaching the individual blankets to the backing fabric to create one enormous installation piece of three panels, which required many more volunteers from local sewing bees, Knitwise and the wider educational team.

The knitted art installation was unveiled over the estate's historic Adam Bridge. It weighed an impressive 130 kilograms (286 pounds), with each of the three panels measuring about six to seven metres (eighteen to twenty-one feet), a joyous kaleidoscope of colour and texture. Since then, the blankets comprising these contributions from around the world have been donated to various charities.

The Power of Making

While knitting is undoubtedly to be celebrated, it seems that anything that involves making has a similar potential to quieten the mind and drown out anxiety. The Crafts Council launched *Make! Craft! Live!* at the end of 2021 to mark its fiftieth anniversary, a year-long programme of nation-wide exhibitions, learning events, fairs and online activities to celebrate craft's ability to empower, enrich and connect society. This marked a shift in the Council's programme, with the emphasis on prioritising the social and environmental value of making and repositioning craft as a vehicle for social change. It echoes its *Market for Craft* report of 2020, which noted the growing public desire to switch off from electronic devices and nurture wellness and mindfulness.

The Men's Sheds' project (which originated in Australia) aims to give socially isolated men a way to connect to their communities through activities such as woodwork, pottery and photography. The UK Men's Sheds Association (UKMSA) provides support and guidance for individuals and groups across the UK in starting and managing Men's Sheds, and in so doing reducing isolation and loneliness. The Sheds movement has been shown to be beneficial to men's health and wellbeing, given that men typically find it more difficult to build social connections than women and rarely share concerns about health and personal worries. UKMSA recently surveyed 500 of its members and found that being a member of a Shed resulted in 96 per cent feeling less lonely; 89 per cent feeling less depressed; 75 per cent feeling their anxiety had decreased; 97 per cent saying they now had more friends; and 88 per cent feeling more connected to their community. In 2022, it launched its Charter for Wellbeing in Craft and DIY, which actively promotes the benefits of such activities in relation to happiness and wellbeing. Its partners on this initiative include Zero Suicide Alliance, which is dedicated to preventing suicide – the biggest single killer of men under the age of forty-six.

It is wonderful to see the viewing figures of programmes such as *The Great British Sewing Bee* (BBC One), *The Great Pottery Throw Down* (Channel 4) and *The Repair Shop* (BBC One) spiral upwards with each season, but how much better if people have a go at making something with their own hands. In fact, for anyone wishing to improve their own mental health, one of the best places to start is learning or developing a craft skill. Many craftspeople run short courses – typically a day or a weekend – to pass on their love and knowledge for what they do and help supplement their fragile incomes. These are not necessarily aimed at professional makers but at anyone who wants to learn the basics.

West Dean College of Arts and Conservation, part of The Edward James Foundation, also runs excellent short courses. Its programme includes over 300 art and craft subjects for all abilities – some online and others at the beautiful West Sussex campus. Many of those featured in this book also tutor at West Dean.

In addition, many of the makers featured in this book also love to teach (see the Acknowledgements for the full list of those that offer courses). Choose from pottery with Clay College (page 23); paper marbling with Lucy McGrath (pages 30–31); sewing with The Royal School of Needlework (page 39); oak swill making with Owen Jones (pages 70–73); hand-printing fabrics with Sarah Burns (page 111); tapestry weaving with Dovecot Studios (pages 208–11); rush weaving with Felicity Irons (pages 112–13); basket making with Annemarie O'Sullivan (pages 107–110); furniture making with Edward Johnson (page 128); shoe last making with Crispinians (page 64); oak spelk making with Lorna Singleton (page 110); kilt-making with Nikki Laird (page 27); bronze casting with Ore and Ingot (pages 62–63); Windsor chair making with Jason Mosseri (see opposite); and lino printing with Hugh Dunford Wood (page 36), to name but a few.

1 The Benefits of Knitting for Personal and Social Wellbeing in Adulthood: Findings from an International Survey by Jill Riley, Betsan Corkhill, Clare Morris.

2 Happy Hookers: findings from an international study exploring the effects of crochet on wellbeing P Burns, R Van Der Meer.

3 Age UK analysis of Understanding Society Wave 10 (January 2018 to December 2019) and ONS mid-2020 population estimates

Above: Jason Mosseri of Hopespring chairs (see page 103) runs outdoor woodworking courses at the end of which participants have made their own Windsor chair.

KNITHUB 24:
Knitting Teachers

Founded by Asif Dhanani and Farah Govani, Knithub 24 is an Islington-based knitwear design studio. Originally set up to help fashion professionals produce their knitwear creations, it took a sharp and sudden change of direction when the COVID pandemic hit. Having just moved to their current premises at the end of 2019, the partners had to think what best to do when it became obvious within a couple of months that they could no longer open their doors to clients.

Recognising the value of knitting as an activity for mental health, they began to create online classes instead. Govani has a wealth of experience and talent, having trained in Textile Design at Central Saint Martins, before specialising in knitwear and going on to work with various fashion brands, including Donna Karan and the re-launch of the Ossie Clark label. She also teaches part-time at the Chelsea College of Arts. She is passionate about hand knitting, machine knitting, crochet and macramé. Dhanani has a background in business, finance and lectur-

Right: A group of Knithub 24 students proudly wearing the hats and gloves they created while on a course learning the basics from Farah Govani.

'Knitting should be seen as an additional way that people can help themselves if they are feeling anxious and stressed.'

ing, so he began working on a plan to involve corporate clients as well. He has also studied a remote-learning course in Global Mental Health and Trauma Recovery with Harvard University and is a certified Mental Health First Aider. All of this knowledge feeds into the Knithub 24 brand and the development of its 'KnitMed' mental health boxes. These include everything someone might need to get started including eco-friendly bamboo knitting needles and vegan crafting yarn.

Today, they have built up an impressive list of corporate clients, who have welcomed knitting alongside other wellness activities for their staff, such as yoga and meditation. Knithub 24 organises half or full-day online workshops, with materials (all of which are fully sustainable) sent in advance to each member of the class with a personalised message. Many of their tutors are fashion and textiles graduates from leading colleges such as Central Saint Martins. This income stream gives the company enough financial stability to keep online courses relatively inexpensive for newbies and hobbyists. It has also enabled them to expand into community projects, including working with an NHS mental health clinic in West London. In the future, they are hoping to donate 'KnitMed' knitting kits to MIND (where Dhanani is a Trustee) and run projects with charities such as Age Concern. During the COVID pandemic, they supported NHS staff with free classes and knitting kits.

They are also determined to promote the fact that knitting is gender-neutral, with men-only beginner classes among their most popular offerings. Here, they have been helped enormously by the profile of Tom Daley OBE as both a gold-medal Olympian and accomplished knitter. As

Left: A student learning stocking stitch at a beginner's class – increasingly, corporate clients have also shown an interest in knitting as a wellness activity.

Govani says, the appeal of knitting is universal, 'Once you have got to grips with the basic technique, it is really relaxing and therapeutic. There is also something wonderful about starting with a simple ball of wool and ending up with a scarf, a hat, a pair of mittens – or even something more complicated once you know how.'

For Dhanani, it is the mission of Knithub 24 to wean people off medication and on to knitting needles instead, 'Knitting's benefits have been proven – it is not some old wives' tale. It should be seen as an additional way that people can help themselves if they are feeling anxious and stressed. Every day Farah and I go to work and ask ourselves the question, "What else can we do to help?" The nation's mental health comes before our profit-and-loss accounts.'

PROFESSOR ALICE KETTLE:
Textile Artist

Below: Sky by Alice Kettle, one of the three works of *Thread Bearing Witness*, the others being *Ground* (see pages 136–137) and *Sea* (see Photographic Acknowledgements for full list of participants).

Textile offers a powerful medium through which to explore themes of cultural heritage, journeys and displacement, steeped as it is in the history of trade routes. Embroidery is also a metaphor for home making and invariably connected with women. In 2016, artist Alice Kettle embarked on an ambitious new arts project, seeking to connect refugees, those seeking asylum, migrant communities, and displaced women artists across the UK and in camps in Europe, by asking them to contribute drawings which would be represented in a series of large-scale stitched art works. This was inspired by her daughter, Tamsin Koumis, who set up an initiative for refugees in Dunkirk, and continues to work for migrant organisations and enterprises. Kettle was profoundly affected by her daughter's experience and the repercussions of this human tragedy.

The result was *Thread Bearing Witness*, which was fully realised at the Whitworth Art Gallery in Manchester in 2018. It comprises various works centred around three monumental eight-metre (twenty-six-foot) long embroideries stitched by Kettle, entitled *Sea*, *Ground* and *Sky*. The latter two include stitched representations of many of the paintings and drawings sent to her, made by the migrant participants. However, she created *Sea* herself as a memorial to those who perished en route and no longer had a voice she could include. One thing that surprised her was the optimism in the imagery that the women of the refugee camps made, showing birds, flowers, trees and hearts. The project also included *Stitch a Tree*, a public-participation work of over 6,000 stitched trees from all over the world, inspired by

'This is a project about universality: the common threads which can be used to create a common ground.'

Left: Alice Kettle at home. She uses textiles to create artworks that explore themes of cultural journeys, migrant communities and displacement.

the Refugee Resilience Collective who used the Tree of Life to inspire resilience and strength in conversations with refugee children. This in turn inspired *Stitch a Tree Karachi*, made by women's groups in Pakistan.

Kettle is internationally renowned for her art form, depicting contemporary events and transformative experiences through her stitched tales. Having trained in Fine Art at Reading University, she took a Postgraduate Diploma in Textile Art at Goldsmiths, University of London. Today, museums and private collectors across the world buy her work, which typically combines intricate needlework with painterly splashes of vibrant colour. Her tradition of thread narrative goes back to the eleventh-century Bayeux tapestry and the histories of all women who have communicated through textiles and stitch. She is represented by the Candida Stevens Gallery in London.

Thread Bearing Witness expressed resilience; how creativity can contribute to dealing with traumas and in creating communities. Kettle did not view herself as the primary force here, but as the narrator and maker through which refugees could tell their stories and unfold the harrowing journeys they had endured.

Of the project she says, 'I did not want to appropriate or misrepresent a story that belonged to others but offer a place for it to be told first-hand and to listen. This is a project about universality: the common threads which can be used to create a common ground.' [1]

1 Alice Kettle wishes to thank colleagues at Manchester Metropolitan University, Hampshire Cultural Trust, the Whitworth at the University of Manchester, the British Textile Biennial, Karachi Biennale Trust, the British Council in Karachi, the Artists Agency and Candida Stevens.

Below: *Family Gathering* explores the important relationships with both family and friends, which provide a bedrock of connectivity, mutuality and support.

8

UNIQUE & PERSONAL

For many people the real joy of working with a craftsperson is the opportunity to create something truly unique and individual. A bespoke piece – whether a chair, a suit, a hand-blocked wallpaper, a pair of shoes, a customised book binding or a backgammon board – is not only made to personal specifications but tailored to someone's precise needs and desires. Commissioning a one-off design is as rewarding and intriguing a process as the object that results from it. This will be a limited edition of one. Whatever the object is, it could include motifs, monograms or witty references that are like a secret language to the client. The best bespoke pieces are those that tell the story of the person who commissioned them.

However, it is also a two-way street that demands commitment and time from both parties. Many people are understandably daunted by the process, as it is the very opposite of online or bricks-and-mortar shopping where someone else has made the initial choices and then it is simply a matter of selecting from what is available. It takes confidence to give precise answers to the many questions that will be asked about material, ornamentation, style and scale. It takes time to look at all the possibilities a bespoke design offers, and it takes patience to wait for it to be completed. The chosen craftsperson will want to create something that surpasses all expectations. He or she can only achieve that with the full support and involvement of the client.

A good place to begin is by collecting as many visual references as possible that give the maker a pointer towards personal taste – perhaps by trawling through magazines, books, websites and social media accounts, and either recording favourites in a notebook or making private Pinterest boards or Instagram collections. If commissioning as a couple, it is essential these indicators are liked equally by both.

Many people find the maker of their choice through word-of-mouth, but there are plenty of specialist craft organisations that can also help (see chapter 1). If possible, put time aside to visit ateliers and workshops, browse libraries of their previous work, and compile questions beforehand that will help decide whether this is the best person or place for the project.

The whole process of designing and making often takes five to six months, so by the time the object arrives most customers are looking forward to it with excited anticipation. One of the most satisfying things about a commissioned piece is that this particular object would never have existed without the person who had the imagination, taste and confidence to request it to be made. Anyone who supports a maker or atelier through bespoke commissions deserves a pat on the back. He or she has stepped out of the crowd and used their own belief and enthusiasm to help create something unique and wonderful.

An alternative option to the fully bespoke is to choose an object that can be customised or personalised in some way. This is particularly relevant when looking for gifts to mark an occasions such as a wedding, landmark birthday or naming day. It could involve taking something relatively inexpensive, such as a much-loved book, and having it transformed into a one-off piece of art by a specialist atelier, such as Wyvern Bindery. At the other end of the scale, it could equally be a limited-edition watch from a company such as Bamford Watch Department,

Right: Embroidered silk wallpaper by Jacky Puzey made bespoke for the client. In Japanese culture koi carp are a symbol of perseverance and endurance.

Left: A skilled bookbinder at Wyvern Bindery in the process of forming the headcap of a full-leather binding by turning the leather on the spine over the head and tail and shaping it.

Opposite: Samples showing the couture work produced by Helen Amy Murray (see pages 214–217), who creates three-dimensional designs from leather, suede and silk. These samples were produced for Rolls-Royce.

where the emphasis on personalisation of time-pieces is part of the company's ethos.

Couture Furniture

One way of judging how good a maker is comes down to the quantity of questions asked. Rather than leading with matters of style, material and finish, the maker should first establish functionality. Where is the piece to go? Who will use it? How often will it be used? Are children also likely to use it? Might pets damage it? Will it be placed in direct sunlight? How wide are the doors into the house and the chosen room (for delivery purposes)? What other uses is it to serve other than the obvious? A desk, for example, may need to be suitable for a laptop and printer, as well as a writing surface. A dining table may double as a working-from-home conference table.

Then come questions centred on aesthetics. The visual references the client has gathered beforehand should help ignite this conversation but are likely to seed more questions. If this is a desk, how big should it be and what shape? How many drawers? A top that lifts? Any ingenious mechanical touches, such as secret compartments? Answers to these help determine the foundations of the piece.

Budget, of course, determines much of the design in terms of the possibilities on offer. Makers are skilled at finding imaginative ways of stretching a budget further, but they can't work miracles. It is important that the client begins the

commissioning journey with a fair and reasonable budget in mind. Margins are tight for every craftsperson and workshop, so it takes the joy out of the process to haggle at every step of the way. While materials obviously affect the price, it is labour that is the biggest indicator of cost. Commissioning is the buying of someone's time: not just the time spent making this object, but the decades of time beforehand invested in becoming exceptional at their craft. It is not that bespoke pieces are necessarily charged at a premium; it is simply that by their very nature they tend to be more complicated and therefore take longer to make.

Specialist upholstery also presents possibilities in creating unique and eye-catching pieces of furniture. Award-winning embroidery artist and designer, Dr Jacky Puzey, for example, creates statement furniture and bespoke wallpaper akin to richly textured artworks, combining a material palette of velvet, silk, fur, feathers, tweed, silk and organza with digital and hand embroidery. The animal kingdom is a constant source of inspiration, with designs that include ravens, hares, koi carp, parakeets and peacocks. Her work may reference allegorical seventeenth- and eighteenth-century still life paintings, but she also encompasses urban themes, such as London's parakeets and the leopards that roam free in Mumbai's suburbs. She particularly loves tracing the symbolism of natural motifs, such as the koi carp once kept in Japanese villages to keep the waterways clean. Koi are a symbol of perseverance and endurance, often featured on Hanten – the Japanese firemen's jackets of the Mejii period (late nineteenth-century) – as a symbol of protection.

Aiveen Daly is one of the UK's most sought-after specialists in technically complicated textile art for interiors and furniture. She trained in traditional upholstery techniques at the London Metropolitan University and sewing at the London College of Fashion. She would often deconstruct centuries-old pieces of furniture as part of her study. This opened her eyes to an age where bespoke furniture was viewed as a luxury item, a sign of wealth and privilege before mass manufacturing became the norm. Her love of craftsmanship and design, combined with a passion to make the skill as relevant today as it was then, has ensured she is in constant demand from architects, interior designers, fashion houses and private clients worldwide.

Combining techniques such as pleating, stitching, embroidery, hand-dyed feathers, fine beading and fabric manipulation techniques, she creates unique compositions of true craftsmanship. Fine fabrics such as silks, Italian lambswool and butter-soft leathers comprise her natural palette, complemented by custom-made metallic details. Her in-house team of textile artists upholsterers works with precision and accuracy to position leather cuts, pleats and ornamentation to within one tenth of a millimetre.

Bespoke to Wear

Of course, furniture is just one example. It is a similar process when commissioning bespoke tailoring, except for the fact that it is the skill of

Opposite: The limited-edition *Infinity Table* by Silverlining furniture (see page 225) features an unusual Reuleaux triangle shape with veneers dyed in vivid colours.

Left: This elegant *Concertina* day bed by Aiveen Daly features hand-twisted leather with lambswool upholstery on a hardwood frame.

Left below: A *Paradise* chair by Aiveen Daly with pleated, emerald green upholstery that has been stitched on the bias and finished with a hand-beaded bronze bird.

the pattern cutter rather than the designer-maker that determines the finished design. It is also a more hands-on, organic process where subtle adjustments can be made with each fitting.

Kathryn Sargent rose to the position of head cutter at the Savile Row tailor, Gieves & Hawkes, the first woman to do so in the company's 200-year history. Having joined as an apprentice in 1996, she opened her business in Mayfair in 2012. Today, she provides a comprehensive offering of bespoke, couture and made-to-measure services for both women and men. From consultation to finished article, the bespoke process takes about three to four months. First, precise measurements must be taken for the intricate pattern-cutting process (arguably the most important of all the skills of a bespoke tailor). Every Master craftsperson who works for Sargent has been trained to the highest standard in time-honoured Savile Row technical and artistic practices. Clients are expected to typically attend two to three fittings, with a little fine-tuning at the end. Properly tailored garments flatter the shape with their perfect fit and are produced to last a lifetime. Fashions may come and go, but the

Opposite: A man's bespoke jacket on display in the showroom of Kathryn Sargent, who trained in the time-honoured Savile Row technical and artistic practices.

Right: Sargent at work in her Mayfair atelier, crafting a pattern for a client's commission. The cabinet behind her is full of clients' paper patterns.

craftsmanship and quality of traditional tailoring can last for generations, making it the most sustainable as well as the most desirable choice.

Daisy Knatchbull, founder of The Deck, was inspired to adapt the traditions of men's tailoring to a women-only clientele after working on the communications team of Hunstman (another Savile Row brand). She and her skilled team are advocates of conscious consumerism – the 'buy better, buy less' philosophy – and offer not only made-to-measure and bespoke options, but also tailored alterations that can breathe new life into much-loved garments. She opened her Savile Row atelier in 2019, the first tailoring house on the street to have a shopfront exclusively for women. The business has found enthusiastic clients of all ages keen to support age-old traditions as well as ethical practices. Recently, The Deck has launched a collaboration with Turnbull & Asser, launching four shirts for women inspired

Opposite left: Three-piece black tuxedo with silk facings by The Deck, which Daisy Knatchbull founded in order to offer women their own Savile Row experience.

Opposite right: Purple tweed suit by The Deck. It also offers a collection of shirts inspired by icons such as Jane Birkin and Katharine Hepburn.

Right: A pair of *Heart Murmur* mid-calf lace-up boots in Alum tawed leather by Caroline Groves, lined with ivory silk and decorated with hand-worked silk embroidery.

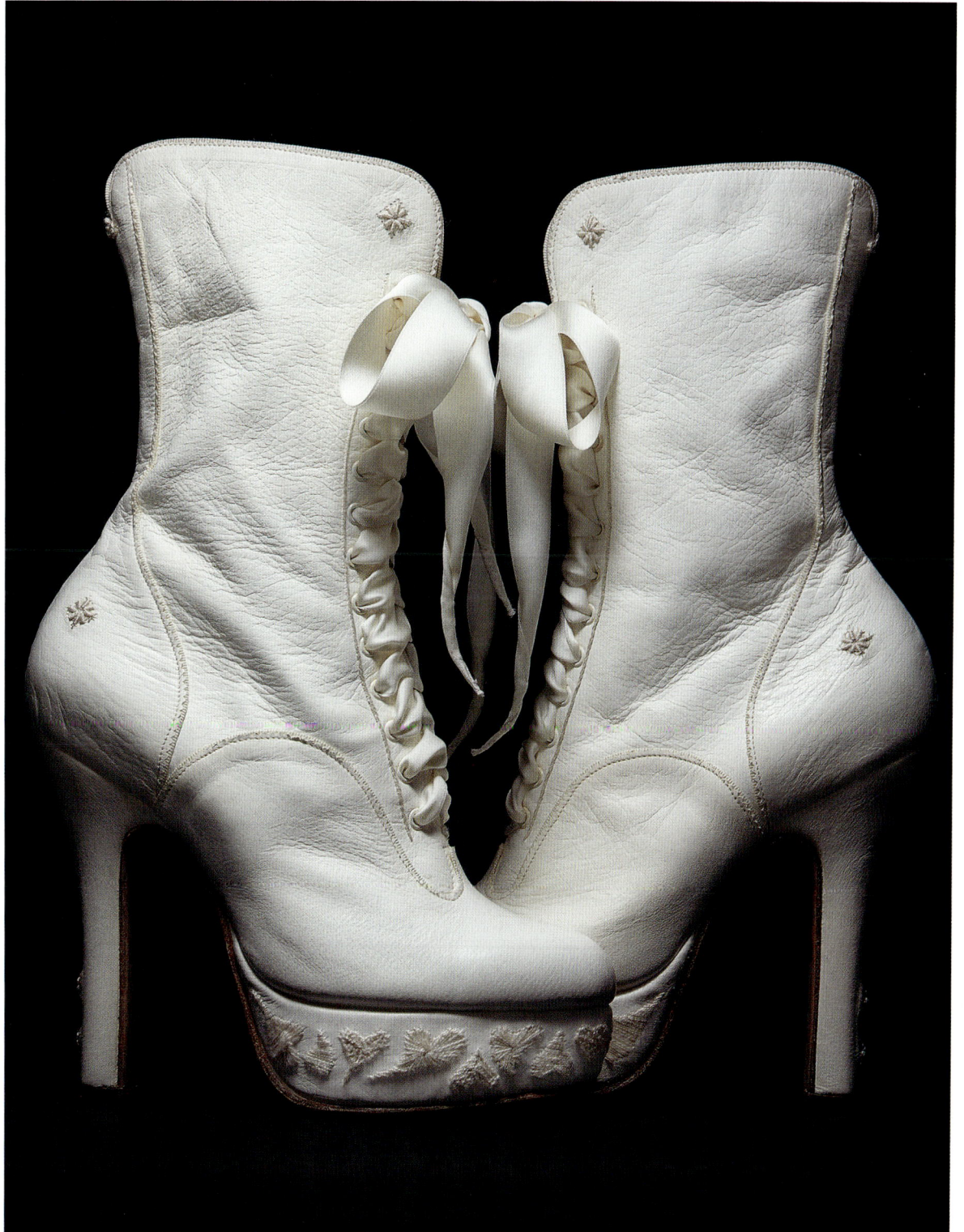

by icons such as Jane Birkin, Christy Turlington, Lauren Hutton and Katharine Hepburn.

Caroline Groves established her couture footwear atelier in 2003. First and foremost a leather worker, her passion is to bring historic, decorative leather techniques into her creations, which are akin to wearable sculpture. She describes the way her shoes are 'built' as similar to the construction of a piece of furniture or a musical instrument. Leather is sourced from the world's finest oak-bark tanneries, with the accreditation to show they have reached the highest standards of sustainabil-

ity and quality. Groves personally guides her clients through the design process from heel heights and toe shapes to trimmings and personal motifs. Shoes are made bespoke in her Cotswold atelier, but she also commissions specialist craftspeople to create unique embellishments. She travels worldwide to visit clients, including private Wardrobe Days where she designs entire shoe collections around the client's extensive wardrobe.

Carréducker is an award-winning shoemakers, with a bespoke showroom, workshop and training school in East London. Founded by

Opposite: A pair of *Neptune* calf and suede button shoes by Caroline Groves, with wool needlepoint embroidery on the heel covers. They were inspired by the client's love of sea folklore.

Right: Shoemaker James Ducker – one half of Carréducker – ploughing an insole at the workbench, pictured in front of a wall of specialist shoe-making tools.

Far right: A bespoke Carréducker loafer in soft, supple, unglazed crocodile epitomises the luxurious qualities of a handsewn shoe with its hand-made tassels and stitched leather sole.

Deborah Carré and James Ducker, they both completed traditional apprenticeships in the craft of handsewn shoemaking before joining forces in 2004. Carré's passion for the craft was ignited when creating her degree footwear collection in collaboration with Tricker's in Northampton. In 1997, a QEST Scholarship enabled her to study shoemaking under Master shoemaker, Paul Wilson, where she met Ducker, who was training as an apprentice at John Lobb (see overleaf).

Today, Carréducker creates bespoke shoes and boots to commission and works with a num-ber of British specialist manufacturers to create limited-edition, ready-to-wear boots. Over the years, it has established an international reputation for combining traditional skills with a contemporary aesthetic – including bespoke trainers. Early on, the two founders recognised the importance of passing on their skills and began training shoemakers through their own Carréducker Shoe and Leather School in 2006. Since then, they have taught hundreds of students from around the world, both in the physical environment of the school and via online resources.

JOHN LOBB:
Boot and Shoemaker

Opposite top left: One of John Lobb's experienced makers hand-scoring the welt, preparing it for stitching. The *maker* builds the bottom half of the shoe from the various components.

Opposite below left: The John Lobb last room in the basement of 9 St James's Street currently houses over 10,000 pairs of lasts, one of the largest collections in the world.

Opposite top right: John Lobb shoes are made to last, meaning they can be returned to be repaired by one of the company's highly skilled shoe makers.

Opposite below right: This original design is based on the John Lobb iconic, single-strap monk style and is hand-crafted from calf leather with thin silver buckles and tapered toe.

John Lobb opened his eponymous shoe shop in 1866 on Regent Street, having created a pair of riding boots for the Prince of Wales (later King Edward VII) of such quality and distinction that they were awarded a Royal Warrant – the first of many for the company. In 1880, he opened a second shop in St James's, allowing greater proximity to his clients who frequented the many gentlemen's clubs in the area. The company has remained in the same family for five generations, each charged with the original commitment to craftsmanship and championing the possibilities of the bespoke. In 2022, it celebrated is 60th anniversary at its current location, 9 St James's Street.

Each pair of handmade shoes relies on the input of a team of specialised craftspeople, all of whom have served long apprenticeships to acquire their skills. First, the feet are measured and examined by the *fitter*. Working from the numerous notes, tracings and measurements that the fitter makes, the *last maker* carves solid blocks of maple, beech or hornbeam into precisely contoured models of the customer's feet – idiosyncratic protrusions and all. These lasts will be added to the thousands on the Lobb shelves, so that subsequent pairs of shoes can be made to the same standards of closeness and comfort. The dextrous *pattern cutter* then cuts a paper pattern to fit the specifications of the lasts and the style of chosen shoe. This is then passed to the *clicker* –

the leather specialist whose vast experience of the various colours, weights, grains and flexibilities of leathers allows him or her to choose the most appropriate hide and cut the eight pieces used in the upper part of each shoe. The *closer* then takes over – sewing, stiffening, lining, shaping and stitching the upper part of the shoes. Uppers and lasts are then passed to the *rough stuff cutter*, whose responsibility it is to select and trim all the materials which make up the bottom of the shoes. The *maker* takes the carefully assembled upper and adds the sole of oak-bark-tanned leather and the layered, riveted heels. The *socker* fits the thin piece of leather to cover the inner soles on which the Lobb name and the Royal Warrant are printed in gold. Finally, the *polisher* brings the shoes to pristine glory, and the *tree maker* fits wooden shoe trees for each individual pair of shoes.

Not only that, but at each stage there are opportunities to introduce bespoke touches, from the type, colour and finish of leather to the style of the toe cap and the stitch of the welt. John Lobb also caters for women, with previous clients including HRH The Princess Margaret and Jackie Onassis.

Director, Jonathan Hunter Lobb, one of the fifth generation of the company says, 'John Lobb has remained true to the essence of its craft throughout its 170-year history. I am confident that if my great-great grandfather were to walk in today, he would recognise everything we do.'

'I am confident that if my great-great grandfather were to walk in today, he would recognise everything we do.'

ALEXANDRA LLEWELLYN:
Bespoke Games Maker

Although she did not know it then, the seeds for Alexandra Llewellyn's business were founded when she made regular visits to Cairo as a child (her step-grandfather is Egyptian) and played the game of backgammon with an elderly man on the street. Although they had no language in common, the game was a way of communicating and enjoying each other's company. As Plato said, 'You can discover more about a person in an hour of play than in a year of conversation.'

At heart, Llewellyn is a story-teller: a fine art-ist who has chosen the medium of marquetry to weave narratives that mean something intensely personal to her clients. She has also single-handedly shaken up the idea that board games are ubiquitous and predictable. Among her most spectacular designs are the *Marilyn Monroe* board made in collaboration with the estate of Milton H Greene, and *Spirit of the Mediterranean*, which interpreted a client's favourite holiday destination into a dazzling display of jasmine, lavender, lemons, oranges, figs and bees. Clients have

Right: Alexandra Llewellyn at her desk in her Belgravia atelier, working on new commissions. Behind her are photographs of some of her most popular signature designs.

the choice of a fully bespoke, one-off piece or the customisation and personalisation of a design from one of Llewellyn's own collections.

Since setting up in 2010, her business has flourished into a team of five working with over twenty specialist workshops around the UK, with at least ten specialist craft skills involved in each bespoke commission. The primary one is marquetry, with her designs translated into varying types and tones of sustainable timbers, combined with hand-painting and fine art printing. Her eureka moment was realising that backgammon is, in fact, a circular game played on a rectangular board, which resulted in her unique circular backgammon table.

Backgammon is still her first love, but over recent years she has also added collections of poker sets, playing cards, chess boards, travelling backgammon sets and games tables to her offer-

ing. While her studio is based in the East End, she opened her first London by-appointment show-room in 2022 in Belgravia.

Commissioned by elite fashion, hospitality and interiors brands to create games for their own clients, Llewellyn also has an impressive list of private clients that includes Hollywood stars, royalty and public figures. She has been recognised by Walpole (the official sector body for UK luxury) as a Rising Star in Luxury and has also received a commendation from the organisation for Excellence in Craftsmanship at the Luxury Briefing Awards.

Her passion for the subject increases all the time, as does her belief in the power of games to unite, just as a small girl in Cairo discovered so many years ago, 'We daydream in the studio that we could achieve world peace by sitting down warring countries and getting them to understand each other better over a game of backgammon.'

Above left: Llewellyn trained in Fine Art and begins with hand-drawn sketches and digital collages of potential designs that are then translated into marquetry veneers.

Above right: Llewellyn's eureka moment was the realisation that backgammon is a circular game played on a rectangular board, inspiring bespoke designs such as this one of the African night sky.

'We daydream in the studio that we could achieve world peace by sitting down warring countries and getting them to understand each other better over a game of backgammon.'

Above: One of her most memorable designs is the Marilyn Monroe board made in collaboration with the estate of Milton H Greene featuring the actress in 1953.

Above: The *Palm* backgammon board flips to a chess board on its other side. As with other Llewellyn designs, it is both elegant and fun on which to play.

9

It takes many years to become a Master of a craft – often decades – and true Masters would say there is never a point at which they feel the journey has been completed. For those passionate about their craft, it is a lifetime exploration of process, material and challenging the technique to its limit. This deep understanding is also why craft objects are often underappreciated in comparison to fine art. It takes a certain level of knowledge to understand why one glass vessel or bone china plate commands a far higher price than another, for example. While craft – often loosely bracketed under the heading decorative art – is attracting more attention than in years past, it does not yet enjoy full parity with fine art.

It is worth reminding ourselves that professional craftspeople choose a life based not on the pursuit of money, but of the pursuit of excellence in their chosen field. Nobody chooses to be a maker for financial gain, although a few do reach the pinnacle that gives them both money and critical respect. Craftspeople are driven by a passion for what they do, dependent for their often precarious income on the appreciation by others of their skill. In this 'fast' age of social media and digital technology, time is the new, valuable currency. When someone buys or commissions a piece of craft, he or she is in effect buying someone else's time: not just the time it took them to make this object, but the decades of experience and commitment that brought it to fruition.

One of the interesting aspects of exceptional craft is that people respond to it so differently compared to fine art. People encounter paintings that they might love, but unless they are professionally involved with the art world, they rarely feel the need to come in close and study brushwork or pigment, and they are understandably discouraged from running their fingers over the surface. The emotional connection a painting can engender is based on qualities such as subject matter, colour, scale and impact. This is true of craft as well, but it is its tactility that often makes it so desirable. When people see beautiful, crafted objects of glass, silver, wood, porcelain – or any other pleasing texture – they want to enjoy it with their fingers as much as their eyes. This haptic desire might make gallerists specialising in fine craft pieces understandably nervous, but it doesn't kill the compulsion to reach out and touch.

Understanding Materials

To help navigate the elevated world of gallery craft, it is worth enjoying a slow immersion into the particular material that most attracts. There are plenty of books, websites, exhibitions and craft fairs to help with this, but the shortcut is to seek help from highly experienced, specialist galleries and guilds, which are happy to share their passion and knowledge. As well as the ones mentioned below, spend time exploring the collections and online catalogues of dedicated craft galleries such as jaggedart, Flow, Contemporary Applied Arts, Oxford Ceramics, Joanna Bird, London Glassblowing and The New Craftsmen.

We have focused here on glass, ceramic, wood and silver but, of course, there are other makers specialising in stone, paper, weaves and willow to name but a few. The best advice for any collector is to find the texture that sings to the fingers as much as to the eyes and enjoy embarking on a parallel voyage of discovery with those who have mastered its beauty and techniques.

Right: The work of Vezzini & Chen is an artful marriage of blown glass and hand-carved ceramics, with collections that tread a fine line between the functional and the conceptual. (Courtesy of Adrian Sassoon.)

Glass

Vessel Gallery was established in 1999 with the mission to be a major destination for those who appreciate contemporary glass and ceramics, specialising in museum-quality sculptural pieces, lighting, and British Studio Glass. Founder Angel Monzon says that he is always searching for a new narrative or innovative technique that pushes the boundaries of glass making, 'We look both for a masterpiece quality of craftsmanship and a story within the piece that has a strong concept and meaning.'

To appreciate glass means first understanding how difficult it is to master the craft, 'You need a lot of patience and perseverance if you choose glass as your material, as it takes at least ten to fifteen years to master it, but more importantly you then have to develop your own style and technique in order to create truly unique works. That takes years of experimentation. Glass artists have

to be tenacious and tireless because there is such a high failure rate with the process. You might lose fifty per cent of your production at any stage, meaning that glass is always on the brink of failure. As well as the possibility of glass shattering at any point, achieving a consistency of colour is also technically challenging. Colour can differ so much according to the particular batch of glass, atmospheric pressure and a myriad other factors.'

When it comes to narrative, he gives the example of Chris Day whose works of glass, clay and mixed media tell stories of social injustices and human tragedy, including referencing the Black Lives Matter movement and the COVID pandemic. For exemplary craftsmanship, he points to the example of Elliot Walker, one of only a handful of glassblowers in the world to practise the *massello* technique, which takes extreme dexterity, speed and precise temperature control to sculpt the molten glass. He cites Samantha Donaldson for the inspiration she draws from the internal structures of naturally occurring geodes, in particular their internal space or *vug*. He also admires Nina Casson McGarva for the parallels she draws in her work between the cycles of nature and the phases of transformation through which glass passes from molten liquid to solid form.

For Monzon, glass will always have an appeal to collectors because of its mesmerising colours and reflective surface, 'Glass is sexy – it has a shiny, sparkly magpie effect that draws people to it, creating a sense of wonder.'

Ceramics

Adrian Sassoon is a world-renowned specialist in eighteenth-century French porcelain, particularly Sèvres and Vincennes. However, his gallery, founded in 1992, is also highly regarded for its focus on contemporary craft works – not only porcelain, but also metalwork, glass, stone, wood and paper. Many of the works he sells are by contemporary greats, such as Professor Felicity Aylieff, Gordon Baldwin OBE and Kate Malone MBE.

Above: Detail of *Collapsed Porcelain Bowl* by Olivia Walker. Her vessels feature lichen-like layers, which seem to eat away at the surface, as if threatening to collapse the form beneath.

Opposite: The detailed and delicate porcelain vessels of Hitomi Hosono (shown here at work in her studio) reference the natural world, in particular botanical specimens. (Courtesy of Adrian Sassoon.)

Above: *Multi-blue Circular Flow* by Fenella Elms is a hypnotically beautiful piece made from individually stained porcelain parts built into a brass frame.

When it comes to assessing the calibre of a work in ceramic, Sassoon is first drawn to the texture, 'I love the sight and feel of an amazing surface under my fingers, whether it is the glaze or the fact it is not glazed. I also know how much work and time goes into making an interesting or flawless texture and that also impresses me. Kilns might have become more sophisticated over the centuries, but porcelain is still as unforgiving to artists as it has always been.'

Having spent much of his long career studying historic objects, he also looks for pieces that speak of their time. 'It's not uncommon to see works by established artists that are beautifully made, but don't appear to have progressed over the last twenty years or more. I want to be able to place something chronologically, so that I can see where it fits into the history of the decorative arts. I like to work with people who are really pushing their technique and being inventive.'

He advises that there is nothing wrong with looking for evidence that other people like something too, 'When you create an object and put it out in the world for an audience, it is important to see how that audience reacts.' For this reason, he recommends visiting the top tier of art, design and craft fairs, even when the work might be financially unobtainable, because it is a chance to get up close to an object and see the hand of the maker at work, 'If you are serious about collecting, find a gallery or a dealer you trust. Don't buy work because the person who made it is considered 'cool' on social media: buy because the work speaks to your eyes and to your fingers.'

Finally, it is alchemy that makes the difference, 'One of the basic tenets of making is that the raw materials delivered to a studio – be it fine

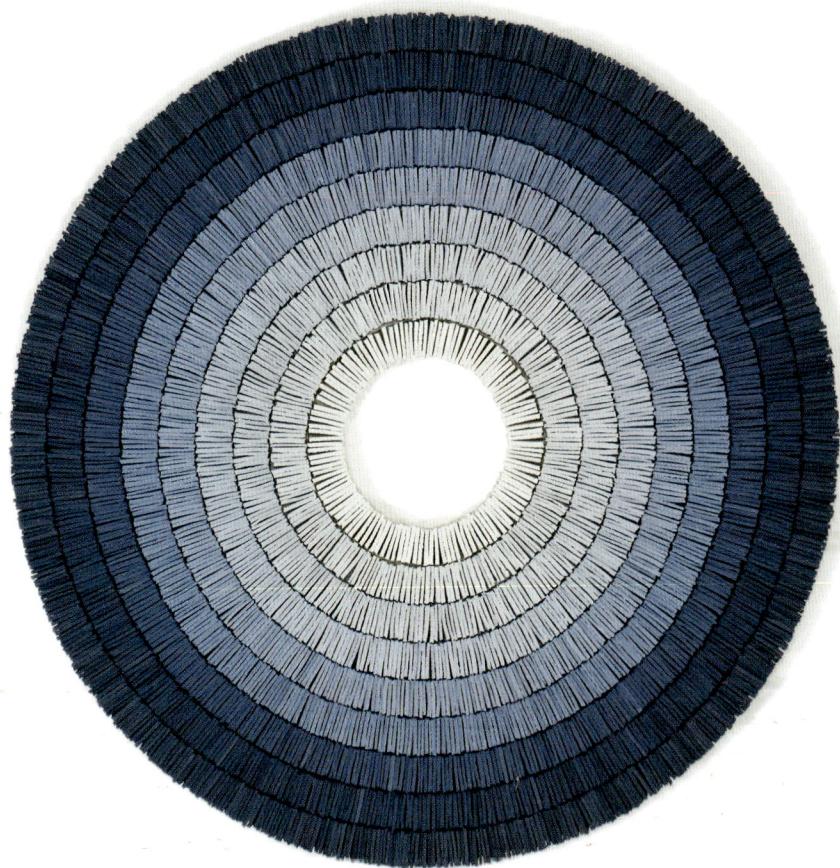

Above: *Coral Island 2* by Lucas Ferreira is constructed from small, hand-crafted porcelain tiles assembled into a circular form. (Courtesy of jaggedart.)

silver sheets, powdered glass, a trunk of wood or a bag of clay – should leave the studio completely transformed. I look for artists who perform miracles every day as a matter of course.'

Wood

Sarah Myerscough established her gallery in 1998, but over recent years has focused particularly on wood and other natural materials. She represents international artist-designer-makers, whose work combines the traditions of craft making with a contemporary eye and innovative approach, such as John Makepeace OBE (left) Gareth Neal (see pages 244–247), Eleanor Lakelin (left), Nic Webb (see overleaf) and Peter Marigold (see page 205).

What she searches for when assessing new works is innovation, 'So often with wood, there is a lack of surprise. As a material, it can be considered old-fashioned, with carving and lathing techniques that have barely changed over centuries. I am looking for sculptural intent, sensitivity and an innate understanding of the material that together create a powerful voice in the context of contemporary culture.'

When it comes to skill, exceptional technique is not enough, 'Unlike many other materials, wood has a life force of its own: it can be spirited, challenging, even argumentative. It relies on the emotional engagement of the maker to harness its beauty and energy. If a piece does not communicate that passion or intellect, then it won't work.'

To anyone new to collecting sculptured wood, she thinks the first step is to clear the head of any preconceptions, 'This type of work is a very far cry from a perfectly veneered piece of fine cabinetry. Artists are often working with raw off-cuts or the heart of the tree; they might be highlight-

Opposite top: *Echoes of Amphora Lidded Vessel 1* by Eleanor Lakelin is made of Horse Chestnut burr, hand-turned on a traditional woodworking lathe; hollowed, sand-blasted and bleached. (Courtesy of Sarah Myerscough Gallery.)

Opposite below: *Trine Cloud Chair 1* by John Makepeace OBE is made of thirteen laminates of scorched English Oak, polished back to expose the cross-grain pattern achieved through the substrata. (Courtesy of Sarah Myerscough Gallery.)

Above left: *Uovo* by sculptor Alison Crowther (see page 204), a private commission that the artist hand-carved from unseasoned English oak using traditional gouges and mallets.

Above: Sensitive to the complex geometry of nature, Crowther observes and responds to her material, taking cues from the grain to create intricate, surface texture and pattern.

Left: *Untitled* i and *Untitled* ii by Nic Webb. These two vessels are of hand-carved and sandblasted oak with a raw finish and flamed interior. (Courtesy of Sarah Myerscough Gallery.)

Opposite: *Hollow In Elm* by Nic Webb is hand-carved and sandblasted elm with a flamed interior. At 120cm high (without plinth), it has a striking presence. (Courtesy of Sarah Myerscough Gallery.)

Left: Solid silver drinking vessels (from left to right): *Tulip Beaker* by Jessica Jue; *Herringbone Beaker* by Rebecca de Quin; *Feather Beaker* by James Dougall; *Solace Cup* by Alex O'Connor; *Fran Champagne Cup* by Elizabeth Auriol Peers; *Song Vessel* by Alex O'Connor; *Leonie Beaker* by Elizabeth Auriol Peers. (Courtesy of Craftmasters gallery.)

Opposite top: Ndidi Ekubia MBE in her studio. The artist's method of making is founded on the idea of pushing sheet metal to its limits, emphasising the vitality of each form. (Courtesy of Adrian Sassoon.)

Opposite below: *Lily Pad* by Hal Messel, made of solid silver. This highly complex work can be assembled as one centrepiece or broken down into components and arranged the length of the table.

ing the grain or echoing the form of how the tree has grown. Wood is commonplace and therefore associated with inexpensive, utilitarian objects. Collectors have to understand that the value is in the process of the crafting and the narrative. There is a privilege in being able to appreciate a piece that does not shout, but instead quietly invites those with a deep understanding to follow the rhythm of each crack, curve or patina. We show work that represents an intuitive love for the material and its connection to the natural world that is very relevant right now.'

Silver

Craftmasters gallery was established in 2020 by Helen Hood to offer an online platform for the best examples of contemporary British silverware and sculpture. It also aims to help silversmiths create sustainable businesses, so protecting skills for future generations. The gallery feeds all its profits back into technical training, whereby Master silversmiths pass on heritage skills to early career makers. Hood has a deep passion for silver, having worked directly with silversmiths both in a curatorial capacity and by supporting organisations such as Contemporary British Silversmiths.

A collector herself, she finds silver addictive, 'There is something magical and primeval about watching a silversmith start work on a new piece. Most begin either with an ingot or a sheet of silver, then employ or combine a number of techniques to create the form, such as raising, soldering, casting and forging. When raising silver, the regular thud of the hammer against metal is meditative and transportive. It is also captivating to see how the metal responds to touch, becoming brittle and hard when worked, then annealed to regain malleability.'

She also loves the fact that silversmithing has its roots in the techniques of the Bronze Age, 'A time traveller would note little difference in the workshops of artisan silver makers 1,000 years apart. However, the design of contemporary silver is dynamic and exciting. A finished object represents total commitment to mastering many complex techniques.'

Her advice to anyone new to silver collecting is to look at the work of established makers first – people who have won awards and been exhibited both nationally and internationally, which gives the confidence to buy, 'As you become more knowledgeable, you can explore the work of emerging makers and be rewarded with the satisfaction of watching their careers grow. Many people also start with collections of one thing, such as silver beakers. Laying a table with these objects looks ravishing and creates a talking point. Of course, silver also has the advantage of being hallmarked for the last 800 years, which is in itself a record of quality.'

Silver can also rise Phoenix-like from the maker's bench, 'As a material, it has exceptional longevity and resilience. Unloved family pieces can be melted down and re-born as new, highly personal designs. There are also a dizzying array of surface finishes – including repoussé, hand engraving, chasing, enamelling or patination.'

One thing she is evangelical about is that silver should be enjoyed, 'When used regularly, silver stays looking beautiful and needs little cleaning. It should never be relegated to the back of a dusty cupboard. There is nothing like holding a piece of silver and experiencing the magic for yourself. No need for white gloves!'

Spotlight on

DAME MAGDALENE ODUNDO:
Ceramicist

Below left: Dame Magdalene Odundo is renowned worldwide for the statements she makes about the plight of women through her voluptuous forms.

Below right: The first firing renders clay red, but the second one turns it black. This colour contrast is part of the powerful message within her work.

Considered to be one of the finest and most inspirational ceramicists working today, Dame Magdalene Odundo produces voluptuous sculptural vessels in a signature palette of rich ochres and black. She hand-builds her forms using a coiling technique, scraping them smooth with a gourd. After the clay is shaped, it is covered with slip, fired and then burnished by hand. Colour is determined by the firing technique: a first firing in an oxidising atmosphere turns the clay red-orange, while a second firing in an oxygen-poor atmosphere renders it black. This method shares its roots with ancient pottery techniques. Many of her forms are reminiscent of the female body, including one of her most recognisable works: a black and ochre vessel with curved base and elongated neck that resembles the swollen belly of a pregnant woman.

Born in Nairobi, Dame Magdalene originally trained in Graphics and Commercial Art as an apprentice with an advertising agency while studying at Nairobi Polytechnic in Kenya. She moved to England in 1971 to take her foundation art course at the Cambridge School of Art, going on to study for a degree in Ceramics, Printmaking and Photography at the West Surrey College of Art and Design in Farnham (now the University

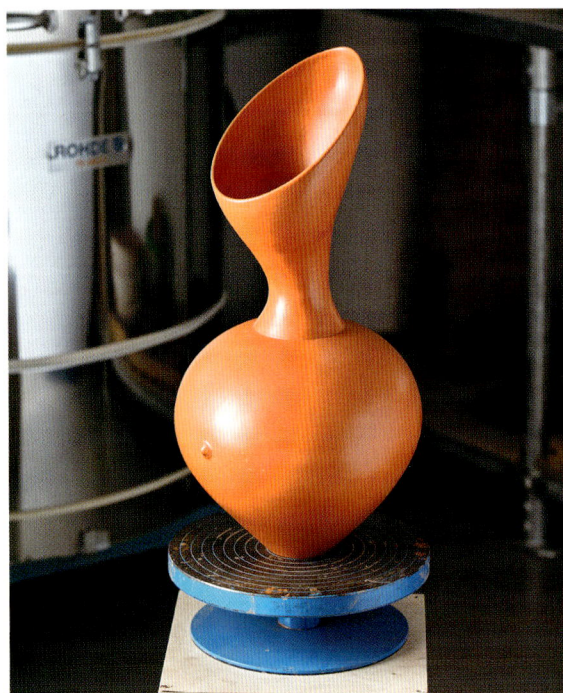

'Working with clay is a universal practice and ... has an empathy that is haptic, and therefore sympathetic, to being moulded in its many forms.'

for the Creative Arts). A three-year period teaching at the Commonwealth Institute in London was followed by her MA at the Royal College of Art, where she specialised in Ceramics, graduating in 1982. Her work won critical acclaim immediately, with invitations to show her work in both group and solo shows. From 1991–1994, she was part of *Africa Explores – 20th-Century African Arts*, which toured across the USA from the Museum for African Art in New York to the University Art Museum of Berkeley, and was then hosted at venues in Germany, Spain, France and finally Tate Liverpool. Indeed, barely a year has passed since she graduated from the RCA without her ceramics being shown somewhere in the world. A long and distinguished career as maker, researcher, lecturer and academic resulted in her being inaugurated as Emerita Professor at the University for the Creative Arts in 2016 and as Chancellor in 2018. Along the way, she has been a generous mentor to many, young aspiring artists, especially those from Africa.

Dame Magdalene's work is now part of the permanent collections of over fifty museums internationally, including The British Museum in London and The Metropolitan Museum in New York. She has also been recognised for her work through the many African and British honours awarded to her, most recently as Dame Commander of the Order of the British Empire (DBE) in 2020.

She says of her passion for her chosen medium, 'Working with clay is a universal practice and the art of ceramics has been appreciated the world over because of its enduring appeal for its expansiveness. It has an empathy that is haptic and therefore sympathetic to being moulded in its many forms.'

Above: Dame Magdalene in her studio in Farnham where she is currently Chancellor of the University for the Creative Arts.

Left: Examples of her highly influential work, which is now included in the permanent collections of over fifty museums internationally.

DANNY LANE:
Glass Artist

Opposite top: Looking into the *Still Water Rising* table by Danny Lane, a unique piece made of ultra-clear float glass. When used in this way, compressed glass is hugely strong.

Opposite below: A pair of forged steel consoles by Danny Lane, which have been acid patinated and waxed. The tops are in fact *scagliola*, made by Thomas Kennedy (see pages 54–55, 57 and 59–60).

Danny Lane's West London studio is a melting pot of industrial glass making, steel forming and forging, stone carving, woodwork and engineering, but it is with glass that he made his name. In the 1980s, he developed a much-imitated process whereby layered industrial glass is cut, drilled and layered on to steel rods. When tightly compressed in this way, glass is hugely strong – about twenty times more so than concrete. He first used this technique to make furniture, such as jagged-edged tables with stalagmite legs and chairs that appear to have been carved from ice, but thirty years ago he began concentrating more on public artworks, such as *Parting of the Waves* at Canary Wharf, the seven-metre (twenty-three-foot) high *Borealis* for the headquarters of General Motors in Detroit, and the thirty-metre (100-foot) long *Balustrade* at the V&A Museum.

Lane was twenty when he moved to England from the USA to study stained-glass under the tuition of the eminent artist, Patrick Reyntiens (responsible for many collaborative projects with John Piper, including major glass fenestrations at Coventry and Liverpool Cathedrals). Having fallen in love with glass, he followed up his studies at the Ruskin School of Drawing and Fine Art at Oxford and a foundation course at the Byam Shaw School of Art, before embarking on a Fine Art degree at the Central School of Art and Design. It was his pragmatic streak that drew him back to glass, inspired by the medieval belief that there need be no distinction between making a fresco for a wall or a table at which to eat.

Having established his studio in the early 80s, he showed work at Ron Arad's One Off design emporium, but then migrated towards architectural-scale sculpture. Today, with a focus on maintaining in-house craft and engineering skills, he orchestrates a team of technicians and students who help him run the furnaces, kilns, workshops and engineering facilities. His clients include public collections, wealthy corporations and private collectors, with every piece unique or commissioned. In 2020, to mark the 800th year since the laying of the first foundation stone, Salisbury Cathedral invited Lane to install *Stairway*, a six-metre (nineteen-foot) high sculpture of glass and steel that metaphorically ascended to the sky, as part of its *Spirit of Endeavour* exhibition. This juxtaposed beautifully with the famous fourteenth-century spire which, at 55 metres (180 feet) high, is the tallest in the UK.

However, what makes Lane remarkable within his field is that he creates huge sculptural pieces with practically no CNC but by working directly with the material, drawing on decades of skill. As he says, 'If I could draw you a map to show how to create something, completely risk free, it would rob the process of its unique essence and vitality. This is about developing each piece organically through intuition and long experience.'

'If I could draw you a map to show how to create something, completely risk free, it would rob the process of its unique essence and vitality.'

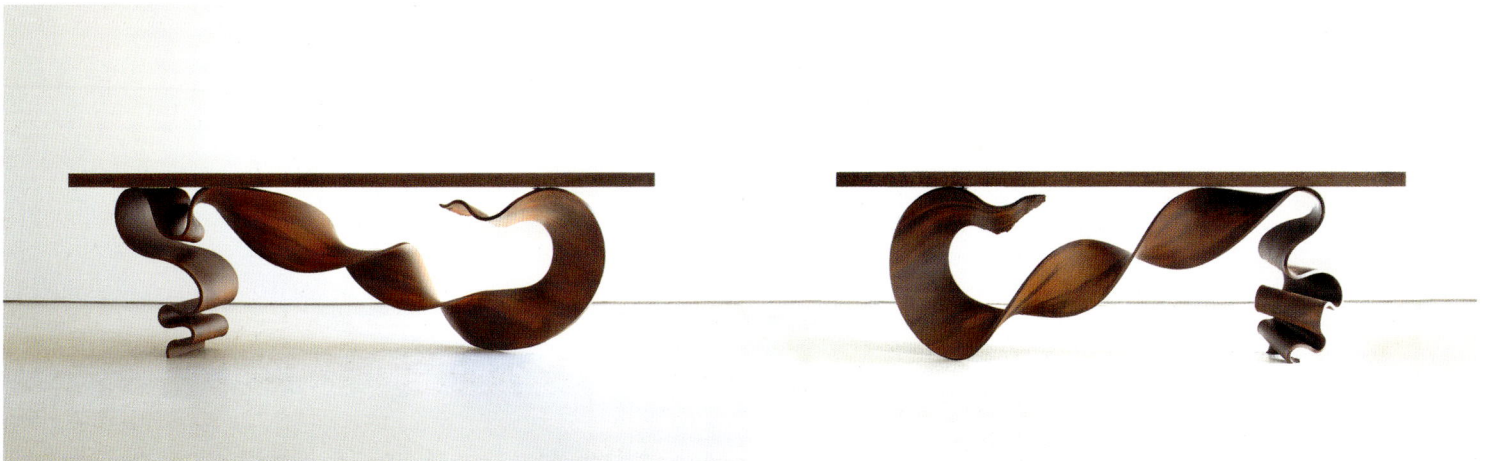

10

COLLECTED & CURATED

At times, it is difficult to delineate with exactitude where craft stops and art begins. There is a whole layer of craft-based work that comes into existence through collaborations with artists, architects and designers.

Sometimes craft is simply a facilitator or fabricator of an artistic concept. One example is the bronze foundries that have been central to many artists' practices since the nineteenth century. Of course, foundries had existed before this time – bronze being an ancient process – but they burgeoned at a time when the demand for bronze statues to commemorate war heroes and political leaders was on the increase. There was a great tradition of bronze founding in France, and a number of skilled French artisans settled in London after the fall of the Paris Commune in 1871. A wave of Italian founders, specialists in the lost wax process, also set up in London, many of whom had trained at the famous Fonderia Nelli in Rome. To name but a few examples, the four iconic lions of Trafalgar Square were the work of Sir Edwin Landseer and cast with the help of Baron Carlo Marochetti. The famous equestrian statue, *Physical Energy*, in Kensington Gardens was made by George Frederic Watts and cast by AB Burton at Thames Ditton. The statue of Prince Albert within the monumental Albert Memorial of Hyde Park was the work of John Henry Foley and his assistant, Thomas Brock, (who took over after Foley's death) and was cast by Henry Prince & Co. of Southwark.

Sculptors of the early twentieth century began to explore ways of translating their ideas into bronze with the help of foundries, including Jacob Epstein, Henry Moore, Barbara Hepworth and Elisabeth Frink. Today, internationally renowned artists such as Tracey Emin CBE, Sir Antony Gormley, Nic Fiddian-Green and Marc Quinn also work with foundries to fabricate works into bronze, often dramatically scaling up the original maquettes. Not that foundries are the only facilitators of art: glassblowers, resin specialists, textile studios, ceramicists, neon benders, lighting engineers and, of course, bespoke framers can all play a vital part in helping to bring an artistic vision to life. Emin, for example, has assimilated craft traditions into her artistic practice that include sewn appliqué and neon bending, elevating them to the same level as the fine art techniques she uses of painting, drawing, photography, sculpture and film.

Stained-glass has also intrigued artists, such as the famous partnership between John Piper and stained-glass artist Patrick Reyntiens, which resulted in twentieth-century masterpieces including the windows of Coventry Cathedral and the Metropolitan Cathedral in Liverpool. More recently, the painter, architectural artist and eminent stained-glass artist, Brian Clarke, has collaborated with luminaries such as Zaha Hadid, Sir Norman Foster and Oscar Niemeyer on projects worldwide, challenging and expanding the boundaries of what the medium can do.

One of the most famous proponents of craft is Grayson Perry who conceived *The Tomb of the Unknown Craftsman* in 2011 and again in 2020, in collaboration with the British Museum. Both sculptures were hung with handmade replicas of British Museum objects to represent the crafts made through the centuries by unknown men and women. In 2015, he created *The Ballad of Julie Cope* – the history of modern Britain told through four tapestries – made for *A*

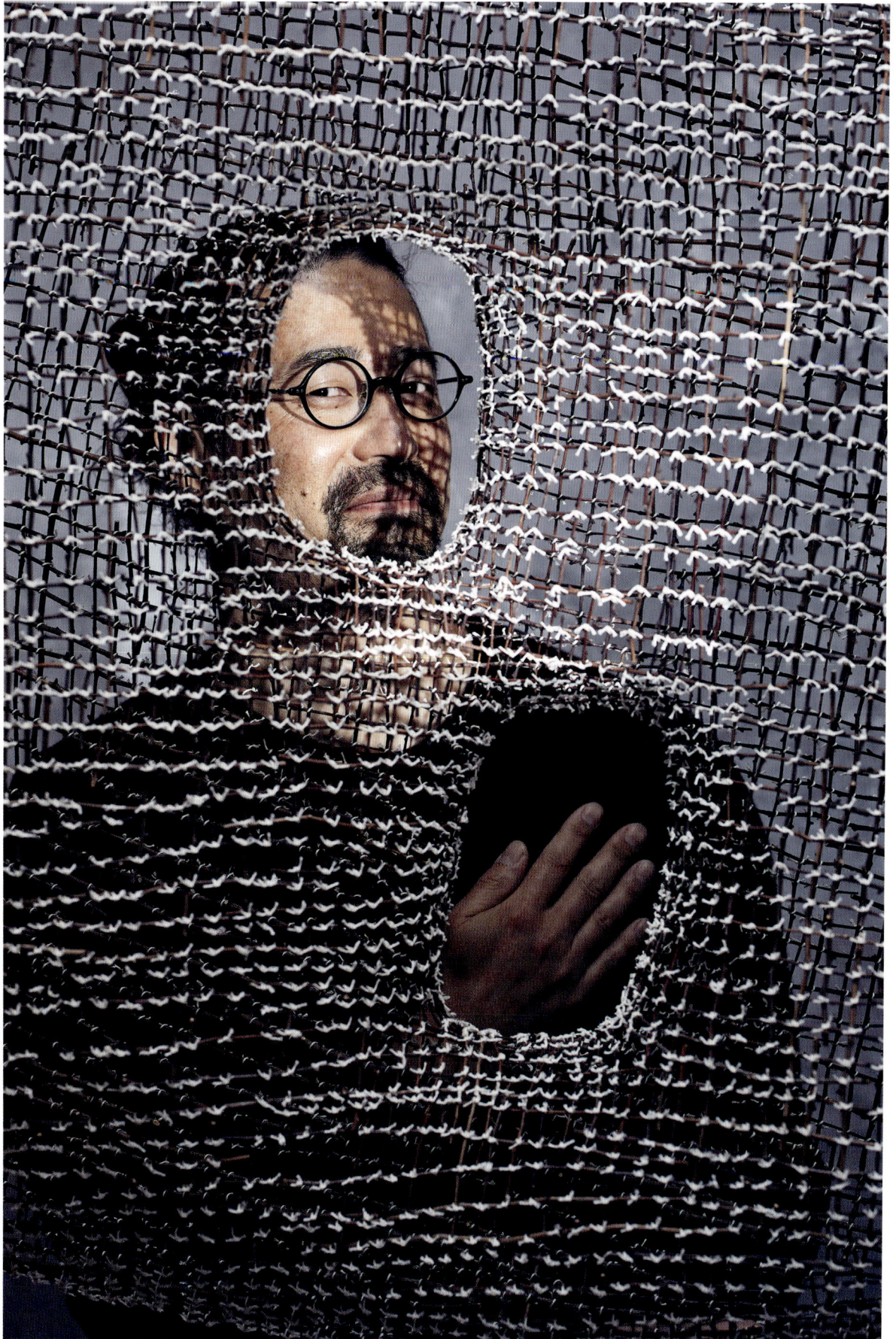

House for Essex (AHFE), the artwork-building designed by Perry in collaboration with Charles Holland of FAT Architecture. AHFE employed traditional craft practices alongside digital fabrication techniques, an equally weighted fusion of art and architecture. As well as the tapestries, the artist designed ceramics, woodcuts, metalwork, textiles, mosaic floor tiles, prints and the distinctive architectural faience of the exterior. These were then produced by various craft specialists, including Darwen Terracotta and Faience, millimetre (metalwork) and Paul Marks (mosaic floor). Two of the large-scale tapestries were acquired by the Crafts Council in 2016 and have since been presented as the travelling exhibition *Julie Cope's Grand Tour* in numerous cultural institutions throughout the country.

Two-Way Street

Just as fine artists are embracing craft as another offering on their palette, a significant number of makers are stepping into the world of fine art. Many show in the context of international art fairs, as opposed to high-end craft fairs, or a combination of the two. They are as likely to be represented by a fine art gallery as one dedicated to the applied arts.

Gagosian in London, for example, represents ceramic artist Edmund de Waal; White Cube represents sculptor Rachel Kneebone, who works mainly in porcelain; Hignell Gallery represents Laura Ellen Bacon (see page 206) whose woven willow works sit right on the cusp of craft and art; Timothy Taylor represents Annie Morris who encompasses tapestry within her work alongside sculpture, painting and drawing; while David Messum of Cork Street represents leading ceramicists Robina Jack and renowned wood sculptor Guy Taplin.

Make Hauser & Wirth Somerset, in Bruton, Somerset is dedicated to contemporary making and the crafted object, bringing together works in clay, textiles, wood and stone inspired by land,

Right: *Wilder than Wildness Itself* (2021) at Make Hauser & Wirth. The installation featured works by textile artist Sophie Rowley and glass artist Jochen Holz.

Right: *Tallgirl* by Saelia Aparicio, a unique piece made of birchwood that has been dyed and stained using Chinese ink. (Courtesy of Gallery FUMI.)

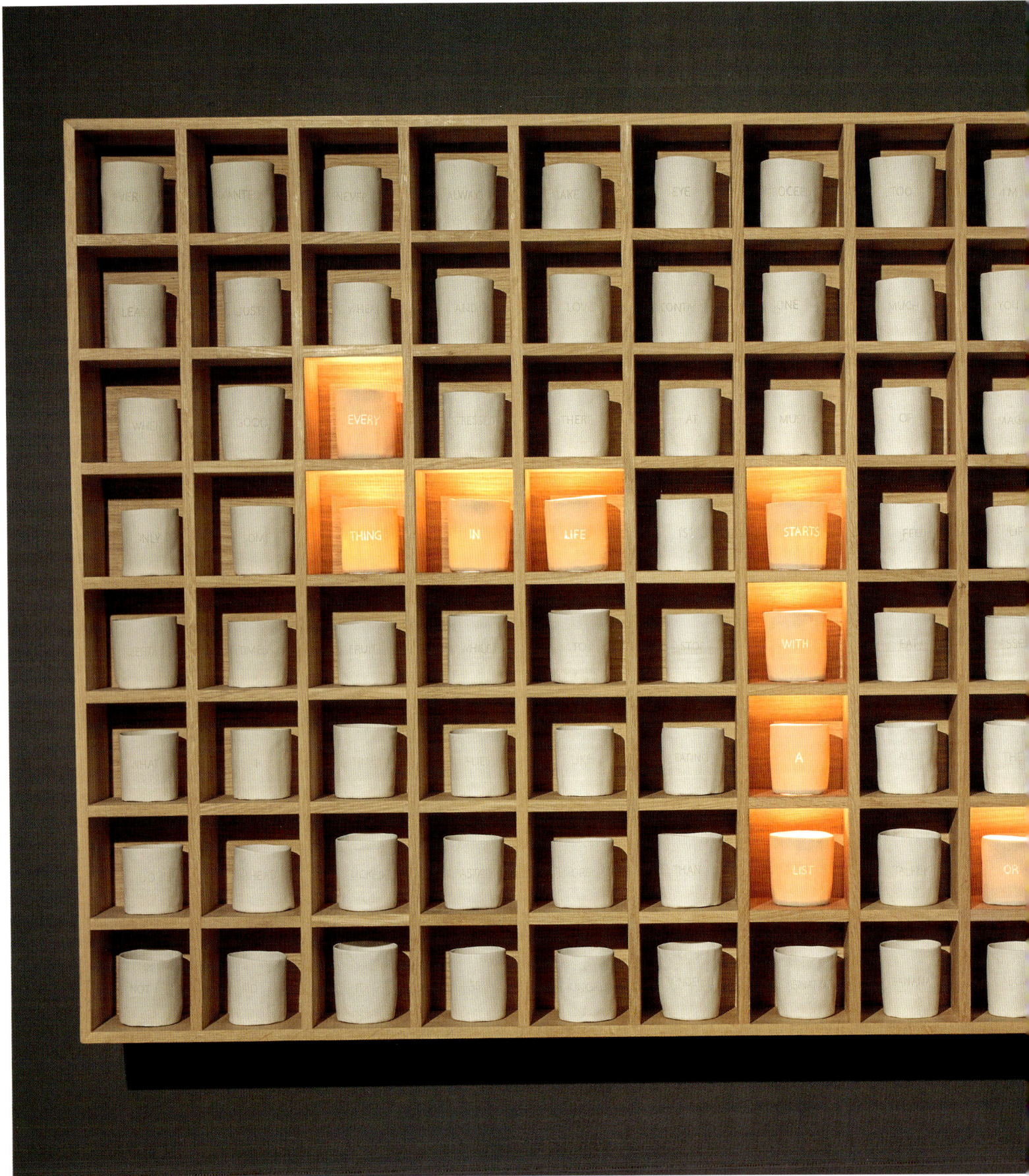

Left: Ceramicist Martha Freud is well known for her witty installations, such as this Mixed Message Box that spells out tongue-in-cheek phrases when illuminated.

Above: The Kit Kemp Design Studio, the creative arm of Firmdale hotels, commissioned this installation from Martha Freud for The Potting Shed in the Dorset Square Hotel, London.

Right: Placuna Pro Dilectione Mea by Rowan Mersh, a unique piece made of sliced and assembled Capiz shells. (Courtesy of Gallery FUMI.)

environment and our relationship to the natural world. Since 2018, it has presented pieces by over 80 artist-makers, many of them using locally sourced materials. Recent exhibitions have included *Wilder than Wildness Itself*, comprising multidisciplinary works in response to 'Oudolf Field', the 'living canvas' perennial meadow created by garden designer, Piet Oudolf at the gallery's main outpost just down the road.

In recent years, Johnny Messum (son of David) has opened regional outposts to the Cork Street gallery, including Messums Wiltshire (Tisbury) and Messums Yorkshire (Harrogate). These larger spaces have enabled the gallery to show an exciting rolling programme of international art, sculpture, photography, craft and performance. Now Messums Creative (Chilmark) has established a new set of studios for making clay, in which artists of all ages and walks of life are invited to explore, learn and thrive.

The New Art Centre at Roche Court near Salisbury is primarily a twenty-four-hectare (60-acre) sculpture park, with a series of awarding-winning indoor galleries designed by the architect Stephen Marshall. The Artists' House is in part inspired by Kettle's Yard, Cambridge,

Right: Asabikeshiinh IV (Dreamcatcher IV) by Rowan Mersh a unique piece made of sliced and assembled Turritella shells. (Courtesy of Gallery FUMI.)

and unites art with craft and design objects. On the top floor is a permanent display of Edmund de Waal's work, while the ground floor hosts temporary exhibitions, which in recent years have focused on names such as Barbara Hepworth, Ian Stephenson, Tess Jaray, Richard Deacon and Nika Neelova. The Design House is configured as the background for exhibitions of ceramics, textile, carvings and sculpture. It has recently hosted work by Ann Sutton, Gary Hume, Barry Flanagan, Fred Baier and Katie Walker (see page 129).

Acclaimed fairs such as PAD, Masterpiece, NOMAD and Design Miami/Basel routinely break down the barriers between art, design and craft, so levelling the field in a very relevant and inspirational way.

Concept and Craft

Increasingly, artists and makers are exploring new ways of expressing powerful messages within the craft process. Concept is now on a par with process. This can be seen in the curation of galleries such as jaggedart and Gallery FUMI where artists are not boxed into one category but encouraged to embrace the dialogue that

EDA (Bough) by Kazuhito Takadoi is made of green grass from the artist's garden with gold leaf on handmade Washi paper. (Courtesy of jaggedart.)

flows between design, art and craft, presenting intriguing narratives within their work.

Take, for example, the work of Peter Ting. Born and raised in Hong Kong China, Ting is a renowned ceramicist and QEST Scholar (now QEST Trustee) whose work bridges East and West. His first experience of working with clay was aged sixteen at his English public school, but his love of the material was instant. Having studied Ceramics at the West Surrey College of Art and Design, Farnham (now the University for the Creative Arts), Cardiff School of Art and Design and Stoke-on-Trent College of Art, he settled in London in 1996, working in-house as a designer for luxury houses such as Asprey and Thomas Goode. He developed a love and deep knowledge of British bone china – as epitomised by companies such as Spode and Royal Crown Derby – working with traditional English styles, such as hand-painted flowers and gold gilding.

However, in 2004, he travelled to Dehua in Fujian Province, known for its centuries-old Blanc de Chine porcelain. Captivated by the hand techniques of Chinese potters, he began to extract motifs from the classical tradition and layer them into his own work, as seen on the cup and saucer of *Buddha Hands*, for example. He has since collaborated with Zha Caiduan, an accomplished porcelain flower maker in Dehua, to create works such as *Flower Cylinder* and *Pearl Vase*. Both *Buddha Hands* and *Flower Cylinder* have been acquired by the V&A Museum in London, meaning that Ting's journey has now gone full circle – a Chinese maker, living in London, with work acquired by an iconic British institution that is honouring the ancient skill of Dehua craftsmanship. He is also co-founder of the Ting-Ying gallery, which in turn is dedicated to artists whose work is inspired by the legacy and history of Blanc de Chine porcelain.

Martha Freud strikes a playful note, often creating entire installations with ceramics embedded with slogans. Since launching her epony-mous studio in 2008, she has won acclaim for the confidence with which she walks the line between tongue-in-cheek wordplay and philosophical reflection, celebrating both the highs and lows of life. She makes simple, organic forms from clay via traditional making practices that are unapologetically slow. Many of her illuminated 'Mixed Messages Boxes' feature up to 200 porcelain cups, each of which is punctured with minuscule holes that form a unique word set within its own box. When electricity is switched on, the cups light up in different sequences, creating pre-programmed compositions that might reference a song lyric, rumination, catch phrase or colloquial expression.

Forest + Found is a partnership between Max Bainbridge and Abigail Booth, who create installations that bridge landscape, material and process. Working with materials sourced direct

from the natural world – both rural and urban – they aim to explore the human relationship with these environments. Bainbridge, for example, consciously seeks out wood that has fallen where it once grew, taking the natural shape and character of the tree in its entirety to inform his sculptural decision-making. In this way, the true essence of the tree is ever-present within his vessels and sculptures, echoing its previous incarnation across surface and form.

Sculptor Alison Crowther, works almost exclusively with English oak sourced from UK woodlands. Sensitive to the complex geometry of nature, she observes and responds to her material, taking cues from the density, grain and growth pattern to create intricate, surface texture and pattern (see page 181). Using tools that range from chainsaws to chisels, she produces work that is sometimes domestic in scale, such as Glyndebourne Kissing Benches and sometimes monumental, as with Scale Tree 1, created for One Shenzhen Bay.

Doctor David Gates makes furniture more akin to pieces of three-dimensional art, exploring ideas directly through the making process. He trained in Furniture and Product Design at Ravensbourne College and also holds a PhD from King's College, London. Cabinets, such as the group of pieces that comprise Yard, are a response to the agricultural architecture of

Opposite left: *Pinned Vessel* in burnished ash (on left in image) and *Land Jar* in spalted beech, both by Max Bainbridge; the textile work is *In Dreams (Dormir)* by Abigail Booth. Collectively, they are known as Forest + Found. (Courtesy of the New Art Centre.)

Opposite right: *At Cliffe 1* and *At Cliffe 2* cabinets by David Gates, made in European oak, bog oak, maple, cedar and steel; shown with vitreous enamel steel vessel by Helen Carnac.

Right: *Cleft Cabinet* by Peter Marigold, a bespoke commission and collaboration with Tadanori Tozawa, in red cedar and black-painted chestnut. (Courtesy of Sarah Myerscough Gallery.)

structures such as silos, sheds and barns, resulting in corrugated, slatted, shuttered and cleft sides. Others are more reflective of industrial architecture, such as the pylons, jetties and depots that inspired *Lodged*. While Gates's cabinets may appear to be purely sculptural forms, in fact they are fully functioning pieces that have been carefully and consciously composed. He also collaborates on some pieces with his partner, enameller Helen Carnac. The rich patinas of her metalwork form much of the design language of the cabinets they make together.

The work of Peter Marigold has encompassed public art works, limited-edition furniture, conceptual artworks and scenography. *Cleft* is a collaboration with Tadanori Tozawa of renowned Japanese atelier, Hinoki Kougei. Based on the form of traditional medicine cabinets, the fronts are made from cleaved wood hewn directly from split logs. Different timbers, such as oak, walnut and chestnut, result in widely varying textures and colours. *Bleed* is a collection of cedar wood cabinets. The painterly patina is created by strategically placing steel hardware on the surface and using acid to strip out the zinc, so the steel reacts over time with tannins in the cedar producing the 'bleeding' pattern. These works set out to present wood that is not overworked, humanised and divorced from the reality of its nature and growth.

LAURA ELLEN BACON:
Land Artist

Laura Ellen Bacon is an artist who uses materials, such as woven willow and stone, to express her distinctive voice. Born and raised in Derbyshire, a landscape that feeds much of her inspiration, she makes quietly powerful statements through her land art and sculpture. Originally she took a foundation year at local Chesterfield College and a degree in Applied Art at Derby University. For her final year, she began experimenting with sculpted spaces inspired by her childhood passion for creating complex treehouses and dens, first using branches (delivered to the university in carloads by her mother) and then willow. With no training in basketry techniques, she began to develop her own instinctive way of knotting, weaving and pulling the stems into forms that are almost muscular in their structure, but also intimate and sensual. The observer is encouraged not only to look but to touch and explore.

In 2004, she was given a Crafts Council Development Award, which allowed her to set up her own studio. Over the last eighteen years, her work has highlighted how art and craft can harmonise to great effect. Not only has she been selected as a Jerwood Contemporary Maker and showed her work at the V&A in London as a finalist in the Woman's Hour Craft Prize, but she has also won artistic recognition for works such as *Natural Course* (2020) at Chatsworth, a sinuous stone sculpture (built with the help of local dry stone wallers) of responsibly sourced stone, that weaves its way through woodland and down a slope into the garden. She is represented by the Hignell Gallery in Mayfair, alongside sculptors such as Sophie Ryder, Helaine Blumenfeld, Peter Randall-Page and Joana Vasconcelos. In 2018, her work *Woven Space* inspired Helen Grime to compose a symphony of the same name, which was subsequently performed at the Barbican Centre by the London Symphony Orchestra conducted by Sir Simon Rattle.

Bacon's works are most often created on site, in both landscape and gallery settings that have included Chatsworth, Somerset House, Jerwood Space, the New Art Centre, Sudeley Castle, Mompesson House, the Holburne Museum in Bath and Blackwell in Cumbria. For the University of Warwick, she created *Don't Let Go*, a huge woven nest wrapped around a tree, designed to both highlight the plight of our insect population and provide a safe and natural habitat for them.

She says that her woven sculptures are addictive and liberating to make, 'I work the way I do because I love the simplicity of the creation process, with no machinery or complex tools needed to create it. The repetitive process of using the materials – and their sheer mass and volume – is always satisfying. I feel hardwired to create spaces and forms that seem rooted to their site.'

'I work the way I do because I love the simplicity of the creation process . . . I feel hardwired to create spaces and forms that seem rooted to their site.'

Right: Laura Ellen Bacon with *The Shape of First Thoughts*, which she created as part of a solo exhibition at the National Centre for Craft and Design in Sleaford.

Below left: A detail of *The Shape of First Thoughts*, which Bacon made from Dicky Meadows willow using her own techniques of knotting and weaving.

Below right: *Course* was an on-site commission for Hall Place in Bexley curated by Artwise and supported by the World Wildlife Fund. The sculpture's physical interaction with the River Cray helped raise awareness of the UK's threatened chalk stream rivers.

DOVECOT STUDIOS:
Tapestry Studio

Dovecot Studios in Edinburgh – originally named The Edinburgh Tapestry Company – was established by the fourth Marquis of Bute in 1912. The building he created for the enterprise was named The Dovecot Studio after the medieval dovecot in the grounds. The Marquis was keen to bring the Arts and Crafts Movement to Scotland and so employed Master weavers,

Gordon Berry and John Glassbrook, who had worked at the Merton Abbey Mills workshops under William Morris, to help set up the studio. Both men were killed in World War I, but they had achieved enough that by the 1920s weavers here were recognised as skilled artisans. By the mid-twentieth century, Dovecot had attracted the attention of artists such as Edward

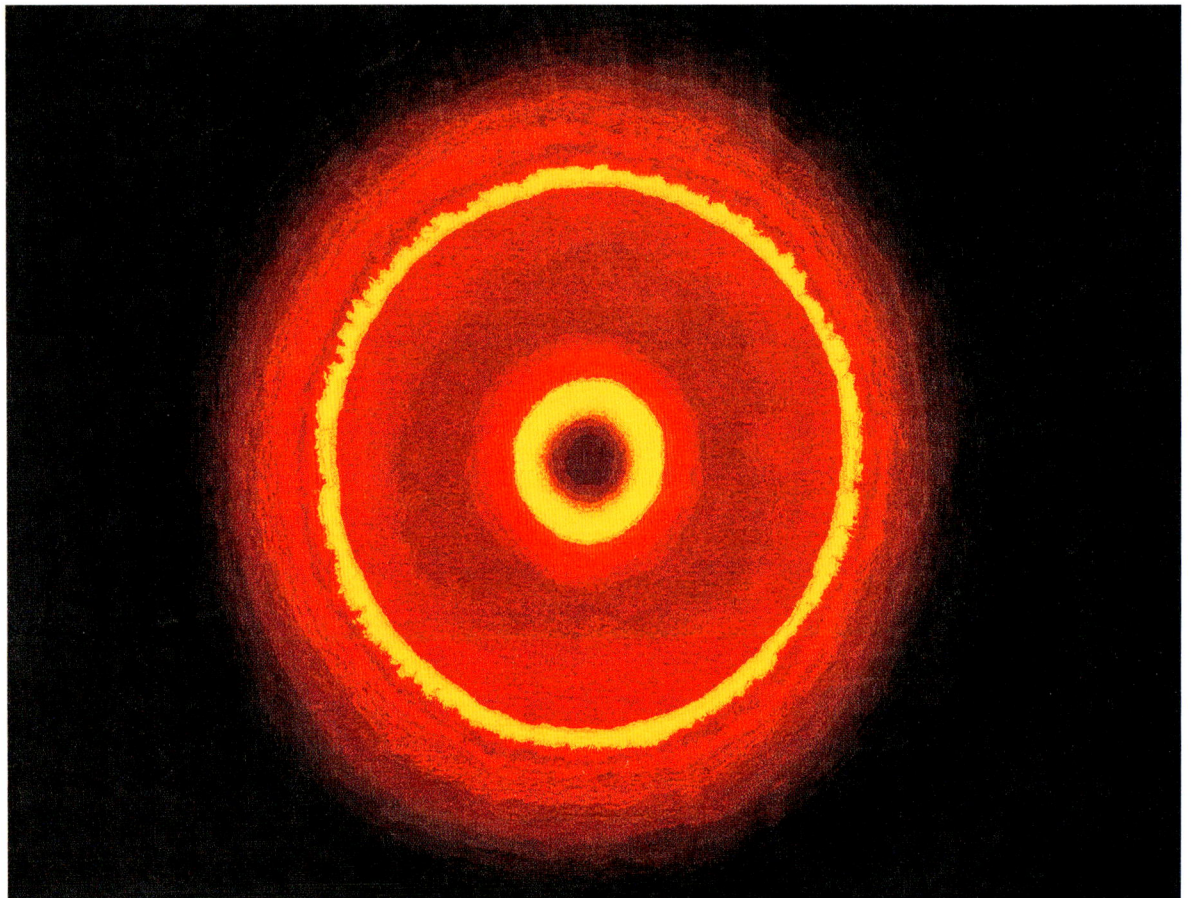

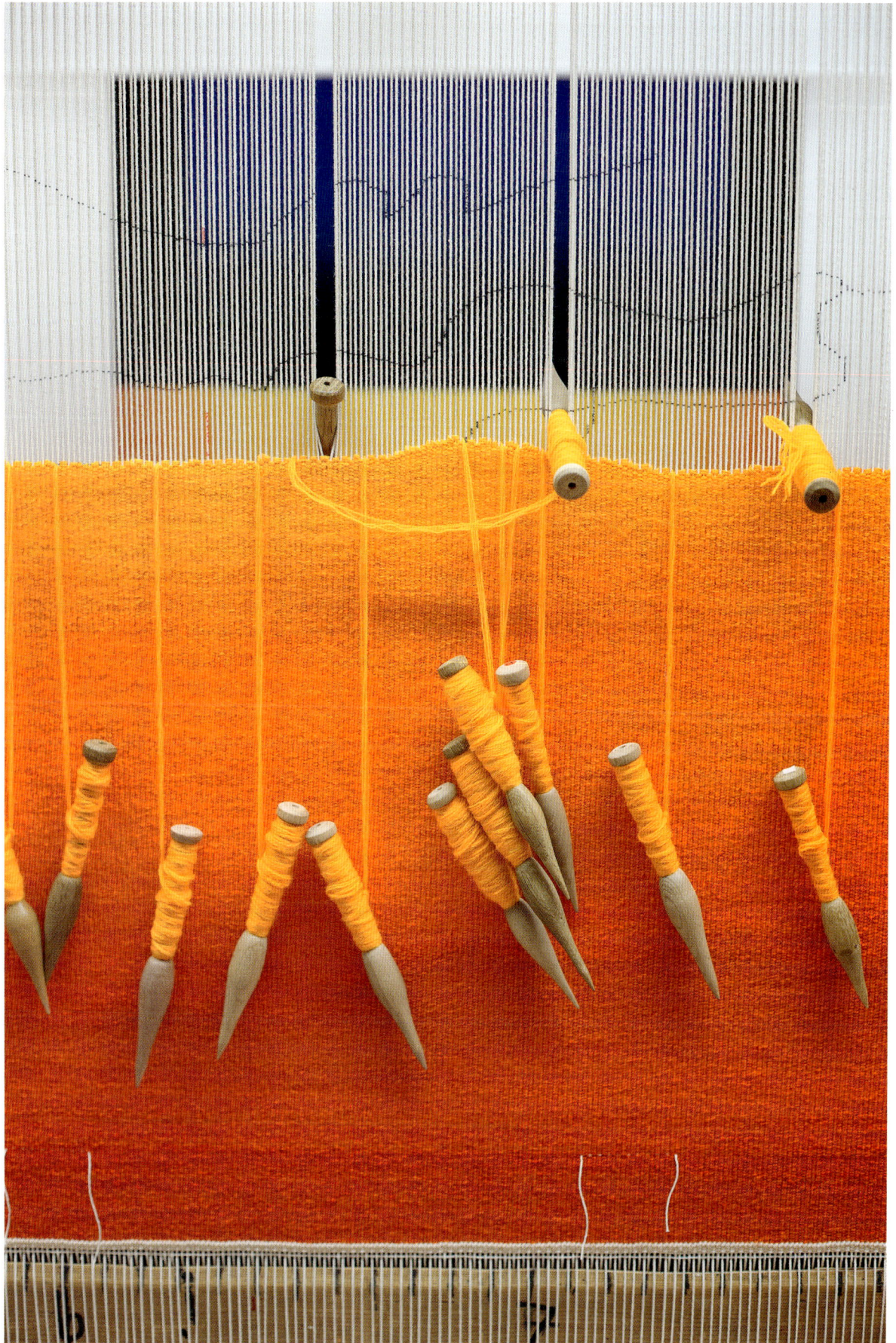

Opposite: *Hearth Rug, Gathered Gold Light* in collaboration with photographic artist Garry Fabian Miller presented the challenge of depicting burning light with contrasting yarns.

Right: The making of *Voyage into the deepest, darkest blue*, which drew upon the weavers' skills to capture the colour purity evident in Garry Fabian Miller's photographic work.

> 'Our collaborations with artists are an opportunity to make new work that engages with bold and contemporary ideas ... and to take Scottish tapestry to the world.'

Wadsworth, Stanley Spencer, Edward Bawden, Graham Sutherland and Cecil Beaton, all of whom designed tapestries, establishing Dovecot's strong and continuing tradition as a collaborator with artists.

In recent years, contemporary artists and commissioners have turned to textiles as a way of exploring new ideas. In 2022, Alberta Whittle and Scotland + Venice Partnership commissioned a Dovecot tapestry by Whittle for the 59th Biennale di Venezia entitled *Entanglement Is More Than Blood*.

July Fields (2021) was a commission to mark the centenary of the birth of Scottish artist Joan Eardley, interpreting her 1959 painting of the same name into a tapestry using woven *haute-lisse* on a high-warp loom. In 2021, the studio also embarked on *Minerva Protects Pax from Mars*, a monumental work inspired by the work of the same name by Leon Kossoff, which in turn was inspired by that of Peter Paul Rubens (1577–1640). However, one of Dovecot's most ambitious tapestries to date is *The Caged Bird's Song* (2021), interpreting a watercolour of the same name by Chris Ofili. Commissioned by The Clothworkers' Company and completed in 2017, it took five weavers nearly three years to complete, and was so technically challenging that it was compared to 'weaving water'.

One of the studio's most recent projects has been *The Mallaig Commission* (2021) with Jock McFadyen RA. This major artwork interprets the artist's gritty vision of Scotland's urban landscape into dramatically intense, inky blues and complex undertones of colour using the gun-tufting process. *Gathered Gold Light* (2020) by photographic artist Garry Fabian Miller is the seventh project that Dovecot has collaborated on with the artist since 2014. It presented the weavers with the challenge of how to represent a disc of burning light against the darkness by combining and cutting contrasting yarns.

Dovecot has also created its own contemporary rug collections, translating works of artists (some living, some deceased) into beautifully executed designs. The richly diverse list of names all have connections to Scotland, Wales or Ireland, including John Byrne, William Crozier, Alan Davie, Nick Evans, Ruth Ewan, Jim Lambie, Alasdair Gray and Rachel MacLean.

Of Dovecot's impressive history and continuing legacy, Director Celia Joicey says, 'As both an international fine art studio and a centre for contemporary craft and design, Dovecot offers an exciting model to sustain British craftsmanship. Our collaborations with artists are an opportunity to make new work that engages with bold and contemporary ideas, to stage exhibitions that allow global audiences to see our skilled approach to making, and to take Scottish tapestry to the world.'

Opposite: A detail of *Minerva Protects Pax From Mars* based on the work by Leon Kossoff, which in turn was inspired from the sixteenth-century painting by Peter Paul Rubens.

Above: The warped tapestry loom used for the making of *Minerva Protects Pax From Mars* in collaboration with the Leon Kossoff estate and Parabola for Edinburgh Park.

II